D0853541

A QUESTION OF BALANCE

A Question of Balance

Charles Seeger's Philosophy of Music

TAYLOR AITKEN GREER

UNIVERSITY OF CALIFORNIA PRESS
BERKELEY   LOS ANGELES   LONDON

University of California Press
Berkeley and Los Angeles, California

University of California Press, Ltd.
London, England

© 1998 by
The Regents of the University of California

Library of Congress Cataloging-in-Publication Data

Greer, Taylor Aitken, 1955–
    A question of balance : Charles Seeger's philosophy of
music / Taylor Aitken Greer.
        p.   cm.
    Includes bibliographical references (p. 000) and index.
    ISBN 0-520-21152-9 (alk. paper)
    1. Seeger, Charles, 1886–1979—Criticism and
interpretation.   2. Music—Philosophy and aesthetics.
3. Musicology—United States—History—20th century.
I. Title.
ML423.S498G74   1998
781'.092—dc21   98-19450
                                                     CIP
                                                     MN

Printed in the United States of America
9 8 7 6 5 4 3 2 1

To Cecilia, François, and Emile

Contents

Acknowledgments

I would like to express my appreciation to the American Council of Learned Societies as well as The Pennsylvania State University for awarding me research fellowships which allowed me the time to begin writing this book. I also gratefully acknowledge the following: the Music Library, University of California, Berkeley, for granting permission to reprint an excerpt from Item no. 18, an unpublished typescript of *Tradition and Experiment in the New Music* in the Charles Seeger Collection; the Department of Special Collections, Oral History Program, University Research Library, UCLA, for granting permission to reproduce seven excerpts from Charles Seeger, "Reminiscences of an American Musicologist"; the Oral History American Music Collection, Yale School of Music and Library, for granting permission to reproduce three excerpts from an interview with Charles Seeger on 16 March 1970 by Vivian Perlis; the University of California Press for granting permission to reproduce figure 2 from Charles Seeger, *Studies in Musicology, 1935–1975,* Berkeley: University of California Press © 1977 The Regents of the University of California, as well as figures 1, 6, and 7, examples 4, 5, 21, 67, 71, 85, 149, 161, and 162, and the list on page 130 from Charles Seeger, *Studies in Musicology II: 1929–1979,* ed. Ann Pescatello, Berkeley: University of California Press © 1994 The Regents of the University of California; and the Theodore Presser Company for permission to reproduce an excerpt from the third movement of Ruth Crawford Seeger's String Quartet, © 1941 Merion Music, Inc., used by permission.

References to specific pitches in this book follow the notation suggested by the Acoustical Society of America: a pitch class is symbolized by an uppercase letter; its octave placement is symbolized by a number following the letter. An octave number refers to pitches from a given C through the B above (e.g., middle C = C4).

There are many people whom I want to thank for their generosity during the course of this project. Michael Broyles, Robert Hatten, and Mark Tucker helped revise several chapters along the way. Scott Burnham, Judith Tick, and Larry Zbikowski all offered invaluable advice during the early stages of my research. Special thanks go to Severine Neff and Joseph Straus who both read the entire manuscript and offered innumerable suggestions. Also I want to thank Lynne Withey, Juliane Brand, and Suzanne Samuel for their consummate skill in shepherding this book through the various stages of production. To my copyeditor, Susan Ecklund, I owe an enormous debt, for she saved me from a mountain of embarrassments. I wish to thank Mike Seeger for all of his help in finding the photograph reproduced on the cover. I am grateful to Penn State University for providing a publication subvention to finance the musical examples and figures, and to David Geyer for creating them with such professional care and good cheer. In addition, I must thank two of my piano teachers over the years—Beth Miller Harrod, for lighting the spark, and Evelyn Swarthout Hayes, for nurturing the flame of my musical imagination.

The spirit of my maternal grandmother, Helen Cook Aitken ("Gigi"), fills these pages, for she always cared so much about ideas and about writing them down with clarity and grace. To my parents I want to express my gratitude for their love and constant faith in me during these many months and years. My heartfelt thanks also go to my sister, Penny, for all she has done, particularly toward the end. My father-in-law, Philippe, I must acknowledge for indirectly helping me meet several crucial deadlines during this project—by providing the incentive to finish my work so that I could join him in our annual cycling tour, that irresistible combination of athletic pain and gastronomic pleasure. Finally, I cannot put into words what my wife, Cecilia Dunoyer, has done over the years to help me finish this book. Her inexhaustible patience, common sense, honesty, and enduring love have been a continuing source of inspiration.

From the very first time I encountered Seeger's writings, I felt innately drawn toward his unique mix of musical curiosity and philosophical reflection. In writing this work, I have certainly discovered as much about myself as I have about him. As I come to the end of this project, I treasure all the more the luxury of pursuing a vocation that seeks to blend art and wisdom. Perhaps Albert Einstein said it best: "The most beautiful emotion we can experience is the mystical. It is the sower of all true art and science. . . . To know that what is impenetrable to us really exists, manifesting itself as the highest wisdom and the most radiant beauty which our dull faculties can comprehend— this knowledge, this feeling, is at the center of true religiousness."

Figures and
Musical Examples

Figures

Musical Examples

Introduction

For over half a century, Charles Louis Seeger (1886–1979) led a distinguished career in American musical life as composer, teacher, author, administrator, and humanist. Once described as a "universalist par excellence," he had an expansive curiosity and brought a wide spectrum of humanistic and scientific fields to bear upon the study of music.[1] The list of disciplines to which he contributed is as long as it is varied, including composition, theory, criticism, historiography, musicology, ethnomusicology, sociology, and philosophy.[2] Seeger's initial writings grew out of his involvement with avant-garde music, first as a fledgling composer himself, and later as a composition teacher and theorist. Among his students in the 1910s and 1920s were Henry Cowell and Ruth Crawford, two of the leading experimental, so-called ultramodernist, composers in America.[3] With the onset of the Great Depression in the early 1930s, Seeger's interests turned to folk and non-Western traditions, as he and Crawford (by then his wife) began collecting, transcribing, and publishing American folk songs. During this period his writings focused on the sociology of music, that is, the study of composition and performance within a broader social and political context. Near the end of his life, Seeger served on the faculty of the Institute of Ethnomusicology at UCLA, where he wrote and revised many of his philosophical and speculative writings about music. In these essays Seeger continued to refine his ideal scheme of musicology—what he called the "unified field theory"—which he illustrated through a series of elaborate maps that integrated every aspect of musical learning into a vast interdisciplinary network. One critic described these schemes of musicology as the "transcendent vision of an erudite and far-reaching mind."[4]

Yet on the whole Seeger's numerous writings have had a rather limited impact on musicians and musicologists in this country. There are three reasons for this. The first is the result of the holistic approach he developed toward the study of music. Seeger's life in music can be described as a marriage of conflicting temperaments: an artistic instinct combined with a rational intellect. In essence, the driving force behind most of Seeger's writings on music was the desire to mediate between these two conflicting impulses. He constantly looked for ways of bringing together the intuitive world of the practicing musician, from radical composer to rural folksinger, with the more intellectual worlds of the theorist, historian, and philosopher. In search of this ideal, Seeger felt drawn toward dualistic models in which an initial pair of opposites would undergo a process of mediation and eventually lead to some greater synthesis. Seeger used these models in a number of ways—to explain how humans compose, criticize, and, indeed, even think about music. For him, striking a balance between diametrically opposed ideas was far more than some abstract exercise in compromise: it was a way of life. The distinctive character of Seeger's thought is less the sheer breadth of his musical and intellectual interests than his idiosyncratic way of mixing these interests together. The challenge of interpreting Seeger's works is that he did not always identify the disciplines or, more important, the discipline-based approaches he was borrowing. Thus, readers may not have always appreciated the subtlety of his interdisciplinary blend. In a climate of increasing specialization, Seeger's holistic way of approaching musical questions has often been viewed as an anomaly, and Seeger himself has been marginalized.

The second explanation for this neglect is the deep split that has developed since World War II between musicologists, those who study Western traditions, and ethnomusicologists, those who study non-Western, folk, or popular traditions. Since Seeger played such a strong role in helping to establish ethnomusicology in America following World War II, his philosophical writings have often been associated with that field alone—as though he were chronicling the growing pains of a new specialized form of musical scholarship. It is ironic that Seeger would be regarded as a specialist, since one of his greatest aspirations was to inaugurate a more universal conception of musicology that would embrace all cultural traditions—both Eastern and Western. Even among ethnomusicologists, Seeger's particular brand of philosophical inquiry has left little legacy; for many, he has been a source more of "inspiration than of substantive instruction."[5] To this day, most composers, theorists, and historians who study European music either do not know Seeger's work or, what is worse, ignore it.

A third reason for Seeger's limited impact is the diffuse organization and labored prose style that often characterize his writing. He was his own harshest critic, struggling to revise drafts of essays and previously published works over and over again. In a recent review of Ann Pescatello's biography of Seeger, Michael Broyles describes his late work, *Studies in Musicology, 1935–1975,* as "a collection of essays whose density was unparalleled in musicological writings."[6] Indeed, in the 1970 symposium "Universal Perspectives of Music" Seeger himself confided that he wrote primarily for himself.[7] Many of Seeger's investigations of musical topics hinge on philosophical principles that he never fully explains or defends. Before Seeger's thought can be fairly judged, it must be presented as clearly as possible and located within the larger historical and philosophical context of the early twentieth century.

The thesis of this book is that Seeger's central contribution to the field of music was his aesthetic philosophy. The theory of knowledge developed in his early treatise entitled *Tradition and Experiment in the New Music* was the seed from which his various writings in music criticism, compositional theory, and speculative musicology all grew. Indeed, it is impossible to fully grasp Seeger's contribution in any of these fields without appreciating the essential role that philosophy served in his thought as a whole. There has been only one book about Seeger: Ann M. Pescatello's biography *Charles Seeger: A Life in American Music.*[8] The book was originally intended to be a collaboration between Seeger and Pescatello; indeed, she succeeds in ably blending his self-reflections into her own narrative. But, as a historian, she focuses more on the rich interplay between his life and works than on the exegesis of his philosophical theories. Other writers have acknowledged Seeger's philosophical leanings, but no study to date has focused on his philosophical theory and traced its relationship to his other writings about music. In short, Seeger's thought has been marginalized because it has been misunderstood.

That said, Seeger was by no means a traditional philosopher. To help clarify his unusual conception of philosophy, it is useful to refer to a recent formulation by the Canadian philosopher Francis Sparshott.

In his essay "Aesthetics of Music—Limits and Grounds," Sparshott observes that the history of music aesthetics has witnessed two contrasting approaches: the inductive and the general. Writers who adopt the first approach begin "with some specific problem, arising out of familiar musical practice or customary ways of describing that practice, which they wish to solve or explore."[9] In such investigations, any general system or scheme of human knowledge is, at best, accidental, being the sum of the individual practical solutions. A good illustration of this aesthetic approach can be found in the thought of the twentieth-century theorist Heinrich Schenker. In his later writings Schenker proposed a theory of "organic coherence" in which all musical meaning resides in the artwork itself and is freed from "every external purpose, whether it be the word, the stage, or, in general, the anecdotal of any kind of program."[10] Rather than investigate such questions as the relation between music and literature or drama or the general nature of artistic experience, Schenker simply ignored them, instead turning his attention to the objective laws governing the tones themselves.

The aim for the second philosophical approach, according to Sparshott, is to develop a broad aesthetic system that can account for all the arts. From this point of view, music serves merely as one among many case studies. An example of such a general approach is offered by the authors of the eighteenth-century French *Encyclopédie* such as Diderot and d'Alembert, who fashioned "great maps of knowledge" and "attempted to take stock of the relations between all actual and possible disciplines of thought."[11]

The unique characteristic of Seeger's philosophy is that at different junctures in his life he employed both of Sparshott's contrasting approaches. In the process of exploring new resources for experimental composition during the 1920s and 1930s, Seeger felt compelled to develop a scheme of knowledge upon which all music speculation would depend. Although he gave up composition in his late thirties, he never abandoned the intuitive viewpoint of a composer or performer. During this period, philosophy was primarily a means of achieving a practical end: to renew composition. But as his passion for the musical avant-garde waned in favor of folk and popular traditions, his taste for philosophical thought also became more systematic. Beginning in the early 1930s, Seeger showed an increasing fascination with developing encyclopedic maps that could illustrate all aspects of human interaction with music. While his philosophical aspirations were never as broad as those of the eighteenth-century French Encyclopedists, the question he returned to again and again was the nature of musical understanding.[12] In his later writings, philosophy served less as a means than an end in itself: to renew musicology by clarifying its philosophical foundation. In sum, Seeger's approach to music aesthetics is a methodological hybrid: part inductive, part general. Indeed, Seeger was as passionate about making music as he was about making sense of it.

My central focus in this study is the philosophical theory Seeger articulates in *Tradition and Experiment in the New Music* [13] and the various critical, compositional, and musicological applications it inspired. It is easy to misinterpret the significance of this early treatise within Seeger's entire output, especially considering that over half of the volume is devoted to technical matters of composition. However, the philosophical views outlined in the initial two chapters are absolutely essential if we are to understand many of Seeger's speculative writings throughout the rest of his life. For example, themes that permeate the last essays Seeger completed in 1977, such as the hazards of the "linguocentric predicament" and the sharp dichotomy between fact and value, all made their first appearance in the philosophical essays of the 1920s that culminated in the treatise. While no single theory could possibly account for all of Seeger's diverse writings in music, the aesthetic philosophy developed in the treatise is indispensable for interpreting his body of writings in criticism, compositional theory, and musicology.

Seeger's treatise had an unusually long period of gestation. Although he completed a revised draft of this magnum opus as early as 1931, it was never published until 1994, fifteen years after his death. Apparently, Seeger had mixed feelings about the work. On the one hand, in a 1966 interview he downplayed its importance, calling it a mere "historical curiosity."[14] Also, in a private letter to Gilbert Chase, Seeger confided that one of his greatest reservations about the treatise was its failure to address folk, popular, and non-Western musical traditions. By focusing so much attention on Western art music, Seeger bemoaned that he "had told only half the story."[15] On the other hand, according to his biographer and friend, Ann Pescatello, "He always retained a regard for that work and harbored a desire ultimately to see it in print—though with revisions, I am sure!"[16] It seems fair to say that the posthumous publication of the treatise was the culmination of an extended musical and intellectual journey that began with his first teaching appointment at Berkeley during the teens, continued in the hotbed of the experimental music scene in New York during the 1920s and 1930s, and finally reached an end while he was teaching at UCLA during the 1960s. In many respects the treatise serves as a map of that journey. The work is divided into two halves, the first of which includes three separate projects: a general theory of criticism, a reappraisal of the six elements of music, and a neumatic theory of melody. The second half is more practical in nature, consisting of a contrapuntal regimen for experimental composers.

The question arises whether a document that was never published during the author's lifetime could have had any influence on musicians or music scholars of his generation. While it is true that until recently the treatise itself was inaccessible, the philosophical ideas outlined in this document lie at the heart of most of Seeger's later writings. Indeed, the opening chapters of *Tradition and Experiment in the New Music* serve as a cipher for clarifying and interpreting Seeger's entire philosophical project. Hence, this work's inaccessibility recedes in importance when one considers the number of Seeger's philosophical writings that were published. The treatise represents a crucial moment in Seeger's development as a thinker for, though his musical and political tastes changed dramatically following 1931, his philosophical orientation became crystallized in this early work and never changed.

My study is also divided into two parts, one devoted to philosophical theory, the other to its application in musical practice. Part 1 focuses on Seeger's theory of music criticism that serves as an epistemological model of knowledge about music. In chapters 1 through 3 I examine the ideas of three philosophers, two European and one American, who helped shape Seeger's idiosyncratic approach to philosophy: Henri Bergson's theory of intuition; Bertrand Russell's philosophical ideal of mediation that balances reason with intuition; and the all-encompassing value theory propounded by Ralph Barton Perry. Chapter 4 consists of a detailed exegesis of Seeger's theory of music criticism. In part 1 I explain the process through which Seeger's philosophical theory developed from his earliest attempt at music speculation in 1923 to its more mature statement in the treatise. While Seeger felt no compunction about borrowing bits and pieces from some of the leading thinkers of his day, the philosophical mosaic he created was all his own.

In part 2 I explore the ways Seeger's philosophical theories inspired specific applications in three fields: music criticism, compositional theory, and speculative musicology. Although he contributed to a much wider range of disciplines than these, his critical, theoretical, and musicological ideas share a common reliance on his philosophical ideals. In all three chapters I assess his specific proposals initially on their own terms and then in relation to the ways in which they realize the theory of knowledge discussed in part 1.

In chapter 5 I examine a selection of Seeger's writings as a music critic from the early 1930s to 1971. While these reviews may initially appear like promotional exercises in the name of "ultramodernism," in fact they demonstrate the depth of Seeger's faith in the philosophical ideal of balance, as expressed in the treatise. I focus on a handful of critical reviews in which Seeger evaluates the music of three avant-garde composers: Ruggles, Cowell, and Crawford. Despite close personal ties to all three, he believes that their music, for different reasons, falls short of greatness. Thus, as eager as Seeger was to champion the cause of experimental music in the 1920s and 1930s, his reviews show an even higher loyalty to preserving the integrity of his theory of criticism.

The principal aim of chapter 6 is to assess Seeger's approach to avant-garde composition within a broader historical context. Despite Seeger's fascination with "new" and experimental compositional techniques, many of the philosophical assumptions on which these techniques depend resurrect the aesthetic ideals of German romanticism. This chapter consists of a detailed study of several questions that Seeger discusses in the first half of the treatise: his reappraisal of the basic materials of music; his adaptation of the theory of harmonic dualism; and his neumatic theory of melodic form. In each of these, Seeger's methodological approach displays a considerable debt to the nineteenth century.

The past decade or so has witnessed a renewal of interest in Seeger's music theoretical writings as well as in Ruth Crawford's music. In a 1986 essay Mark Nelson explored Crawford's use of palindrome and other compositional devices in relation to Seeger's concept of heterophony.[17] In his book *American Experimental Music, 1890–1940,* David Nicholls was the first musicologist to examine Seeger's principles of dissonant counterpoint in any depth, skillfully tracing various ways in which they shaped the music of Carl Ruggles, Henry Cowell, and Ruth Crawford.[18] The only shortcoming of these two studies is the limited number of sources that were available to them. Until the trea-

tise appeared in 1994, the only published account of Seeger's views on
experimental technique and aesthetics was a seven-page essay published in *Modern Music* in which he provides a rather laconic overview
of several chapters of the treatise.[19] What is needed now is a fresh look
at Seeger's compositional theories not only in light of the newly published treatise but, more important, in the context of his broader
philosophical and speculative program.

In recent years there has been a virtual renaissance of interest in
the life and music of Ruth Crawford including editions, recordings,
conferences, and scholarship. Joseph Straus recently completed a compelling monograph on Crawford's music in which he exhaustively analyzes six of her compositions in part by using various categories from
Tradition and Experiment in the New Music.[20] Judith Tick's comprehensive biography provides a vibrant portrait of Crawford's life as
composer, arranger/transcriber, mother, and wife and the ways in
which she intertwined them all.[21] While it is true that Crawford arrived at her own synthesis of Seeger's compositional theories, his
unique blend of speculative theory and experimental practice is worthy of study in its own right.

In the introduction to his study Straus raises the question of how
much Ruth Crawford contributed to *Tradition and Experiment in the
New Music.* She certainly played an instrumental role in assembling
the document, considering that she typed while Seeger dictated the
entire first draft at the family farm estate near Patterson, New York,
during the summer of 1930. However, her exact role in the formation
of the content itself is not clear. On the one hand, Seeger certainly felt
the book was a collaboration, since he suggested that she be listed as
a coauthor, an offer that she refused.[22] On the other hand, we do know
that Seeger decided to ignore a number of her recommendations for
revising the text, since in the recent edition of the treatise Pescatello
transcribed the marginalia in Crawford's hand that appear in the most
complete version of the manuscript.[23] (Incidentally, Seeger's decision
is unfortunate, since Crawford had an uncanny gift for clear thinking
and writing.) What no one knows is how many of her suggestions for
writing and/or revising the text Seeger did follow. Also, there is the
question of whether Seeger composed the music examples accompanying the commentary, especially since so many examples from part 2
resemble Crawford's distinctive idiom.[24] Because my study focuses on

a set of philosophical ideas that not only appeared in the treatise but continued to absorb Seeger for the rest of his life, I will assume that he is the principal author.

Finally, chapter 7 is devoted to one of the continuing leitmotifs of Seeger's musical speculation: his ideal scheme of musicology. I compare four different maps or schemes of the discipline presented in essays written between 1939 and 1977, both in the context of music historiographical developments at the turn of the century and in relation to Saussure's theory of language. Two themes emerge from this comparison. First, throughout his life, Seeger insisted on combining his protest against musicologists' indifference toward new music with his comprehensive panorama of musical scholarship. In that respect, he sometimes allowed his personal musical tastes to influence his conception of systematic musical knowledge. Second, his bias against historical interpretation, first evident in the treatise, gradually diminished over time, and in the models of musicology published in the 1970s the spirit of his philosophical ideal of mediation was at last fulfilled.

Throughout this study my point of view is like that of other historians of philosophy; that is, I assume that any philosophical problem arises out of and, indeed, is defined by a particular set of historical conditions. This is why I devote as much attention to the muses that shaped Seeger's unique approach to aesthetics as to the ideas about music it eventually inspired. The discipline of philosophy has traditionally been preoccupied with its own past. My hope is that by focusing on the formation of Seeger's philosophical ideas as much as the ideas themselves, it may help us rediscover our own musical philosophies.

Before proceeding with the story of Seeger's philosophical ideals and their expression in various fields of music, we must begin with another story: Seeger's life itself. A brief biographical sketch is particularly important in the case of Seeger, for some of his earliest experiences as a musician and teacher played a direct role in shaping his unusual conception of philosophy.[25]

Born in 1886, Charles Louis Seeger, the oldest of three children, came from an old New England family whose ancestors can be traced back over two hundred years. Until reaching the age of sixteen, Charles and his whole family shuttled every few years between Mexico City and New York City, where his father ran an import-export business. During these idyllic years Charles and his brother, Alan (who later became a notable American poet) developed a lifelong fondness for Latin American culture.[26] Whereas much of his early education was conducted at home by tutors, in 1902 he enrolled in a private Unitarian school in New York in order to prepare for entrance into college.

It is with his arrival at Harvard that Seeger began to manifest a passion for composing that would later become an essential component of his unique approach to musical speculation. His parents assumed that, upon graduation, he would pursue a business career and eventually become a partner in his father's company. However, since Seeger's rebellious streak was just as strong as his hatred of business, he decided instead to major in music, with the intention of being a composer. Early on, Seeger showed a cynical and contemptuous attitude toward school. In order to devote as much time as possible to composition, he neglected all of his classes in the sciences and humanities, for which he received low grades. As for his music courses in harmony, counterpoint, canon, fugue, song writing, and so forth, Seeger could barely tolerate his professors. He held so little respect for music history that he refused to take a single course in it.

It struck me that these books on music were just hopelessly out of the real mainstream of music. My claim was that when a man sat down to compose or when he sat down to perform or to listen to music, nothing in those books figured at all. . . . So I considered myself really pretty much apart from that sort of thing.[27]

Instead Seeger and his classmates were fervent lovers of contemporary music, which, for them, meant Debussy, Strauss, Mahler, Scriabin, and Satie. He regularly attended rehearsals and performances of the Boston Symphony Orchestra, eventually aspiring to mix composition with conducting. In 1908 Seeger graduated magna cum laude in music, and left to seek his musical fortunes in Europe.[28]

What is significant about this chapter in Seeger's life is the explicit anti-intellectual bias that characterized his approach toward school. Adolescent rebellion aside, his only passion during this period was to be a practicing musician: composing, performing, and eventually conducting. Although he would later overcome this bias and discover that he, indeed, had a love for learning and the life of the mind, it never-theless remained a fundamental part of his artistic makeup.

His sojourn in Europe lasted over two years, during which he worked as an assistant conductor at the Cologne Opera, composed, and occasionally traveled to Paris and Berlin. But, because of a gradual loss of hearing, he eventually discovered that he would never have a pro-fessional conducting career. Soon after returning to New York in 1911, he met a talented young violinist named Constance Edson, protégée of the Damrosch family and student of Franz Kneisel, and became her piano accompanist. A romance blossomed, and on December 22, 1911, they were married. In the first few months Seeger and his bride eked out a meager existence by performing at various private parties and resorts in the Northeast. Within the year, however, an opportunity arose that would dramatically change both of their lives. In May 1912 Benjamin I. Wheeler, the president of the University of California, of-fered Seeger, upon the recommendation of the Harvard music faculty, a position as full professor with the assignment to inaugurate a new music department. Seeger accepted and that fall reentered the halls of academe.

Considering Seeger's recalcitrant attitude toward school as an un-dergraduate, his first few lectures must have been rather comical. About his inaugural lecture Seeger writes:

I felt so sure of myself that I went to my first lecture without any preparation whatever. I found out after twenty minutes I had nothing more to say, so I dismissed the class. I'd never opened a book on the history of music. . . . For-tunately in the library there were a couple of dozen books on music, mostly elementary textbooks. . . . in my second lecture I was able to discourse learnedly upon Greek music and Early Christian music. I didn't lack things to talk about for the rest of the year.[29]

Soon he found his stride as a classroom teacher, choir director, and even impresario, as he inaugurated a series of chamber music concerts on campus. Of particular note was the emphasis he placed on folk tra-ditions in his summer school course in music history, for which a local soprano performed songs in seventeen languages.

Although Seeger's work in the music department was generally suc-cessful, he eventually became, as he puts it, "keenly aware" of his "deficiencies in general education."[30] He met Herbert E. Cory, a bud-

ding poet and an instructor in the English department, whose vo-
racious appetite for reading was a perfect complement to Seeger's
newfound enthusiasm for learning. Together they devised a lengthy
reading list and a regimen of self-tutoring, which they augmented by
auditing their colleagues' classes and seminars. In a series of interviews in 1968, Seeger chronicled the course of his intellectual development during this period, which included studying history with
Frederick Teggert and anthropology with Alfred Kroeber, and reading Karl Kautsky on political theory and Karl Pearson on the nature of
science,[31] as well as the Veda, the sacred books of Hinduism.[32]

Seeger's autodidactic efforts are noteworthy not only because he
explored a wide cross section of disciplines outside of the arts but also
because of the idiosyncratic way in which he did so. For instance, while
Seeger's survey of the history of philosophy included several contemporary thinkers such as Bertrand Russell and Ralph B. Perry, the latter of whom delivered a series of lectures on campus in 1918, it omitted such eighteenth-century figures as Immanuel Kant, whom Seeger
found too abstruse.[33] During this period and throughout his life, his
intellectual curiosity was as eclectic as it was enthusiastic. The threads
of inquiry that Seeger began connecting between music and other
fields in the humanities and sciences would later be woven into lumi-
nous tapestries depicting his ideal schemes of musicology.

The other major development in Seeger's musical life during this
period was his work as a private composition teacher: his first student
was Henry Cowell. In 1914, when the precocious sixteen-year-old arrived for his first lesson, Cowell was "the most self-sure autodidact"
Seeger had ever met,[34] for by that time Cowell had already completed
over a hundred compositions. Together they agreed on a program of
study that bore Seeger's pedagogical stamp: they would alternate between studying the traditional disciplines of harmony and counterpoint and cultivating Cowell's own compositional ideas in the context
of contemporary music. During this period Seeger also devised for his
prodigious student the first version of his regimen of dissonant counterpoint.[35] This combination of classifying and interpreting past traditions while at the same time experimenting with new resources for the
present is a microcosm of the approach Seeger would later adopt in the
treatise. Following his lessons with Seeger, between 1916 and 1919
Cowell organized some of his new compositional ideas in the form of

a treatise called *New Musical Resources,* which he later revised and published in 1930.[36]

In late 1918 Seeger took a sabbatical leave of absence. Partly because of his differences with the administration over American involvement in the war in Europe (he had registered as a conscientious objector) and partly because of an emotional collapse, he never returned to the university. Seeger's departure marked a twelve-year period of transition and redirection in his life. Living mostly in New York, he stopped composing and instead concentrated on teaching at the Institute of Musical Arts (a forerunner of the Juilliard School) and the New School for Social Research, while developing his new philosophical and musicological ideas in a handful of articles. In an interview with Vivian Perlis he admitted that he had reached a point of paralysis where "music that moved me I had no respect for. I couldn't admire. What I admired I couldn't be moved by."[37] Whereas he still harbored a deep admiration for musical masterpieces of the past, he believed that modern composers were crippled by the theoretical and artistic traditions they had inherited. In 1927 his marriage with Constance began to sour, leading to a divorce five years later.

Yet during this same period Seeger renewed his commitment to avant-garde experimentalism, initially through his involvement with such groups as the League of Composers and the International Composers Guild and later through his private composition teaching. Through Cowell, Seeger met a handful of other experimental composers, including Carl Ruggles,[38] Dane Rudhyar, and later Ruth Crawford. Ruggles and Seeger soon became fast friends. Ruggles not only spent the summer of 1921 at the Seeger home in Patterson, New York, but also dedicated both versions of his orchestral work *Angels* (1920–21; revised 1938) to Seeger and even confided that Seeger was "a father to him."[39]

Seeger's ties with Crawford proved to be even more profound. In 1929, when she moved to New York, she was an experienced composer and pianist, having studied composition with Adolph Weidig at the American Conservatory in Chicago and piano with Djane Lavoie-Herz. Cowell introduced Crawford to Seeger, who became her private composition teacher until she left for Europe on a Guggenheim Fellowship. This encounter was a significant turning point in his life, for Crawford not only was a talented student but also became his intellectual companion and, three years later, his wife. In the summer of 1930 they combined the material from her private composition lessons with his own previous philosophical speculations and assembled the first draft of *Tradition and Experiment in the New Music.* During this period and throughout the 1930s, Seeger wrote critical reviews of the music of Ruggles, Cowell, and Crawford.

Upon their return to New York in 1931, the onset of the Great Depression renewed Seeger and Crawford's strong social conscience and led them both to turn away from avant-garde composition. Disenchanted with the rarefied world of new music, Seeger took up the banner of the Composers' Collective, a group of composers seeking new ways of expressing a socialist aesthetic for music. During this period Seeger also dabbled in music criticism, writing occasional reviews under the pseudonym Carl Sands (or C. S.), for the *Daily Worker.* It is curious that even while composing socialist anthems, Seeger found time to continue cultivating his traditional musicological interests. In 1930, along with Otto Kinkeldey, Joseph Schillinger, Joseph Yasser, and Henry Cowell, Seeger established the New York Musicological Society (the precursor to the American Musicological Society), served as secretary, and later edited the first volume in a new series of monographs sponsored by the society.

In 1935 Seeger underwent another dramatic transformation, which has been described as trading the "rhetoric of revolution for reform."[40] He became immersed in the idealism of Roosevelt's New Deal, enjoying a distinguished career initially as a technical adviser in the Resettlement Administration and later as second in command at the Federal Music Project within the Works Progress Administration. In 1941 he became head of the Music Division of the Pan American Union, where he served until 1953. A longtime student of Mexican culture, Seeger began to champion the cause of Latin-American music, fostering exchanges among countries in North America and trying to gain support for Latino composers. At about this time the Seegers met John and Alan Lomax and became passionately involved in the study and transmission of American folk music. From the late 1930s until her death, Ruth Crawford worked like a dynamo, transcribing, arranging, and/or editing five major collections of folk songs.[41] During this period Seeger also became fascinated with applying the tools of ethnomusicology to the American folk song. In one study, by comparing seventy-six different performances of a single song, "Barbara Allen," Seeger contributed to a new understanding of orally transmitted music.[42]

Shortly after his retirement from government service, Seeger helped collaborate in developing a machine called the "melograph," which provided a graphic representation—in terms of frequency across time—of melody. While this instrument initially had great promise as an ethnomusicological tool for studying oral musical traditions, it was later supplanted by more sophisticated means. In the 1950s he spearheaded an attempt to organize an American counterpart to the International Musicological Society, which had been forced into extinction during the 1930s. His efforts led to the founding of the Society for Ethnomusicology, which eventually elected him its president in 1960–61 and later honorary president. Tragically, in 1953, Seeger lost his second wife and professional partner, Ruth Crawford, to cancer.

Seeger's final years were spent searching for ways to put into practice his vision of a truly universal scheme of musicology. In 1961, at the age of seventy-five, Seeger accepted a position as research professor in the newly formed Institute of Ethnomusicology at the University of California, Los Angeles, where he remained for nine years. In his faculty colleagues—Mantle Hood, the institute's founder, and Klaus Wachsmann—Seeger found kindred speculative spirits, and the interdisciplinary and hard-nosed dialogue of their joint seminars became famous.[43] It was here that Seeger wrote and refined his holistic studies of the nature of musicology, returning yet again to the continuing theme of a lifetime of musico-philosophical variations. Charles Louis Seeger died in Bridgewater, Connecticut, on February 7, 1979.

During his ninety-two years Charles Seeger had a total of seven children, three by Constance—Charles III, John, and Peter—and four by Ruth—Michael, Peggy, Barbara, and Penny. Among them, three have developed significant musical careers of their own. Since the 1940s the name of Pete Seeger (b. 1919) has become almost synonymous with the American revival of folk music as a means of social protest through his association with the Almanac Singers, the Weavers, and People's Songs, Inc. Two other Seegers have also made noteworthy contributions to the world of folk music: Mike (b. 1933), through his solo performances, his work with the New Lost City Ramblers, and his field recordings of traditional music, especially of the rural Southeast; and Peggy (b. 1935), through her efforts as singer and scholar, alone and with her husband, Ewan MacColl (1915–1989), in perpetuating British and, more recently, American folk music.

One of the recurring themes in the secondary literature about Charles Seeger is his paradoxical nature. In her recent biography Pescatello describes him as follows:

Charles was contradictory in nature and spirit. . . . On the one hand he was a traditionalist and preserver of traditions, while on the other he was a creative genius and a champion of the new and untried. His approaches to music were both cognitive and affective; he wrote the densest essays on systems and ideas in music, while at the same time promoting lyrical tunes.[44]

This assessment is consistent with that of Henry Cowell, who in 1933 wrote that Seeger "is personally a bundle of contradictions."[45] Judith Tick describes him as a "post-Victorian rebel" suspended between two worldviews: Victorian and modernist.[46]

There are several possible ways of interpreting this inclination toward paradox and contradiction. First and foremost, Seeger's unique style of thought is the inevitable outgrowth of his Janus-like temperament: part of him always remained loyal to the intuitive and practical world of musicians, and the other part flourished in the abstract world of ideas. Beginning with the autodidactic regimen he undertook while teaching at Berkeley, Seeger was always searching for ways to mix intuitive experience with empirical confirmation and logical analysis. Yet this two-sided temperament was not always internally harmonious, as can be witnessed in his emotional breakdown during the late teens and twenties. Even though he felt a calling for musicology, he shared neither musicologists' fascination with older musical styles nor their collective indifference toward contemporary music. Thus, a certain predilection for paradox found its way into the culminating document of this early period, the treatise. This predilection became even more pronounced in his later philosophical writings. He often prefaced his latest revision of an exhaustive method of describing music by warning that verbal language and musical experience were ultimately incompatible.

Viewed more broadly, the paradoxical nature in Seeger's writings also resonates strongly with the forces of change that were at work in other fields during this period. In one sense, Seeger was a conservative; his reliance on dualistic models to explain musical experience is ultimate proof of his intellectual debt to the nineteenth century. Yet in another sense he was also discontent with the musical legacy he had inherited. The title of the treatise itself reflects the breadth of Seeger's aspirations: *Tradition and Experiment in the New Music;* he was as eager to question the traditions of the past—whether speaking as a philosopher, theorist, historian, or composer—as he was to revive them. The story of Seeger's ideal of blending music and philosophy is an eloquent testament to the modernist spirit that transformed all of the arts during the early twentieth century.

Part One

·   ·   ·   ·

Philosophical Theory

Chapter One

. . . .

Bergson's Intuition
and Seeger's Predicament

Introduction

In order to introduce Seeger's unique approach to the aesthetics of
music, it is useful to identify three distinct aspects of his life: his attitudes toward religion, science, and politics. Although Seeger wrote
little about his personal spiritual beliefs, he must have been attracted
to the mystical way of life for he refers to it frequently in his philosophical writings. He usually describes his spiritual feelings in artistic
terms as an intrinsically musical experience that transcends language.
By contrast, the methods of empirical science began to have a strong
appeal for Seeger during the 1920s as one dimension of his theory of
music criticism. This scientific dimension also played a key role in his
later writings when he developed a comprehensive method of describing music from any cultural tradition. Finally, Seeger's political
beliefs are symbolized by the conversion he underwent during the
1930s, when he discovered folk and non-Western musical traditions,
and by his later passion for developing a general scheme of musicology that would embrace them.

These same three aspects also defined the character of Seeger's
philosophical theory, and for each Seeger borrowed and adapted the
ideas of a leading early-twentieth-century philosopher: those of Henri
Bergson, Bertrand Russell, and Ralph Barton Perry. Bergson believed
that the faculty of intuition was a way of seeing into the very essence
of things — something akin to mystical revelation. His sharp dichotomy
between intuition and reason mirrors perfectly Seeger's conviction that

musical experience and verbal description are incompatible. Oddly enough, the philosopher in this trio most interested in the precision of logical analysis, Bertrand Russell, influenced Seeger less by his logic than by his ideal of combining it with mystical faith. In an early essay outlining his rational approach toward religion, Russell extols the virtues of the principle of mediation that would later help inspire Seeger's conception of musical criticism. Perry supplied Seeger with two things: a critique of Hegel, which Seeger adapted to explain the relation between music and language; and, more important, a philosophical approach that enabled Seeger to assimilate all of his interdisciplinary interests in music within a single overarching framework. Despite Seeger's often-stated contempt for philosophers who lacked musical expertise, time and time again he drew inspiration from these three thinkers, only one of whom ever wrote about music (Bergson), and then only in passing.

The purpose of part 1 is threefold: (1) to summarize the ideas of these three philosophers that helped shape Seeger's own philosophical project; (2) to examine the rather sporadic evolution of his various philosophical theories that began in the essays written in the mid-twenties and culminated with the revised version of the treatise; and finally (3) to submit Seeger's theories themselves to a close exegesis. The task of identifying the historical roots of Seeger's philosophy is particularly important, since some of the theories he borrowed can be traced back to ideas of a much older vintage.

William James, a popular American philosopher at the turn of the century, also had strong beliefs in the same three areas—religion, science, and politics—which he brought to bear upon his philosophical reflections. In a revealing portrait of James, Bertrand Russell marvels that James's philosophical approach could be nourished by so many sources: "The best people usually owe their excellence to a combination of qualities which might have been supposed incompatible, and so it was in the case of James."[1] The same can be said of Charles Seeger, and the following pages are devoted to uncovering exactly how these supposedly "incompatible" qualities all converged in his aesthetic philosophy.

The Question of Influence

The story of Charles Seeger's attempts to establish a new philosophical foundation for the study of music must begin with Henri Bergson.

Although the thought of this charismatic French thinker plays a significant role in the development of Seeger's ideal conception of musicology, for some readers his presence may be difficult to detect. As a rule, Seeger seldom provided any documentation for ideas that he either borrowed directly or adapted to suit his own purposes: his reliance on Bergson is no exception. Yet there is considerable evidence, both direct and indirect, that Bergson exercised an influence on Seeger's conception of philosophy. This evidence includes (1) references to the same synopsis of Bergson's thought in three different autobiographical memoirs; (2) two different summaries of Bergson's thought that Seeger most likely encountered sometime before 1931; and (3) internal resemblances between Bergson's and Seeger's ideas themselves. Each will be summarized in the following.

As we saw in the introduction, while Seeger was a professor of music at the University of California, he became obsessed with expanding his general knowledge of philosophy, history, and other fields outside of music. Thus it comes as no surprise that in the reading list for his inaugural senior seminar in musicology in 1915–16 he included a recent work by the English philosopher Bertrand Russell.[2] In an interview near the end of his life Seeger recalled, "One of the prescribed books that my class—an introduction to musicology—had to read, was Bertrand Russell's *Mysticism and Logic.* I had never heard of such a thing when I graduated from Harvard."[3] Seeger mentions this work in two other autobiographical materials: an extended interview entitled "Reminiscences of an American Musicologist" and an unpublished foreword for *Principia Musicologica.*[4] Since Russell wrote two works by the same title—a single essay written and published in 1914 and a larger collection of works published four years later that begins with the 1914 essay—Seeger could be referring to either one. However, a careful inspection of the collection reveals that none of the other nine essays could have served as a source of inspiration for Seeger's critical theories.[5] Most important, the first essay in the collection, "Mysticism and Logic," is unique in Russell's entire list of publications, for it includes a detailed summary and, what was rare for him, a sympathetic critique of Bergson's theory of metaphysics. Since we know that Seeger must have been acquainted with this essay by Russell by the time he assigned it to his music seminar at Berkeley, there is every reason to believe that he was exposed to the thought of Henri Bergson through the writings of Bertrand Russell (chapter 2 includes a detailed summary of Russell's essay and its significance for Seeger).

There are two other possible sources for Seeger's knowledge of Bergson. The first is in a series of lectures that Ralph Perry delivered between January and May 1918 at the University of California, Berkeley, which he published later that year as *The Present Conflict of Ideals: A Study of the Philosophical Background of the World War*. Perry provides a sixteen-page summary of Bergson's basic ideas in the context of a comprehensive panorama of recent developments in moral, political, and religious philosophy.[6] In his reminiscences Seeger describes the impact that Perry's lectures had on him:

> One day . . . a professor from Harvard named Ralph Barton Perry was advertised to give a lecture in Wheeler Hall on the general theory of value. . . . His first lecture was an eye- and ear-opener to me. There *was* such a thing as the study of value! It had been conducted mostly by psychologists and economists in Austria, and I hadn't learned of their existence.[7]

Although Seeger never explicitly mentions Perry's treatment of Bergson, it is more than likely that he either heard Perry's lecture or later read a chapter in Perry's book on the subject.

The final source is a manual on music criticism written by M.-D. Calvocoressi in 1923 to which Seeger refers in the revised version of the treatise completed in 1931. Calvocoressi discusses Bergson's conception of intuition in the context of a wide-ranging discussion of the nature of judgment.[8]

The evidence from Russell, Perry, and Calvocoressi points toward one conclusion. Whereas it is true that Seeger never mentions Bergson's theories in his philosophical writings during the 1920s and 1930s, it is more than likely that he encountered Bergson's work sometime in the teens, and that the French thinker's ideas helped shape his own philosophical theories.

Let us now turn to the ideas themselves. Before one can appreciate the profound impact that Bergson's philosophy was to have on Seeger's aesthetic ambitions, it is necessary to provide some overview of his theory of knowledge and its relevance for aesthetics.

Bergson's Theory of Intuition

It is impossible to overestimate the impact of Henri Bergson (1859–1941) in Europe during the first part of this century, which reached its zenith in the years leading up to World War I and then waned dramatically by 1945: "In the eyes of Europe's educated public he was clearly *the* philosopher, the intellectual spokesman *par excellence* of the era."[9] Born to Polish and English parents, Bergson graduated from the Ecole Normale in 1881, and in 1900 he was awarded a chair of Philosophy at the Collège de France, where during the next twenty years his reputation as a lecturer was legendary. Among the many distinctions he received are election to the prestigious Académie des Sciences Morales et Politiques and in 1927 the Nobel Prize for Literature. His best-known philosophical writings include *Time and Free Will* (*Essai sur les données immédiates de la conscience*), *Matter and Memory* (*Matière et mémoire*), and *Creative Evolution* (*L'Evolution créatrice*). His writings also sparked considerable controversy among philosophers and theologians alike, as is shown by the fact that in 1914 his publications were all placed on the Index of prohibited works by the Roman Catholic Church.[10] Combining an unusual literary gift with a keen knowledge of contemporary biological and psychological theories, Bergson developed a unique philosophical outlook that had a strong, if short-lived, influence on European and American thought during the early twentieth century.

There were two prevailing currents in French intellectual life in the late nineteenth century. The first, which can be called "scientific humanism," continued to foster the philosophical ideals of the Enlightenment.[11] Advocates of this persuasion, including Auguste Comte, relied on a naturalistic understanding of the world in which reason, order, and balance prevailed; for them, all physical or mental phenomena could be investigated with the tools of empirical science. Opposed to this view was a movement known as "religious humanism" (or "vitalism," as it was later called), whose members initially sought to revive and protect the spiritual heritage of the church. This movement reacted strongly against the ideas of the Enlightenment, arguing that activities of the mind, as witnessed in the principles of free will and spontaneity, could never be reduced to mere physical explanations. Not only did two of Bergson's teachers belong to this movement,[12] but Bergson himself continued this vitalist tradition and gave it new life.

One of the curious historical twists about Bergson's thought is that the controversies over the nature of reason and intuition he ignited in the early twentieth century reenacted some of the same philosophical debates that had occupied the German and English romantics at the turn of the previous century. In that respect, Seeger, Bergson, and Russell shared a special kinship because of the strong intellectual bond that linked them with the nineteenth century.

The best place to begin an introduction to the work of Henri Bergson is a lecture he delivered in 1911 entitled "Philosophical Intuition." In his many years of teaching the history of philosophy, he came to the conclusion that every "philosopher worthy of the name has never said more than a single thing."[13] When one studies closely a philosopher's writings, regardless of how arcane or complex they may initially appear, they can always be reduced to one simple insight that Bergson calls an "intuition." He then makes the further observation that, although philosophers may be capable of discovering some insight, they often are the last to know it, for most are unable to express the insight clearly in language. After having initially sketched out this essential intuition in writing, most philosophers undergo a lengthy process by which they correct the original formulation, and then correct the correction and so on until their intuitive point of departure has become obscured, if not lost entirely. Bergson finds it ironic that the more an author writes, the less likely he or she is to succeed in communicating the initial insight.

At first glance, Bergson appears to be attributing great importance to a mere cliché—as if he were trying to transform a commonsense notion about simplicity into a new principle of historical method. Yet the ultimate significance of this lecture is less about the history of philosophy than about Bergson's *own* philosophy.[14] This lecture serves as a telling introduction to the concept of intuition, which performs a crucial role in all his theories. The lecture also demonstrates his unusual style of thought, for he managed to integrate many disciplines— metaphysics, biology, and, to some extent, aesthetics—into a unique philosophical approach. It is this integrative and holistic approach toward philosophy that was to have such a strong influence on Charles Seeger.

One of the clearest presentations of Bergson's ideas can be found in a short treatise published in 1903: *Introduction to Metaphysics.* Bergson begins with a portrait of the human mind in which various faculties and the types of knowledge they yield are presented in opposition to one another. He draws a sharp distinction between what he calls "relative" and "absolute" knowledge. As an illustration, he considers the concept of motion. If we were to witness an object moving in space, our perception of it would vary depending on whether we ourselves were in motion or at rest. Likewise, our description of that motion would also be subject to change, depending on what symbols or system of coordinates we used to represent it. Thus our perception and resulting knowledge of the object would never be fixed but instead would be relative to the countless circumstances of each act of perception. Despite the usefulness of such "relative" knowledge in the practical world of science and in everyday life, Bergson is not content with it. Against this type of knowledge he contrasts a more immediate way of knowing that never wavers regardless of what point of view is adopted. The symbolic representation of this knowledge never becomes an issue because, for Bergson, such immediacy cannot be expressed in words or symbols. He refers to this second way of knowing as "absolute," and it is the sine qua non of metaphysics. In the *Introduction to Metaphysics* he waxes eloquent about this approach toward philosophy:

> If there exists any means of possessing a reality absolutely instead of knowing it relatively, of placing oneself within it instead of looking at it from outside points of view, of having the intuition instead of making the analysis: in short, of seizing it without any expression, translation, or symbolic representation—metaphysics is that means.[15]

Immediate knowledge achieved through intuition was the aim to which philosophers should all aspire.

For Seeger, the ultimate significance of "relative" and "absolute" knowledge has less to do with questions of physics than with the mental faculties that generate them: intellect and intuition. During the 1920s Seeger would borrow this dualistic model of the human mind and place it at the heart of his theory of music criticism.

To appreciate Bergson's conception of the human intellect, one must understand how much his entire generation was fascinated by Darwin's theory of natural selection and its potential for explaining questions outside of biology. One of the most distinctive features of Bergson's approach is the way he combines a highly personal interpretation of Darwin's theories with philosophical speculation. The intellect, he claims, has been forged by the fires of necessity, by the sheer will to survive, and the result is that it perceives itself and the world around it exclusively as a means toward some practical end. Human beings know only what they need to know. Efficiency and simplicity are the watchwords for this kind of knowledge, which Bergson describes as follows:

Life is action. Life implies the acceptance only of the *utilitarian* side of things in order to respond to them by appropriate reactions: all other impressions must be dimmed or else reach us vague and blurred. . . . My senses and my consciousness, therefore, give me no more than a practical simplification of reality.[16]

Ultimately, the cost of this practical cast of mind is the ability to grasp the true nature of things.[17]

Against the intellect, Bergson contrasts the faculty of intuition. He believed that in an earlier stage of human development intellect was balanced against a different faculty, namely instinct, which man shared with the rest of the animal kingdom. As the human species had continued to evolve, however, these animal instincts gradually were transformed into a more elevated activity called intuition that was "disinterested, self-conscious, capable of reflecting upon its object and of enlarging it indefinitely."[18] This process of transformation also meant that intuition was freed from the contingencies of the practical world and could instead turn its full attention to a form of understanding that was immediate. Intuitive knowledge requires a certain intellectual sympathy whereby the observer grasps the object from within as if the two were one. For him, intuiting is an immediate and apparently infallible activity by which "one places oneself within an object in order to coincide with what is unique in it and consequently inexpressible."[19]

It is significant that Bergson regarded such acts of mental "coincidence" as incompatible with the traditional methods of science. In his monograph on Bergson, A. R. Lacey encapsulates the opposition between science and metaphysics as follows: "Science becomes limited to the study of matter, with intelligence as its method, and metaphysics to that of mind, with intuition as its method. . . . science employs measurement, while metaphysics aims to 'sympathize' with reality."[20] Furthermore, the traditional methods of science, such as empirical observation as a means of confirming or refuting operating hypotheses, are equally flawed. By relying on overly static concepts and amassing evidence to support them, scientists end up distorting the very phenomena they are trying to explain. Indeed, Bergson goes so far as to say that cultivating intuition requires a radical reshaping of mental habits that are dominated by reason: "The mind has to do violence to itself, has to reverse the direction of the operation by which it habitually thinks, has perpetually to revise, or rather to recast, all its categories."[21]

One consequence of Bergson's strict dichotomy between intelligence and intuition is that he has little faith in the language of formal logic and mathematics. One reason for his lack of faith was that he believed logic was incapable of accounting for change. Any logical explanation was predicated on the value of analysis: the process of breaking things down into their constituent parts. Bergson explains this limitation as follows: "For the human mind is so constructed that it cannot begin to understand the new until it has done everything in its power to relate it to the old."[22] Genuine change or evolution, then, is utterly foreign to the human intellect. Bergson describes this orientation as "cinematographic," likening it to a movie camera that transforms motion into a series of fixed and static frames.[23]

Aesthetic Theories

Bergson's writings on aesthetics, though limited in number, provide a fascinating portrait in miniature of his mature philosophy. They consist primarily of a short book published in 1900 entitled *Laughter: An Essay on the Meaning of the Comic* (*Le Rire*) and various supplemental remarks scattered throughout his works.[24] As its title implies, *Laughter* is a treatise on comedy, where Bergson presents a simple but controversial theory of humor, applying it mostly to drama, and then expands his focus to consider broader aesthetic matters. In many ways, all of Bergson's philosophical writings were cut from the same cloth. Although there is no evidence that Seeger read the essay on comedy, throughout his early writings he applied Bergson's basic definitions to the question of musical perception.

Bergson begins by contrasting the creative artist's understanding of the world with that of the rest of humanity. For the vast majority, Bergson believes that a "dense and opaque veil" has been interposed that limits their view of nature and even of themselves.[25] This blindness is due to the intrinsic limits of the nonartist's intellect, which is solely occupied with survival and practical gain. Viewed against this backdrop, the artistic sensibility is a virtual miracle:

So art, whether it be painting or sculpture, poetry or music, has no other object than to brush aside the utilitarian symbols, the conventional and socially accepted generalities, in short, everything that veils reality from us, in order to bring us face to face with reality itself.[26]

Yet, the "natural detachment" that artists possess, a kind of "virginal manner" of perceiving,[27] is limited to one sense alone. For each artist it is as if the curse of pragmatism had been only partly dispelled, the "veil" had been lifted only halfway. By proposing that these artistic gifts were distributed to different senses in different individuals, Bergson was able to account for the full diversity of the arts.

Later in the same essay Bergson identifies two characteristics of artistic intuition: its individuality and its incompatibility with conventional language. These two characteristics were to bear the richest fruit in Seeger's critique of musicology.

For Bergson, a work of art is neither a statement of universal truth nor a vision of mystical unity in which the artist becomes one with the universe. Instead, an artwork captures some finite, particular aspect of "reality" that is utterly unique, whether of the natural world or the inner psychological world of its author. Again, it is a question of the artist's highly developed powers of perception, since the "*individuality* of things or of beings escapes us, unless it is materially to our advantage to perceive it."[28] What the musician composes, the poet writes, or the architect designs, all, by definition, elude any form of generality. The products they create cannot be represented by any symbol, type, or category.

The second characteristic is a consequence of the mind's natural orientation toward pragmatism. The rational intellect invented language for the same reason that it organizes and classifies the things around it: to derive the greatest profit. In short, practical intelligence *precedes* language. Thus Bergson argues that speech, as a whole, reinforces the innate human tendency to generalize and simplify. Thus, it comes as no surprise that when faced with the task of describing works of art or the process that created them, language is utterly powerless. The individuality of an artist's vision escapes classification and resists generality. Over and over again, Bergson employs turns-of-phrase and metaphors that focus on some secret internal life that artists are able to convey. He says "It is the inner life of things that [the artist] sees appearing through their forms and colors."[29] Artists evoke "certain rhythms of life and breath that are closer to man than his inmost feelings," and these rhythms have nothing in common with language. Whether it be a radiant color, a pattern of verse, or a "rhythm of life," the artwork is able to transmit the unique character of these things in a way that words alone cannot. Artists are endowed with the ability to "compel us, willy-nilly, to fall in with [their vision], like passers-by who join in a dance."[30]

Seeger's Writings

Seeger's early ideas about the nature of musical knowledge are documented in three sources: two short essays entitled "On the Principles of Musicology"[31] (hereafter abbreviated as "Principles") and "Prolegomena to Musicology: The Problem of the Musical Point of View and the Bias of Linguistic Presentation"[32] (hereafter abbreviated as "Prolegomena") and the treatise on composition. When examining these works, one might expect a gradual pattern of evolution to emerge as Seeger encountered the ideas of three contemporary philosophers— Bergson, Russell, and Perry—and then, one after another, adapted them to his theory of knowledge. In fact, Seeger's philosophical project matured at an uneven pace: some aspects of his theory of knowledge appear only in the treatise, whereas others are evident in prenascent form as early as "Principles." Thus, for simplicity's sake, here and in chapter 2 I will focus on how the work of one philosopher influenced a single early essay: Bergson in "Principles" (1924) and Russell in "Prolegomena" (1925). Chapter 3 explores Perry's influence in both essays, and chapter 4 traces how all three philosophers helped shape the formation of *Tradition and Experiment in the New Music.*

Seeger opens his essay "Principles" with a diagnosis of the current state of musicology. He observes that

no adequate statement of the premises (fundamental assumptions), no satisfactory definition of its data, nor of the scope of [musicology] has ever been made, and no organised [*sic*] study of music comparable to the study of language, physics, biology, astronomy, etc., can be said to exist.[33]

In his mind, since most musicologists are blind to the limits, as well as the possibilities, of thinking about music, they have no guiding spirit or philosophical purpose. It is this gap in the "higher organization of the study of music" that he hopes his essay will help fill.

Needless to say, Seeger's characterization of the discipline as disorganized and without any guiding spirit is somewhat off the mark. By

the mid-1920s, musicology had already developed into a rich humanistic tradition, beginning in Germany during the eighteenth century
and continuing into the nineteenth and twentieth centuries in England and France. Indeed, the very title of a watershed essay by the
Viennese music historian Guido Adler, "Umfang, Methode und Ziel
der Musikwissenschaft," includes precisely what Seeger claimed previous musicologists had ignored: namely, scope, method, and purpose
(chapter 7 explores Adler's thought in greater detail).[34] If Seeger had
limited his comments to the state of musicology in America, he would
have been closer to the truth, for during the 1920s the discipline in
this country was still in its infancy. Such hyperbole on Seeger's part
can most likely be attributed to an excess of polemical zeal.

Next Seeger provides a brief inventory of the human mind by outlining what kinds of mental faculties are involved in *any* field of inquiry. Although scholarly studies may vary in their premises or methods, Seeger concludes that the one thing they all have in common is
the act of "judgment," which he divides into two parts: an "intuitive"
aspect and a "deliberative" or, what might be called, a rational aspect.
Next he considers two kinds of people who actually write about music, each with their own special aim: musicians write about music in
order to benefit the art itself, and philosophers write about music with
the aim of extending and refining "the universe of discourse."[35] In this
section of the essay Seeger blames both groups for overemphasizing
the "deliberative" or rational aspect of judgment at the expense of the
mind's intuitive capacity for music. He is disturbed that, over and over
again, musicologists fail to adopt a point of view that reflects the interests or experiences of the practicing musician. Instead, he argues,
they usually borrow the methods and approaches of disciplines outside of music to talk about their art.

Seeger's analysis of these two groups underlines the dualistic character of his vision of musicology. The basic assumptions of this vision
can be summarized in the form of three dichotomies or oppositions:

1. musical versus nonmusical
2. rational versus nonrational
3. musical versus linguistic

Even though in his critique of musicology Seeger never presents these
dichotomies as separate entities, he nevertheless places great empha-

sis on the first and third, and the second is implied throughout his commentary. It is my contention that all three show the profound influence of Henri Bergson on Seeger's theory of musical knowledge, and, furthermore, that any analysis of Seeger's philosophical works that fails to take them into account is inherently misguided.

Musical Versus Nonmusical

The best place to begin examining the basis for this dichotomy is to determine the precise meaning of each term. Seeger was of two minds about the matter of definition. At several junctures in his two essays he explicitly avoids any clear definition of "musical," preferring to speak in tautologies and, thereby, shroud the concept in mystery. Yet at other times he offers a more existential approach, assuming that any practicing musician should know what it means to be "musical." Taken together, the two definitions shed considerable light on the intuitive roots of Seeger's philosophical approach.

In the essay "Principles," Seeger speaks in an oracular tone about the "musical" point of view, as if it were some kind of obscure prophecy that needs to be deciphered. Music, he proclaims, "is not something else, whether it be expressed by one word or a host of them"; elsewhere he says, "To the musician, music is music." [36] At first glance, this statement is puzzling—an exercise in tautology more than musicology. But the structure of the utterance itself suggests that Seeger is borrowing one of the traditional methods of mystical thought. In a footnote in his essay "Prolegomena" Seeger summarizes the various ways in which mystics use language to communicate their insights:

Broadly speaking, . . . the mystical use of language is characterized by paradox, contradiction and unfettered meaning. The mystic speaks for effect, primarily: accuracy in meaning is irrelevant. Mysticism is intentionally non-logical and non-methodical. [37]

In this aside Seeger provides a veritable catalogue of the writing styles and rhetorical postures that mystics employ. If we apply this catalogue to the statement "music is music," we see an author speaking "for effect," with little interest in communicating a precise message. The fact that Seeger neglects to define the terms in this dichotomy may have been a conscious strategy of avoidance rather than an oversight, as though the act of definition were a challenge against the very point he was trying to articulate.

By contrast, in the essay "Prolegomena" Seeger presents another definition. Whereas the notion of "musical" cannot be expressed or communicated in words, it can be understood by *engaging* in some musical activity:

If an enquirer does not know what the musical point of view is, he should study music until he does. He cannot expect to find out by studying language.[38]

One discovers the musical point of view more by deeds than by words. In other words, to find out the meaning of the term "musical," an individual must perform some "musical" task, which is "the complex of habit, foresight, feeling, etc. of a skillful musician during the act of musical composition, performance or audition."[39] This statement tells us that Seeger regards this notion as a curious blend of disparate elements. Apparently, to be musical is to combine the practical with the emotional; that is, the various skills required in executing a piece of music must be mixed with the rich emotional response that such music might evoke.

Rational versus Nonrational

The second dichotomy, rational versus nonrational, is the most elusive of the three. Although in his early writings Seeger was content to suggest or hint at his attitude toward rational discourse, this dichotomy is essential if we are to appreciate the consequences of his ideal conception of "musical." In the essay "Principles" he treats the term "philosophy" as a synonym for all nonmusical fields in the natural and social sciences as well as the humanities. He asserts that commentators from outside of music, or, as he prefers to call them, "philosophers,"[40] generally lack musical fluency and technique, and, conversely, that musicians lack fluency in fields outside of music. He concludes that "the philosopher's ignorance of music and the musician's ignorance of language dance a strange jig indeed."[41]

This "dance" of mutual ignorance reveals much about Seeger's underlying attitude toward science and rational thought in general. He begins by claiming that he holds no prejudice against the sciences per se and, more important, that he recognizes the legitimacy of employing methods that are appropriate to achieve the unique demands of each science.[42] However, his opinion of scientific endeavors that have some bearing on musical experience is much less charitable. He warns that, until the findings of the sciences are adapted so as to take musical technique into account, they cannot be accepted as genuine contributions to the field of musicology. In order for scientists to satisfy Seeger's criterion of "musical," they must speak the language of music, not of mathematics.

For musicologists who knowingly borrow the methods of the natural sciences or humanities Seeger shows even less tolerance. Despite whatever new and fascinating aspects of musical experience such research might uncover, these pursuits all suffer from the same shortcoming. For example, inasmuch as the physicist studies music as a phenomenon of sound, the psychologist examines the nature of musical cognition, the sociologist explores the social factors of a performance, or a philosopher uses a musical work to illustrate an aesthetic theory, none of them treats what Seeger regards as the music itself. In all four cases, music "acquires predicates and becomes . . . *something else*," either sound waves, a behavioral pattern, a social value, or a manifestation of the sublime.[43] Thus the opposition between musical and nonmusical ultimately depends on a fundamental opposition between rational and nonrational thought. When musicologists appropriate the methods of any of these various fields, they betray their calling as musicians. Like Esau, they are willing to sell their musical birthrights for a mess of scientific pottage.

With the overview of two of Seeger's three dichotomies now complete, it is appropriate to draw some initial conclusions. By characterizing the problem of musicology as a failure to address purely "musical" questions, Seeger is mixing apples and oranges. In the name of a self-proclaimed standard to protect the purity of the art, he attacks virtually any form of cross-fertilization between music and other fields of knowledge. According to him, composers, performers, and listeners who use mathematical logic are anathema. Likewise, the concept of musical becomes a yardstick with which he measures the worth of any musicological undertaking. Yet, surely he does not expect all scholars, whether of the sciences or the humanities, to think like practicing musicians. Criticizing an acoustician for not addressing questions of musical technique is like criticizing a composer for committing an error in arithmetic. Compositions need not be judged by standards that apply to mathematical logic or the sciences; by the same token, scientific experiments, whether in acoustics or musical anthropology, need not be judged by aesthetic standards that apply to composition.

Musical versus Linguistic

The third dichotomy Seeger employs in the early essays is more of a refinement of the first dichotomy than something altogether new. He distinguishes between musical experience itself and the language used to describe that experience, or, more simply put, between music and language.[44] Besides logic, the use of language is the only other common denominator that unites all the fields of knowledge that Seeger has dubbed "non-musical." He writes, "The musician, in so far as he talks and writes and reads about music, comes to regard it from a non-musical point of view."[45] Language is the fly in the musical ointment, so to speak, and the greatest impediment to achieving the prize of purely musical knowledge. Verbal accounts of an individual's musical perception can neither express its unique character nor transmit that character to anyone else. Hence, as a mirror of musical experience, language distorts as much as it reflects. Despite the insights an acoustician, a music physiologist, or an aesthetician may have about some musical phenomenon, their insights lose what Seeger regards as their purely "musical" value the moment they are written down.

Seeger is also troubled that society as a whole prefers language over music for the simple reason that more people are fluent with words than with notes and rhythms. What Seeger fears most is the impact of this widespread bias on the field of musicology. Problems ensue when musicologists are unaware that their mode of discourse is controlled by the habits and conventions of language. He characterizes the situation with a political metaphor: "This naturally tends to confirm the . . . view of music as a lower class for which the higher class, language, can legislate."[46] One of Seeger's ultimate goals in developing a philosophical basis for musicology is to restore a relatively equal balance of power between an individual's musical perceptions and the linguistic tools available to describe them.

Seeger then goes one step further in his diagnosis of the incompatibility between music and speech. He points out that, inasmuch as music is a nonlinguistic art, and that the only means of discussing it is in language, we are caught in an insoluble dilemma. To dramatize this dilemma, Seeger invents a new term, the "linguo-centric predica-ment," which, in his mind, is the quintessential philosophical problem of the discipline.[47] His attraction to the notion of a "predicament" or dilemma represents one aspect of his thought that was highly influ-enced by the early twentieth-century American philosopher Ralph Barton Perry (1876–1957). It will be useful to discuss Perry's ideas in some detail before we consider in what ways Seeger adapted them to his own ends.

Born in Vermont, Perry was educated at Harvard, where he even-tually taught for forty-four years. A prolific author, he wrote over two hundred essays and two dozen books, and during his lifetime was re-garded as the greatest authority on the thought of William James. Perry's two most notable contributions to philosophy were his virulent attacks against neo-Hegelian idealism, the most prevalent philosoph-ical movement in England and America during the early twentieth century, and his later attempts to create an all-encompassing theory of value. Both were to play a crucial role in the formation of Seeger's ideal conception of musicology.

As was true for many intellectuals during the late nineteenth cen-tury, Perry's training as a philosopher coincided with an enormous re-vival of Hegel's "idealist" theories that swept across Europe and America. One of the fundamental tenets shared by any "idealist" ap-proach is that the natural world exists only insofar as there is a human mind to perceive or, in some sense, to know it. Perry, however, could not accept this "idealist" view of the world, and he has been credited with firing "the first literary gun in the notable campaign . . . against idealism."[48] In his essay "The Ego-Centric Predicament" he attacks Hegel's idealist system using a principle of inductive logic known as the "Method of Difference," which was first devised in the nineteenth century by John Stuart Mill. This method requires that a state of af-fairs be imagined first with a given property and then without it in or-der to determine what difference the given property makes.[49] Perry uses this method to determine whether the fact that an object is or is not perceived by a human subject changes that object in any way; to put it another way, whether a given object's existence depends on the relation between the knowing subject and the known object.

In order to discover if possible exactly how a thing is modified by the cogni-tive relationship, I look for instances of things *out* of this relationship, in or-

der that I may compare them with instances of things *in* this relationship. But
I can find no such instances, because "finding" is a variety of the very relationship I am trying to eliminate.[50]

Since the self can never gain the objectivity required to view its own
acts of consciousness, Perry is faced with a paradox, or what he calls
the "ego-centric predicament." Such a predicament shows that one of
the fundamental premises of the idealist theory of knowledge is beyond confirmation. Perry ends up arguing that this lack of confirma-
bility undermines one of the crucial tenets of all idealist philosophies,
thereby sounding the death knell for that approach once and for all. If
Perry's point is correct, then the only way anyone could accept the
idealist view of human knowledge would be on the basis of sheer faith.
To Perry, such an approach would no longer deserve to be called
philosophy.

The differences between Perry's and Seeger's conceptions of a philosophical "predicament" tell us much about the underlying motivations
of each author. The first difference concerns a contrast in scope between the two notions of "predicament": Perry's is broad, Seeger's is
narrow. Whereas Perry concentrates on the act of knowing itself,
Seeger focuses on two particular ways of knowing music: "thinking
about music," which involves some form of language, and "thinking in
music," which by definition excludes the use of language.[51] To put it
another way, Seeger retains the basic structure of Perry's argument,
but he substitutes a "speaking subject" in place of Perry's "thinking
subject." In so doing, Seeger reconceives this epistemological problem so that it is more relevant to a nonverbal art form such as music.

Ultimately, the most profound difference between the two thinkers
is less the way each applies the "Method of Difference" to a specific
philosophical problem than the way each interprets the results. For
one, it serves as a means of refuting a widely accepted theory; for the
other, a means of stimulating the development of a new theory. When
Perry discovers that he cannot verify the reliability of an assumption
about human knowledge, he abandons the assumption; when Seeger
discovers that he cannot verify the reliability of a verbal statement
about music, he abandons the criterion of verifiability. Seeger regards
the discrepancy between music and all verbal accounts of it as a genuine insight into human knowledge rather than as a flaw in his own
theory of knowledge. Rather than using the "linguo-centric predicament" as a means of proving that a basic assumption about musical ex-

perience is untenable, Seeger accepts the predicament itself as a modus operandi. What is a predicament for one is a basic premise for the other.

But what if Seeger's application of the "Method of Difference" to the discrepancy between music and language were interpreted differently—more in keeping with the approach Ralph Perry takes in his original article? Perry's strategy for repudiating the late-nineteenth-century followers of Hegel could be reenacted against Seeger himself. One could test the reliability of Seeger's claim by employing the "Method of Difference," whereby a situation is first imagined with a given property and then compared to the same situation in which that property has been removed. However, when one tries to imagine some thought about music that is nonlinguistic and then compare it to the same thought expressed in language, it is impossible. Indeed, language is the very means by which the "Method of Difference" is carried out. This mental experiment would yield yet a new paradox that could be dubbed the "musico-centric predicament." It could be argued that Seeger's conception of "musical" must be abandoned before we could expect to produce any genuine insights into the nature of musical knowledge.

Yet such a logical inconsistency about our view of language would be grist for Seeger's music-critical mill. Does not this line of reasoning tell us more about the limits of the "Method of Difference" itself than about language? It could be argued that the "musico-centric predicament" proves only that Perry's mental test is inadequate as a means of evaluating one's preconceptions about language. One needs a new kind of objectivity, at least something different from that offered by the "Method of Difference," to be able to explore fully the nature of language. In fact, such a neutral point of view, one that resists the natural limitations of language, is precisely what Seeger was trying to find.

Influence on Seeger

Having completed this overview of Bergson's and Seeger's ideas, we are now in a better position to study the relationship between them. There are two principal similarities between their approaches, each of which will be discussed in brief: the incompatibility between the immediacy of artistic experience and its expression in language; and a fundamental distrust of science and rational thought. Despite Seeger's persistent attacks against philosophers for their ignorance of the arts, this comparison reveals that he relied on contemporary philosophical thought as a foundation for his vision of musicology.

Henri Bergson and Charles Seeger were both fascinated by the possibility of the mind's immediate apprehension of an object: immediacy is as essential for Bergson's theory of intuition as it is for Seeger's conception of "musical" knowledge. Even more important, for both thinkers, this kind of immediate knowledge is ineffable. According to Bergson, the principal reason that words alone can never express what is unique about an artwork is that uniqueness contradicts the basic function of language: to simplify and generalize. Although Seeger focuses less on the uniqueness of musical works, he, too, believes that musical experience is intuitive and can never be fully expressed or communicated to others by means of language.[52] Seeger's skeptical attitude toward speech is encapsulated in his notion of the "linguo-centric predicament."

The second point of similarity between Bergson and Seeger is that both harbored a deep distrust of science and the traditional tools of scientific research. The strict opposition between intellect and intuition is one of the basic axioms of Bergson's philosophical outlook. Yet this same opposition lies at the heart of Seeger's objections to traditional musicology. Though in his writings Seeger never emphasizes the dichotomy between rational and nonrational thought, nonetheless it is strongly implied by his repudiation of musicologists who borrow from fields outside of music such as acoustics, cognitive psychology, or linguistics. Since the one thing these fields have in common is that they all conform to the standards of scientific investigation, it is fair to conclude that in the mid-1920s Seeger regarded science and, indeed, any form of rational thought, as incompatible with the realm of purely "musical" knowledge.

A comparison of Seeger and Bergson could not be considered complete if it did not take into consideration those ways in which the two thinkers' work diverged. Where they differ most is in the scope of their overall project and the role that immediacy plays in it. Bergson maintains the widest possible definition of the term, applying it as readily to the natural and artistic world as to the psychological world of the self. His interest in such direct knowledge is part of a broader ambition to study all activities of the human mind. Seeger's project, by contrast, is more limited in scope. Although he explores some of the same epistemological questions that occupied Bergson, he does so within the context of musical perception. Whereas Bergson addresses all branches of art and the special sensibility they inspire, Seeger confines his attention to a single artistic medium.

During the years since Bergson first published his ideas, several fundamental objections have been raised against the concept of intuition and its relation to his philosophy as a whole. While, needless to say, this is hardly the place to assess Bergson's overall contributions to philosophy, a brief look at one of the most common criticisms raised against it helps place Seeger's intuitionist theory in a new light.

Any reader of Bergson knows how appealing his method of presentation can be. He introduces his theory of intuition without any logical argument, as though the idea were so convincing by itself that no evidence was necessary. What he does provide in the way of explanation is usually confined to metaphors and analogies. Indeed, Bergson is remarkably adept at describing an experience which he claims is indescribable. His narrative style is so spellbinding, the images he conjures up so provocative, that the reader ignores the contradiction between medium and message. There is no little irony in the fact that Bergson uses the written word to proclaim his prophecy about intuition—that it cannot be expressed in words.

The question arises whether Bergson's theories, strictly speaking, even belong to the discipline of philosophy. In a colorful survey of early twentieth-century intellectual history, George Santayana provides an apt description of the French philosopher: "He is persuasive without argument. . . . he moves in the atmosphere of science and free thought, yet seems to transcend them and to be secretly religious."[53] In fact, Santayana does not consider Bergson's work to be philosophy at all but rather something closer to "literary psychology" or even "mystical poetry" masquerading as philosophical reflection.[54] It is worth remembering that Bergson received the Nobel Prize in 1928 for his achievements in literature, not philosophy.

The question of style certainly distinguishes Bergson's work from that of Seeger. Any student of Seeger's writings knows that he possessed neither the poetic inclination nor the literary grace for intimating the unfathomable. His writing style could be characterized as earnest if not labored, and, though he occasionally relied on a metaphor to make his point, he certainly did not possess Bergson's knack for suggestive imagery and turns-of-phrase. If, as Santayana argued, Bergson was guilty of crafting "mystical poetry," then the worst thing Seeger could be accused of would be writing "mystifying" prose.

However, Santayana's scathing critique touches on a fundamental difference between the two thinkers. If Bergson's ultimate purpose is to present a new theory of reality revealed by intuition, Seeger's aim is to use intuitive insight as the point of departure for a theory of knowledge about music. The difference is that, for Seeger, intuition is the beginning of a vast musical and philosophical journey, not the final point of arrival. Whereas Bergson believed that intuition held the ultimate secrets of human knowledge, Seeger contended that it was merely the first stage in an ongoing critical process that would eventually employ mental faculties other than intuition. Just as reason is incomplete without the leaven of creativity, so imagination alone can never succeed without the tempering force of reason. That mixture of imagination and reason is the subject of the following chapter.

Chapter Two

.   .   .   .

Russell's Synthesis
of Mysticism and Logic

In the introduction to his vast compendium, *Tradition and Experiment in the New Music,* Charles Seeger reveals a new dimension in his ideal conception of musicology:

We may grant that there is much about the art of composition that cannot be reasoned about—much that cannot even be spoken about in any way. But we also hold that there are certain aspects of it that can be, and—in view of the customs of our day—that must be organized in the most rigorously logical manner possible.[1]

Thus far the picture I have painted of Seeger's musical-critical approach has been strongly colored by his fascination for the powers of intuition. Yet a portrait of Seeger's early speculations on music would not be complete if it did not include his devotion to matters of the rational intellect. As will be recalled from chapter 1, he felt that mathematical logic and the methods of science constituted an impediment to discovering the true foundation of musical scholarship, and his early writings are suffused with a skeptical attitude toward rational thought. But by the time he wrote the initial draft of the treatise in 1930–31, Seeger had undergone a virtual conversion in his attitude toward science. The skepticism he had manifested in the early essay "Principles" had all but disappeared, and in its place was a much more balanced view of the virtues and the limits of science.[2] Seeger understood that reason was indispensable to a philosophical investigation of musicology and, ultimately, to the countless practical tasks of the working musicologist. The challenge he faced was to find some way of exploiting the tools of language and logical analysis without having to compromise his ideal of musical intuition. The solution to this challenge was to be found in an unlikely place: the religious writings of Bertrand Russell. This chapter presents an overview of Russell's early writings on the relation between spirituality and philosophy, and then explores the influence of these ideas on Seeger's approach to aesthetics. Following this there appears a brief assessment of the thought of Karl Pearson, a prominent nineteenth-century advocate of "positivism," as well as a summary of the curious parallels between Seeger's theory of music criticism and William James's theory of pragmatism.

Seeger's relationship with Bertrand Russell has several dimensions. He first encountered Russell's writings at Berkeley during the intellectual "journey" he embarked upon with Herbert E. Cory, a young English professor, through a broad landscape of humanistic disciplines including philosophy. As mentioned in chapter 1, there is substantial evidence that Russell's essay "Mysticism and Logic" had a formative influence on Seeger. Not only did Seeger include this collection on a required reading list for his senior seminar in musicology in 1915–16, but over fifty years later, in the final section of his article "Preface to a Critique of Music," he refers to one of the key arguments of the opening essay in the collection.[3] Seeger also provisionally named a retrospective collection of critical essays *Principia Musicologica* in honor of Russell's groundbreaking study of mathematical logic, *Principia Mathematica.* In addition, during his last years in Berkeley, Seeger held Russell in high esteem for his outspoken commitment to pacifism—one critic has even described Russell as Seeger's "special spiritual mentor."[4] Although it is impossible to determine how many of Russell's numerous publications Seeger may have read, it is fair to say that at least one of the Englishman's essays served as a source of inspiration throughout his life.

Bertrand Russell was among the most outstanding British thinkers of the twentieth century, renowned for his contributions in mathematics and philosophy, as well as for his passionate and often controversial views on various moral and political issues of his time. His initial interest in philosophy grew out of his study of logic. In *Principia Mathematica* (1910–13), which he coauthored with Alfred North Whitehead, he attempted to prove that the laws of mathematics could in principle be stated in terms of and, hence, reduced to logic. Later Russell joined G. E. Moore to lead a revolt against neo-Hegelian idealism, the predominant philosophical school in England at the time and, in its place, helped pioneer what has come to be known as the "analytical" approach. For them, the proper method of philosophy should be analysis, a kind of enlightened common sense, by which any problem can be reduced to its constituent parts and, more important, any proposition about the world can be confirmed in isolation. Yet it was Russell's popular writings that earned him the greatest fame. An aristocrat by birth, he published numerous iconoclastic essays on religion, war, sexuality, and education that captured the public imagination and occasionally landed him in prison. He has been hailed as a "prophet of liberal humanism, a hero of those who regard themselves as rationalists, . . . devoted to the cause of human freedom . . . and of social and political progress."[5]

One of the curiosities of Russell's intellectual temperament is that, alongside his passion for philosophy and mathematical logic, he also harbored a fascination for the nature of religious belief. Whereas he later gained notoriety for his bitter attacks against organized religion through a series of essays and speeches such as "What I Believe" (1925) and "Why I Am Not a Christian" (1927), his early writings display a generally sympathetic attitude toward religious faith. Russell's interest in religious contemplation and its relationship to reason flowered during the most productive and, in some respects, most tumultuous years of his life: 1902–1914. His interest in mysticism was more than a passing fancy; in fact, it was based on personal experience. In 1902 and 1911 he underwent extraordinary experiences (some describe them as "conversions")[6] that deepened his curiosity about mystical thought.

During the early 1900s Russell had gradually become estranged from his first wife, Alys, and, upon meeting Lady Ottoline Morrell, a fellow aristocrat and a lover of the arts, he discovered a new realm of human emotion. In a letter written during the summer of 1911, Russell confides that he had found an "inward harmony"; he adds, "All I have felt and thought is fused into a whole, in which I can live without constraint."[7] Whether mystical or not, this experience served as the inspiration for an outpouring of literary activity that not only was far removed from his interests in logic and analytical philosophy but also touched a wide variety of genres including novella, allegory, essay, and autobiography.[8] This outburst of creativity culminated in two works: "Prisons," an unfinished manuscript outlining a rational conception of

religion, and "Mysticism and Logic," an essay that was to have a significant impact on Charles Seeger.

"Prisons" is without question the most mystical piece of work that
Russell ever initiated. Originally, it was to be a joint project with his
mistress, Lady Morrell, in which they hoped to translate their emotional and spiritual bond into a vision of a nondogmatic and nonsec-
tarian religion. In "Prisons" he hoped to record the fruits of their fre-
quent and impassioned religious debates and, in the process, to
accommodate her mystical faith with his own skeptical doubt. However, when the fires of their summer romance eventually burned out,
Russell's enthusiasm for trying to rationalize religion had also begun
to wane. Although the original manuscript of their collaboration,
numbering over 129 pages, is now lost, Russell reiterated its central
thesis and even incorporated entire passages from it in various other
writings during this period.[9]

Russell's letters reveal that the Dutch philosopher Benedictus de
Spinoza (1632–1677) also helped shape his spiritual ideas during this
period. Russell had admired the thought of the seventeenth-century
philosopher beginning as early as 1894 when he wrote to his wife:

> I wish I had got hold of Spinoza two years ago instead of Thomas à Kempis:
> he would have suited me far better: he preaches a rich voluptuous asceticism
> based on a vast undefined mysticism, which even now has seized hold of my
> imagination most powerfully.[10]

Russell's interest in Spinoza was renewed in the course of writing two
reviews of recent works by and about Spinoza for *The Nation*.[11] Though
Russell found Spinoza's ethical theories rather elusive, he took solace
in what he regarded as a kindred view of mysticism: "a function balancing reason and emotion."[12]

Several years later Russell returned to the subject of mystical
thought but with a more detached and objective frame of mind. In the
winter of 1914 he wrote a speech entitled "Mysticism and Logic,"
which he delivered five times in all, twice in England and three times
during his first trip to America.[13] Later that year the speech was published in the *Hibbert Journal,* and it is in this form that Seeger must
have first encountered it.[14] In 1918 Russell included the speech as the
opening work in a collection of essays bearing the same name. The essay explores the nature of mystical insight and its relationship to math-

ematical logic, and though Russell is more at home with the latter, his remarks reveal an unmistakable respect for the mystical cast of mind.

Over the course of his life, Seeger, though curious about mystical ideas and systems of thought, never became a practicing mystic. What interested Seeger most about Russell's essay was the epistemological assumptions he adopted, that is, his model of the human mind as a balance between conflicting forces. Since the same ideal of mediation helped these two thinkers solve such different problems—a rational view of religion, on the one hand, and a theory of music criticism, on the other—it is worth discussing the essay in some detail.

In "Mysticism and Logic" Russell proposes an ideal synthesis of two fundamental and conflicting human impulses: the mystical and the rational. In his view, the history of philosophy serves as a textbook of the different ways in which these conflicting impulses have been fused: "The greatest men who have been philosophers have felt the need both of science and of mysticism." [15] Although in the essay's introductory section Russell illustrates this ideal with excerpts from the writings of three ancient Greek philosophers, Heraclitus, Parmenides, and Plato, his overall purpose is less historical than analytical. The heart of the essay is an analysis of the limits of mystical thought.

Russell isolates four characteristics that he believes all mystical doctrines share: (1) a strict opposition between the faculties of intuition and intelligence, and a belief that the former is superior to the latter; (2) the principle of monism or pantheism, that is, the belief in the underlying unity of all things in the universe; (3) the denial of time; and (4) the denial of the distinction between good and evil. With this catalogue in hand, Russell proceeds to refute all four characteristics. For my purposes, Russell's commentary on the first characteristic is the most important, for it would serve as one of the philosophical seeds that later took root in Seeger's theory of musical knowledge.

Russell attacks the assumption that the cognitive faculties of reason and intuition are exact opposites and, by extension, that the worlds of science and mystical religion are incompatible and mutually exclusive. He chooses Henri Bergson as the prototype of a mystical philosopher, and, following a brief summary of the French philosopher's principal arguments, provides a refutation of each one. Russell's choice of Bergson is no accident, for in March 1912 he had delivered an exhaustive and derisive repudiation of Bergson's philosophical theories at a Cambridge academic society called "The Heretics," which apparently launched Russell's career as a public speaker.[16] Yet, while the first and third sections of "Mysticism and Logic" can be interpreted as an abbreviated reenactment of his earlier lecture, the tone is more subdued and conciliatory. Russell's arguments will be briefly summarized in the following.

As his point of departure, Russell questions the premise that intelligence is a purely practical faculty. He takes Bergson to task for relying so heavily on Darwin's biological theories, since it is only by means of reason and scientific inference that such theories could ever have been developed in the first place. Instead, he argues, assuming that Darwin's theory of natural selection is correct, then *all* our mental faculties, not merely the intellect, must have been developed as the species struggled to survive.[17]

Next Russell reassesses Bergson's definition of the two faculties in question and, in the process, presents what he considers an honest account of the merits and shortcomings of each. Intuition, he proposes, "is greater, as a rule, in children than in adults, in the uneducated than in the educated."[18] It is most effective in practical matters such as distinguishing between friendship and hostility or especially in judging the subtleties of human character and personality. If love or self-preservation is at stake, for example, Russell admits that intuition "will act sometimes . . . with a swiftness and precision which are astonishing to the critical intellect."[19] Despite this uncanny skill of discrimination, however, intuition is not immune from error. By contrast, the faculty of reason is indispensable as a way of tempering and otherwise guiding the insight initially discovered through mystical revelation. The most obvious advantage of our reasoning capacity arises in the event that two intuitions of a single object, whether by different people or by the same person at different times, contradict one another. If each intuition is accepted as absolutely true, then how can a dispute between conflicting "truths" be settled? Russell's answer to this question is that reason can be a force of mediation, an agent of arbitration "which tests our beliefs by their mutual compatibility, and examines, in doubtful cases, the possible sources of error on the one side and on the other."[20]

Having completed his reappraisal of the two human faculties, Russell then concludes that reason is more appropriate for philosophical reflection. To be successful, the philosopher must be liberated from the life of instinct and attain "a certain aloofness from all mundane hopes and fears."[21] Since philosophy, for most people, has never been a means of ensuring either their survival or their discrimination of human character, it is hardly the best arena for intuition to prove itself. Russell is led to the conclusion that, in matters of philosophical contemplation, intellect is superior to intuition.

Yet, in saying this, Russell is by no means claiming that intuition is better left in the nursery. Ideally the two faculties should be interdependent, one counterbalancing and complementing the other. Thus, the most painstaking scientific investigation "may be fostered and nourished by that very spirit of reverence in which mysticism lives and moves."[22] As an absolute creed about the world, mysticism alone is inadequate, but as an occasional attitude, emotion, or source of inspiration, it is priceless.

> It is common to speak of an opposition between instinct and reason. . . . But in fact the opposition . . . is mainly illusory. Instinct, intuition, or insight is what first leads to the beliefs which subsequent reason confirms or confutes; but the confirmation, where it is possible, consists, in the last analysis, of agreement with other beliefs no less instinctive. Reason is a harmonizing, controlling force rather than a creative one. Even in the most purely logical realm, it is insight that first arrives at what is new.[23]

In Russell's model these two mental faculties are linked in a symbiotic union.

In this overview of "Mysticism and Logic" I have focused primarily on Russell's own fascination, at least until World War I, with mystical revelation. The manuscript "Prisons," which he and his mistress left unfinished, reflects his desire to transform their mutual passion for mystical contemplation and for each other into a rational conception of faith. If "Prisons" was born out of the twin fires of romance and spiritual rapture, then "Mysticism and Logic" sprang from the dying embers of the same flames.

Since 1914 Russell's ideal synthesis of mysticism and logic has received scant critical attention. The question arises: What is the significance of Russell's early writings on religion, since they disagree so violently with his general philosophical temperament? Alan Wood, author of the first biography of Russell, captures well the incongruity between "Mysticism and Logic" and the rest of Russell's writings on religion:

This is the great paradox of Russell. All his instincts were on the side of the "rationalists"; his greatest hatred was for those who exalted emotion, or any sort of mystic intuition, at the expense of reason. But because Russell was the greatest rationalist of all, he had to admit that reason cannot prove the mystics wrong. In fact, in some private moods he was a mystic himself.[24]

Here Wood implies that since Russell was such a fervent champion of reason, he was all the more aware of its limits.[25] In the introduction to Russell's collected papers, Richard Rempel and his fellow editors offer some insight into the philosopher's personality: "There is a bipolarity in Russell's nature which makes it difficult but necessary to discuss the toughness of his intellect along with the tenderness of humane and even religious feelings which on occasion almost overwhelmed him." They observe that one reason his religious writings are so appealing "comes from watching Russell struggle with the two sides of his nature, the contemplative and mystical and the rational."[26] Even more important, it was these writings that Seeger, himself in the throes of a spiritual and aesthetic crisis, read and applied to his own theory of musical knowledge.

Influence on Seeger

In the essay "Prolegomena" Seeger unveils the first version of his ideal conception of musicology, which grew out of the philosophical meditations he had initiated in Berkeley and continued in New York. As its Greek title indicates, a "prolegomenon" is an introduction or preface to a larger and more ambitious work. Whereas the namesake for his essay, Immanuel Kant's *Prolegomena to Every Future Metaphysics* (1783), appeared after its author's philosophical masterpiece, *The Critique of Pure Reason* (1781), Seeger's short essay preceded by five years his later compendium of philosophical and practical knowledge, the composition treatise. This essay has some degree of overlap with Seeger's first essay, "Principles." After repeating his earlier warnings about the dangers of language in discourses about music, Seeger develops a strategy for limiting its impact. His proposal for musicologists to mediate between the competing demands of reason and intuition reveals the extent to which Russell's thoughts on religion influenced his thinking.

Seeger begins his meditations with an informal prelude to the heart of his argument. He posits a distinction between two approaches: "monism" and "pluralism." "Monism" is a mystical orientation in which all conflicts arising from the differences between music and speech disappear; "pluralism" is a logical orientation in which such conflicts are identified and indeed cultivated. Seeger associates these two orientations with distinct cultural traditions: the former with the Orient, the latter with the Occident. Although the object of Seeger's study is limited to Western music, he is determined to augment and otherwise overcome what he has characterized as the "Western" orientation of logical thought. As his discussion unfolds, the relationship between these two orientations becomes complementary rather than mutually exclusive.

Seeger's desire to exploit a middle ground between these two extremes is the first sign of the degree of Russell's influence. Seeger begins his exposition by reiterating Bergson's fundamental distinction between the mind's innate faculties, intuition and intellect, but he prefers to use Russell's terminology. In comparing the two orientations, he says that "arrogance is the mystic's strength: humility, the logician's";[27] elsewhere he elaborates on the "monistic" approach: "For to the mystic there is no dilemma nor any difference between ways of talking such as mysticism and logic."[28] Seeger illustrates the most extreme expression of each faculty, what he calls "simon-pure," as religious poetry, on the one hand, and pure mathematics, on the other. The best musicology can hope for lies somewhere between these two extremes.

Following in Russell's footsteps, Seeger proposes that the two cultural orientations should somehow be assimilated: "Between an ingrown monism and an ingrown pluralism there is nothing to choose. Eventually they must and will be, I believe, reconciled or fused."[29] He then goes one step further by saying that each orientation and the corresponding mental faculty is somehow implied by the other. Thus logical standards presuppose a mystical attitude; likewise, a mystical mood or attitude presupposes some kind of logical standard: "For in our ignoring of the Yogas, for instance, we are as false to our logical standards as is the conservative Oriental who combats our sciences

false to the best tradition in mystical thought."[30] By defining the two
faculties as mutually dependent, Seeger unveils a model of the human
mind that is quite sympathetic with Russell's synthesis of reason and
intuition. Nothing, he claims, is gained:

> By setting mysticism and logic at loggerheads or by preferring one against
> the other. . . . The stand-pat logician, as indeed the stand-pat mystic, is like a
> man with two good feet who insists upon hopping around on one. This is
> strengthening to the foot hopped upon but withers the unused one and lends
> to but a precarious footing.[31]

The assumption is that logical thought and mystical feeling are both as
indispensable to the interpretation of art as one's own limbs. If musicologists hope to maintain their interpretive "footing," they must cultivate both approaches equally.

To realize this intercultural union, Seeger imagines a discipline
where two art forms—music and language—are blended together.
Such an ideal blend requires an equal degree of proficiency in musical and literary technique. There is only one problem with this newfound synthesis: namely, the linguo-centric predicament (this "predicament" is explained more fully in chapter 1). Before such an ideal
is remotely possible, it is imperative to explore the ways in which the
nature of human speech controls or even distorts the study of music.
To write or talk about music, Seeger feels, by necessity compromises
and therefore changes the essential character of that experience. Anyone who denies such a change is reinforcing "the subordination of one
art to another."[32] If Russell's ideal union of mysticism and logic is ever
to be realized for the art of music, then the discrepancy between musical experience and the description of it in language must be confronted.

Seeger's strategy for overcoming the predicament may be divided
into three parts: (1) a detailed comparison of the art of music and of
language; (2) a method of balancing the knowledge gained by music
and language that preserves the autonomy of each medium; and (3) the
principle of "presumptive adjustment."

In the first stage of his analysis Seeger compares the similarities and
differences between the art of music and language, thereby shedding
new light on the two key ingredients in his ideal musicological blend.
He focuses on the resemblances between the traditions of education
and criticism in both fields, calling their relationship a "homology." To
give them greater emphasis, he develops a list of terms, arranged as

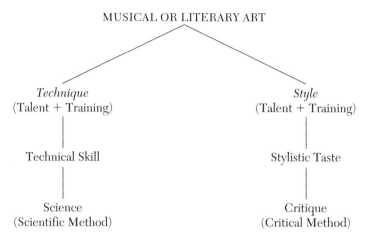

Figure 1. Comparison of music and language

three pairs of opposites, that apply as much to music as to literature: technique versus style; skill versus taste; and science versus critique. The hierarchy of terms is displayed in figure 1.

Musical and literary "technique" are a combination of native skill and professional training. Likewise, "style" in either music or literature refers to those technical developments that have achieved the "greatest value, universality and permanency."[33] Increased ability in technique is called "skill"; increased ability in "style," in turn, is referred to as "taste." The study of "technique" or "style" in either art form, in turn, obeys its own rules and requires its own methods. Seeger contrasts science and all the associated procedures of empirical observation and logical analysis with a "critique," which he defines rather vaguely as "the application of a critical method."[34]

Seeger's views regarding the differences between these two arts are even more intriguing. He begins by distinguishing between two processes, "thinking about music" and "thinking in music." Initially, he repeats the now familiar refrain that, for the most part, "thinking in music" is beyond description. He then considers differences that are crucial if his musicological reforms are to succeed. Seeger believes that his ideal blend of art forms has several distinct advantages. First, the discipline of "thinking in music" enables musicologists to view the tools of language with a newfound objectivity and impartiality. In short, to understand the limits of speech, one must abstain from speaking. Second, and more important, such an objective vantage point allows musicologists to discover hidden assumptions or biases that might distort or otherwise inhibit the process of translating musical experience into words.

Seeger then identifies two further differences between music and language that are inspired by structural linguistics. The first is an outgrowth of the previous distinction between "monism" and "pluralism": "Language is essentially a pluralising instrument. . . . it is double-acting: its sound has a *meaning.*"[35] To better explain Seeger's distinction, it is useful to borrow Ferdinand de Saussure's model of language. Although Seeger was not acquainted with Saussure at this time, he later expressed admiration for the Swiss linguist and adapted several key concepts for his musical theories.[36] Any linguistic act, which Saussure calls an utterance, can be divided into three parts. Two of these three are the "signifier," the agent that signifies, and the "signified," or the thing that is being referred to or signified. The third part is the point at which these two converge, which Saussure called the symbol itself, or the "sign." The two aspects Seeger refers to in his term "double-acting" are the "sign" which he treats as aural in nature, and the thing being signified, which he calls the sound's "meaning." Music, by contrast, is "single-acting" and *"it does not have meaning. Its sounds are not symbols."*[37] Stated in Saussure's terminology, musical sounds are "signs" that have nothing to signify.

Another crucial difference between language and music is that the law of noncontradiction, one of the primordial laws of symbolic logic passed down from Aristotle—indeed, part of the very foundation of Western thought—does not exist in music. Hence, whatever opposition may be pointed out in a composition, for example, the difference between a fugue subject and its statement in inversion, the relationship is contrasting but never, strictly speaking, contrary. Seeger says, "Opposition, as the term is used in music, does not imply contradiction."[38] One of the consequences of this difference is that in the province of truly "musical" inquiry, the criterion of logical validity or, what is more loosely known as logical truth, does not exist. However, this does not mean that musicologists should abandon the search for truth altogether.

Truth is the chief goal of logic and a basic, often unspoken, assumption of mysticism. But it cannot be applied to music because music does not have meaning. In musicology, then, truth is only to be sought as a characteristic of the language side.[39]

Seeger's point is that while, strictly speaking, there are aspects of musical experience which elude logical analysis, there are other aspects which a logical investigation, in either spoken or written form, *can* reveal. A few years later, when preparing his comprehensive treatise, Seeger would elaborate further on the limitations of logical discourse.[40]

The second stage of Seeger's analysis suggests two ways of overcoming the inherent priority of language over music. First he recommends alternating between two ways of approaching musical experience: "thinking in language" and "thinking in music," thus creating "a sequential, comparative process in which what is [being] talked or written [about] is referred constantly back to actual musical work."[41] The second method, somewhat more virtuosic, consists of engaging in musical and linguistic forms of knowledge *simultaneously.* Seeger believes that, unlike critics of most other fields, musicologists are in a good position to cultivate this two-dimensional thought process, since most have already developed a similar ability in musical terms: they are accustomed to perceiving two or more melodies in contrapuntal textures at the same time. Both methods offer a means by which the marriage of music and language can be attained.

The enormous contrast between these two recommendations tells us much about Seeger's style as a thinker. One of these two methods is a genuine procedure that can be realized in practice; the other is essentially an exercise of the imagination. To liken this simultaneous process of thinking in music and critiquing in language to a texture of two-part counterpoint is, to say the least, rather whimsical. That Seeger would introduce these two methods in the same breath shows the extremes to which he was willing to go in his struggle to find some way of overcoming the dominant role of language in musical study. The reason Seeger ultimately places a higher priority on the sequential than the simultaneous method stems from his desire to preserve the autonomy of each art form. He reminds the reader that:

The principle of balance . . . means *not* blending [oppositions] in an obscure attempt to create a monistic philosophy, but making use of each opposite in turn equally and *by itself.*[42]

In the end the goal of Seeger's synthesis, like that of Russell, is to respect the autonomy of reason as well as intuition.

The third question that Seeger pursues in "Prolegomena" concerns a strategy for engaging in musical speculation despite the limitations of the "linguo-centric predicament." As will be recalled from chapter 1, the "predicament" arises whenever an individual wants to describe a nonverbal experience, such as music, but the only descriptive tools available are linguistic in nature. Apparently, Seeger realizes that neither his nor any other philosopher's fears about the distorting effects of language will ever bring the entire discipline of musicology to a standstill. What he ends up proposing is less a solution to a philosophical "predicament" than a practical compromise—a way for musicologists to proceed with their daily activities, but from an enlightened point of view. Given the dualistic structure of the world, Seeger needs some strategy for exploring one member of a given pair of opposites without necessarily fully embracing it. In short, he proposes a principle of "presumptive adjustment." By the term "adjustment," Seeger means a kind of prejudgment in which one of the two options posed by a dilemma be accepted *for the time being* and then reappraised at some future point. The music-interpretive process becomes a series of provisional decisions in which musicologists are free to weigh various aspects of each member of an opposition before accepting it. Examples include "beginning and ending, seeming and being, appearance and reality, fact and value, science and criticism, matter and mind, subjective and objective, identity and difference, determinism and teleology—an almost endless list."[43] The principle of "presumptive adjustment" allows a musicologist to begin an investigation of the relation between music and language, and then let the method of alternation determine in what way it will proceed. The only difference between this account of mediation and the version Seeger would later propose in his treatise is that here he identifies it with a somewhat misleading term.

Seeger's proposals in the essay "Prolegomena" warrant several comments. First, using Russell's essay as a model, Seeger envisions a marriage of opposites in which he tries to reconcile the strict dualism between intuition and intellect. Yet Seeger substitutes new partners in the marriage: music in place of mystical intuition and language in place of reason. The only problem with this substitution is that the new partners are not in the same relationship as are their counterparts in the original. Whereas the analogy between mystical insight and Seeger's definition of musical experience is relatively easy to imagine, the analogy between language as a whole and the specific skills involved in logical analysis is by no means clear. It is a question of mistaking the part for the whole. The problem with Seeger's approach is that it defines language too narrowly. He treats a single rhetorical style, the expository or polemical, as though it were the distinguishing characteristic of all linguistic utterances. For Seeger, the purpose of any act of speech is to prove a point, or to link cause and effect. But the phenomenon of human language encompasses a far broader range of types, purposes, and rhetorical styles than he is prepared to admit. At times, Seeger himself appears aware of this problem, contrasting the mystical and logical *use* of language as opposed to the acts of mystical insight and logical deduction themselves. Nevertheless, a continuing source of confusion in Seeger's proposals for reforming musicology is his tendency to treat a single manner of writing or speaking as though it were language as a whole.

Another problem in Seeger's formulation is his initial distinction between "thinking in music" and "thinking in language." Some aspects of purely "musical" activities such as composition and performance, in fact, rely on logical concepts and can be discussed and even improved through the use of verbal discourse. Reading music notation is an example. Few would argue that a student's innate musical gifts offer any help whatsoever in learning to read unfamiliar musical notation. The attributes of perfect aural memory or spontaneous feeling are quite useless if an illiterate musician is faced with a page of meaningless symbols to interpret. To master traditional music notation requires a certain degree of mathematical capacity—for instance, to be able to comprehend the arithmetic proportions between different rhythmic symbols. Considering the advantages of logic for acquiring fluency in reading notation, one wonders if the two mental processes are initially as separate as Seeger claims.

This point leads us to reconsider Seeger's "homology" between music and language (see figure 1). For the most part, he focuses on such issues as education and criticism. The problem is not that these issues are insignificant in themselves but that his treatment of them is overly superficial. He posits basic elements of similarity such as "technique" or "style" as if to encourage the apprentice musicologist to try to master both fields. Several questions suggests themselves. Can "technique" and "style," and the concomitant terms "skill" and "taste," be truly separated and studied in isolation? If a writer or composer is blessed with

the talent necessary for recognizing and creating subtle differences in
"style," is not that gift inextricably bound up with technical "skill"?
More important, are the failures of past musicologists due more to the
intrinsic limits of language or to the limits of a given individual's literary technique? Could the disappointments in previous musicological
studies have been due to their practitioners' lack of musical technique
rather than the inherent ineffability of musical experience? Just because, in Seeger's opinion, no musicologist has ever transmitted musical experience into words does not mean that, by definition, it cannot
be done. Considering all of these questions, Seeger's attempt to draw
exact correspondences between musical experience and its expression
in language is more of a rough outline than a specific plan of action.

Near the end of the essay, Seeger summarizes his thesis and, in the
process, enumerates three specific aspects of his philosophical ideal:
"We must keep our balance, our poise: between two arts . . . ; between
two ways of using language—mystical and logical . . . ; between two
methods—scientific and critical . . . ; in short, between all the opposites that the art of language presents to us in its dilemmas."[44] Here
Seeger makes abundantly clear his debt to Russell's principle of mediation and, more important, his desire to apply that principle to music speculation.

I have two final comments about the debt Seeger's theory of music
criticism owes to Russell's ideal fusion of mysticism and logic. First, it
is significant that the essay from which Seeger drew inspiration over
and over again for his philosophical pronouncements is so loosely organized. A close reading of Russell's essay shows that in the course of
his meditations on mysticism, he actually defends four different philosophical positions: an ideal of philosophy from ancient Greece, the role
of imagination in modern scientific thought, a seventeenth-century
conception of ethics, and an early twentieth-century theory of intuition. His essay is a like a guided tour of various provinces of mystical
thought. Even more important, the methodology he employs is anything but precise: an ideal of negotiation between complementary
mental faculties is more of a strategy for emphasizing the overall unity
within the human mind than a precise philosophical system. For instance, Russell never establishes rules for settling differences among
conflicting intuitions, instead reassuring his readers that reason will
somehow find a way to strike a balance. His essay is a preliminary
sketch, a kind of high-spirited manifesto announcing a new philosoph-

ical discovery that, one assumes, he will refine and explain more carefully at a later time.

However, this lack of precision is not only understandable but laudable, considering Russell's intended audience and his reason for writing in the first place. After all, this lecture was originally designed for the general public, not for a community of professional philosophers. Furthermore, the ideal model of mediation that Russell offers is less a new philosophical breakthrough than a personal and, as it turned out, provisional solution to help resolve the spiritual conflict in his own life. Indeed, after delivering this lecture in America and publishing it, Russell had a change of heart, never again writing about the mystical impulse with as much sympathy.

But what is even more interesting is that Charles Seeger not only borrowed the same basic idea of mediation but also placed it at the very foundation of his philosophical theory of knowledge. The point is not that Seeger was less of a professional philosopher than Russell; indeed, Seeger not only would have conceded such an accusation, he would have been proud of it. Rather, Seeger had a different audience than Russell—musicians with a philosophical leaning—and he wrote for a different purpose. Ultimately, Seeger's attraction to the loose-fitting framework of mediation must be judged in relation to the many applications he envisioned for it in various fields of music: criticism, compositional theory, and musicology. For him, philosophical speculation was not only an end in itself; it was also a means of stimulating new directions among musicians and musicologists alike.

My second comment concerns a possible misinterpretation of Seeger's model of mediation, which is partly fueled by a remark he himself made in the introduction of the textbook on harmony he wrote with Edward Stricklen. There he writes:

Ideas long current in literary and scientific work are being projected into the chaotic waters of modern musical life which may lead upward and onward in true Hegelian fashion, to higher, more complete and more comprehensive forms—not forsaking the old, but reaffirming transcending and embellishing it as each new fragment of dissonant chaos is conquered and found beautiful to the eyes of a more universal consciousness.[45]

Seeger's reference here to a "universal consciousness" suggests that the German idealist philosopher G.W. F. Hegel (1770–1831) may have been a model for his philosophical theories. In particular, there is a de-

gree of resemblance between Hegel's dialectical model of consciousness and Seeger's dualistic model of the human mind. One could easily
imagine the following neo-Hegelian scenario: intuition alone pervades
the listener's first glimmers of musical perception; then reason, its an-
tithesis and rival, intervenes, and the two engage in conflict; eventually, their conflict leads to a higher synthesis of musical understanding.

But on closer scrutiny such a resemblance is rather superficial.
The profound differences between the two approaches outweigh any
apparent similarities. First, two thinkers who figured prominently
in Seeger's philosophical catechism—Bertrand Russell and Ralph
Perry—shared a strong desire to find an alternative to the dominant
model of the late nineteenth century: German idealism. One common
thread uniting the English "analytic" movement led by Russell and the
American "new realist" movement to which Perry belonged was their
complete rejection of Hegelian dialectics. Second, Hegel's dialectical
method is more strict than anything Seeger would have tolerated; indeed, Seeger's methodological approach has more in common with
the ancient Greek view of dialectics.[46] Hegel's view of human knowledge is closed. Any individual's thoughts or perceptions are like tiny
cogs within a great cosmological wheel. Once set in motion, Hegel's
dialectical chain of triads, thesis-antithesis-synthesis, continues past
the moment of our collective self-knowledge and culminates in the
unity of Divine Spirit. Seeger's philosophical aspirations, by contrast,
are much more modest; his sights are set on revealing the individual's
consciousness rather than the eternal Consciousness—the difference
between a lowercase and uppercase "c." Seeger's own Bergsonian leanings were too strong; that is, he believed that the potential for each individual to discover a particle of musical truth, however small, was
more meaningful than trying to reveal the grand design of the cosmos.
The philosophical stakes of Seeger's investigations were not as high as
those of his German predecessor. Seeger envisioned an unlimited process of action and reaction within the sphere of the individual's mental faculties, not within the arena of the all-encompassing journey of
the human spirit.

Nineteenth-century Positivism

Thus far I have treated the word "science" in an ahistorical fashion, as
though there were only one model of the natural sciences, first estab-

lished in the seventeenth century and preserved intact up to the mid-1920s. To better appreciate what particular concept of science Seeger believed would alternate with intuition in his ideal model of knowledge, it is necessary to briefly characterize the intellectual landscape of the late nineteenth and early twentieth centuries. In this overview I will trace the direct influence of an English philosopher of science, Karl Pearson, whose writings Seeger praised. In addition, I will point out some curious resemblances between Seeger and one of the most popular American philosophers of his generation, William James.

In the 1840s a French thinker named Auguste Comte pioneered a new philosophical movement called "positivism," which had an immediate impact on virtually all scientific and humanistic disciplines. Modifying Comte's views, later philosophers such as John Stuart Mill, Karl Pearson, and Ernst Mach argued that philosophy was merely an extension of science, the primary aim of which was to discover the general principles common to all the sciences and to use them as a basis for guiding human conduct. As a result, positivists opposed all forms of metaphysics or any other procedure that could not be reduced to scientific principles. In his book on Bergson, Robert Grogin describes this new credo:

The reigning positivist orthodoxy inherited from the Second Empire declared its unbridled faith in the power of experimental science to challenge all traditions, beliefs and institutions, and to hold them up to the pure light of reason. . . . Furthermore, in a century dominated by positivism, natural science was raised to the level of a determinist metaphysics and gradually assumed the status of a new religion—scientism.[47]

The ideas germinated by the early positivists would later come to fruition in a wide range of philosophical views by such twentieth-century figures as Ludwig Wittgenstein and Rudolph Carnap.

Seeger's understanding of science was drawn largely from one of the leading spokesmen for positivism in England: Karl Pearson (1857–1936). While Pearson's reputation as a scientist rests largely on his pioneering work in modern statistical theory, his most famous work was *The Grammar of Science,* a primer on scientific method which he published in 1892. Addressed to the specialist and the layperson alike, this volume went through three editions in the space of twenty years. In a 1968 interview Seeger had nothing but praise for Pearson's work, which he first encountered while teaching at Berkeley:

Science was . . . designing concert halls and instruments, analyzing [what] we call musical sounds, and there were beginning to be psychologies of music. . . . I fortunately had . . . Pearson's *Grammar of Science,* which became my Bible for the next few years.[48]

Though Seeger's devotion to the *Grammar* was anything but religious, Pearson's ideas would play a significant role in the development of his theory of music criticism.

Pearson considered himself an enemy to the prevailing approach in the universities—neo-Hegelianism—and one goal in writing the *Grammar* was to eclipse the influence of this tradition. Once described as an effort at "intellectual house cleaning," Pearson's book attempts to define the aims and limits of scientific inquiry, as well as clarify its relation to other fields of endeavor.[49] Two aspects of Pearson's manual are significant for our understanding of the roots of Seeger's philosophical theories: Pearson's model of the "scientific method," and the wide range of disciplines in which the model could be applied.

Like his empiricist predecessors, Locke and Hume, Pearson believes that all knowledge can be divided into two fundamental types: immediate sense-impressions and memories of, or what he calls the "remaining impresses" of, past sense-impressions.[50] Having stated these basic premises, he then outlines his three-step version of the scientific method.

1. Careful and accurate classification of facts and observation of their correlation and sequence;
2. Discovery of scientific laws by aid of the creative imagination;
3. Self-criticism and the final touchstone of equal validity for all normally constituted minds.[51]

My discussion will focus on the last two steps.

It is in his approach to "law" where Pearson shows his true philosophical colors. He insists that our sense-impressions have no necessary one-to-one correspondence with the physical world. In fact, he is content to reject causality altogether, instead relying on the principle of association. In this context, a "law of nature is but a simple *résumé,* a brief description of a wide range of [human] perceptions."[52] Scientific laws, he cautions the reader, do not explain the physical world but merely describe it.

Once the facts have been collected and arranged in their appropriate categories, however, something more is needed to arrive at the concept of a law. Pearson believes that reason, by itself, is insufficient and needs to be balanced by an imaginative or aesthetic sensibility. All great scientists have demonstrated an imaginative gift, the rare knack for synthesis, which enables them to transform an assemblage of facts into a law: "The discovery of some single statement, some brief *formula* from which the whole group of facts is seen to flow, is the work, not of the mere cataloguer, but of the man endowed with creative imagination."[53] In the third stage reason plays one final role in the development of scientific laws by guarding against the potential excesses of the imagination. Pearson emphasizes that a newly proposed law must be severely tested and criticized by its discoverer to see that it covers a wide range of individual cases.

The other proposal in Pearson's *Grammar* that is sympathetic with Seeger's and Russell's thinking involves the relation between the natural sciences and other fields of the humanities and social sciences. Pearson believed that his conception of method was by no means restricted to the physical sciences.

The field of science is unlimited; its material is endless, every group of natural phenomena, every phase of social life, every stage of past or present development is material for science. *The unity of all science consists alone in its method, not in its material.*[54]

Since all that was required for an approach to qualify as "scientific" was that it follow a prescribed method, Seeger must have felt that, if Pearson had been alive, he certainly would have given his blessing to an ideal of "scientific" music criticism. It is rather ironic that in Pearson's attempt to define more sharply the boundaries between disciplines, he effectively broadened the province that could be considered science.

With this overview of Pearson's plan complete, it is now possible to compare the two thinkers' approaches. The similarities between Pearson's and Seeger's theories of knowledge are unmistakable. Each assumes that the faculties of logic and intuition (or imagination) complement and depend on one another. Although Seeger harbored little interest in the process through which scientists discover and confirm new laws per se, his and Pearson's methods of explanation rest on the same epistemological grounds.

Pragmatism

Seeger's adaptation of Russell's idiosyncratic treatment of religion raises a curious parallel between his approach and "pragmatism," a philosophical movement that was popularized at the turn of the century by the American philosopher William James. Although there is no direct evidence that Seeger ever read the works of the leading pragmatic thinkers, the strong resemblances between the ideas themselves are worth considering.

Pragmatism is a rich philosophical tradition that first emerged during the 1870s in the writings of the logician and mathematician Charles S. Peirce, whose primary aim was to develop a method for clarifying and interpreting the meaning of signs. William James later revived Peirce's ideas and, in the process, transformed them into his own unique synthesis: a theory of truth mixed with a foundation for moral reasoning. Finally, John Dewey gave the pragmatic philosophy new life in his attempts to bridge the gap between his theory of logic and its implications for science and morality.

The work that is most relevant to our discussion of Seeger is a collection of James's lectures entitled *Pragmatism,* published near the end of his life. When this work appeared in 1907, it immediately became a best-seller and catapulted its author into public acclaim and international honor. Since it is intended for the general reader rather than the specialist, it serves as an excellent précis of James's basic approach. In the opening lecture, "The Present Dilemma in Philosophy," he lays the groundwork for his proposals. He remarks:

The history of philosophy is to a great extent that of a certain clash of human temperaments.... Of whatever temperament a professional philosopher is, ... [it] gives him a stronger bias than any of his more strictly objective premises. It loads the evidence for him one way or the other.... Of course I am talking here of very positively marked men, men of radical idiosyncrasy, who have set their stamp and likeness on philosophy and figure in its history. Plato, Locke, Hegel, Spencer, are such temperamental thinkers.[55]

James then illustrates the concept of philosophical temperament with two broad categories: the rationalist, which he associates with idealism and religion, and the empiricist, which he associates with materialism and doubt. To dramatize the differences between these types, James assembles two lists of attributes, arranged as pairs of opposites

Tender-minded	*Tough-minded*
Rationalistic	Empiricist
—(going by "principles")	—(going by "facts")
Intellectualistic	Sensationalistic
Idealistic	Materialistic
Optimistic	Pessimistic
Religious	Irreligious
Free-willist	Fatalistic
Monistic	Pluralistic
Dogmatical	Skeptical

Figure 2. List of traits for two philosophical temperaments, based on William James, *Pragmatism* (1907)

(see figure 2). Although in practice the difference between these two types is a question of emphasis rather than of kind (as he says, "no one can live an hour without both facts and principles"), this contrast in emphasis nevertheless can generate considerable hostility.[56]

Faced with these two alternatives, James is profoundly discontent. For him the purely empirical philosophy is not religious enough; conversely, the purely religious philosophy is not empirical enough. He hopes for some way of blending attributes from both lists.

You want a system that will combine both things, the scientific loyalty to facts and willingness to take account of them, the spirit of adaptation and accommodation, in short, but also the old confidence in human values and the resultant spontaneity, whether of the religious or of the romantic type.[57]

His solution is the philosophy of pragmatism, which he conceives as "a method of mediating between the extremes of competing conceptions of reality and truth, between rationalism and empiricism, between contrasting temperaments of 'tender' and 'tough-minded.'"[58] Above all, James conceives of this new approach as a method of settling disputes. It consists of considering each alternative and "tracing its respective practical consequences. What difference would it practically make to anyone if this notion rather than that notion were true?"[59] If no difference can be found, then the two alternatives mean the same thing, and the dispute disappears. When such a method is applied to the original dilemma between temperaments described earlier, reconciliation is possible. James concludes: "Science and metaphysics would come much nearer together, would in fact work absolutely hand in hand." [60]

Near the end of his life, when James's innovative approach to philosophy became more broadly known, it was subjected to intense scrutiny and criticism by the philosophical community. For one thing, Peirce, an old college friend and professional colleague, disavowed any connection with James and, more important, insisted on referring to his own contributions with the ungainly term "pragmaticism" in order to distinguish them from James's "pragmatism." Others objected to the lack of clarity in James's conception of "practical consequences"; one critic enumerated thirteen distinct ways in which the approach could be interpreted. [61] In all fairness to James, however, his late writings and lectures should be regarded as rough sketches or outlines of a general theory he never lived to complete.

Equipped with this brief overview, we can offer some provisional comparisons with Seeger's philosophical ideas. Considering that there is no indication that Seeger read any of James's works, the resemblances between the two are almost uncanny. Seeger's dualistic framework and his ideal of mediation seem like pages torn out of James's late essays. While the terms in Seeger's pair of opposites may differ from those of James—music and language instead of "tender-" and "tough-minded"—the underlying strategy of mediation is the same. Even though the resemblance may be more accidental than some kind of direct influence, it is fair to say that Seeger's ideal of musicology as a balance between opposites has an unmistakable "pragmatic" cast.

Chapter Three

. . . .

Perry's Philosophy of Value

In our innermost beliefs and convictions, those deeper
things we live for, we stand more or less apart . . . but with
no clear understanding of one another. . . . What are the
deeper ideal bonds that unite us? What are the irreconcilable differences of belief and conscience that divide us? I
should like to be able to construct a world-map of convictions, creeds, ideas, like the maps which ethnologists make
showing the distribution of racial types in Europe; or like
the maps economists make to show the distribution of the
corn crop. I should like to make a map with intellectual and
moral meridians, with degrees of latitude, trade-routes of
thought, and great capitals of faith.

This is a comprehensive undertaking; you may be
tempted to say that it is an *impossible* undertaking. But that
is what you must expect of a philosopher.

Ralph Barton Perry, *The Present Conflict of Ideals*

The Science of Value

During the late nineteenth and early twentieth centuries, a controversy developed around the concept of value which cut across the traditional boundaries of philosophical inquiry. The distinguishing feature of the philosophy of value or axiology was the desire to start with
the concept of ethical value and then generalize it to embrace many
fields from the humanities such as ethics, economics, and political theory within a single framework. The common thread unifying these
disciplines was the fact that all of them concerned matters of human
values as opposed to matters of fact, and that all could be studied using the methods of science.

Beginning in the late teens Seeger was fascinated by this concept,
and for the rest of his life it was one of the recurring themes in his philosophical writings. His source for the philosophy of value was Ralph B.
Perry, the same author whose concept of the "ego-centric predicament" had so influenced Seeger several years earlier (see chapter 1).

The preceding excerpt is drawn from a series of lectures designed for a popular audience that Perry delivered at Berkeley in 1918, some of which Seeger heard. Disturbed by the world war then in progress, Perry undertook a comprehensive survey of recent intellectual history in search of its underlying causes. Although Perry's "world-map of convictions" is more of an evocative dream than a genuine philosophical argument, Perry's aspirations to develop a comprehensive and ethical study of human motivation are abundantly clear. Perry's magnum opus, *General Theory of Value* (1926), has been described as "the most complete and systematic treatment of the subject in English and probably in any other language."[1] Inspired by Perry's approach, Seeger proposed a new, more comprehensive view of musicology that included moral judgment—something usually associated with ethics. In a series of essays written between 1931 and 1977, Seeger presented ideal schemes of musicology in the form of elaborate visual models— as though he were realizing Perry's dream of fashioning a map of "intellectual meridians" but now translated into music-theoretical terms (In chapter 7 I explore a wide range of Seeger's maps of musicology). Seeger's holistic vision of musicology as a discipline that unites other disciplines was unique in American musicological writings during the early twentieth century.

Before proceeding to Perry's specific theories and Seeger's adaptations of them, it is necessary to establish a workable definition of "value," and then to briefly outline the history of the philosophical debate that has surrounded it. Unfortunately, any study of value is handicapped by the vagueness of the term itself. To help overcome this problem, let us explore four meanings of the term. Historically, "value" has been used to refer to anything that has worth, usually in an economic sense. By contrast, since the nineteenth century, philosophers have employed the term in a much broader sense to denote any form of obligation, beauty, or even holiness. Rather than studying each of these questions in isolation—as would be typical in the disciplines of ethics, aesthetics, and theology, respectively—philosophers of this persuasion ask whether these questions all share something in common, and, if so, whether that common element transcends human affairs and is more spiritual in nature. In modern parlance the term has preserved some of this general character. These different meanings are illustrated in the following four examples:

1. A violin's value in an auction;
2. A violinist's expressive values as conveyed in performance;
3. The aesthetic values shared by all humans within a given cultural tradition;
4. General human values.

Phrases 1 and 2 exemplify the economic and commonsense meanings of the term, respectively; phrase 3 is the aesthetician's "daily bread"; and phrase 4 is the domain of the value theorist. Throughout this study, unless otherwise specified, the term "value" will refer to either the third or fourth definition.

The tradition of studying human values can be traced back to the sophist school of philosophy of ancient Greece during the fifth century B.C., particularly in the life and work of its most famous proponent, Socrates. The primary source for our knowledge of Socrates' teachings, the dialogues of Plato, are full of ethical reflections about human conduct, including such questions as What is goodness? What is justice? What is beauty? Even though the seeds of virtually every controversy that has arisen in modern value theory are already present in Plato, nowhere does he treat the questions of goodness, justice, beauty, and so forth, as though they all belonged to the same family. Such a unified approach would have to wait until the nineteenth century.

The next chapter in the history of the concept of value appears in the writings of the eighteenth-century English philosopher David Hume (1711–1776). Of all the traditional branches of philosophy, the one that bears the closest resemblance to value theory is ethics. In his masterpiece *A Treatise of Human Nature,* published in 1739, Hume makes an observation about the nature of ethical thinking that in later years would have a strong impact on the study of values. He observes that somewhere in every moral argument a crucial shift occurs whereby the author stops talking about matters of fact and begins talking about matters of moral judgment. This shift can be immediately detected, he feels, in the very language the author employs: the word "is" disappears in favor of "ought."[2] Hume argues that the sudden introduction of this word and the accompanying shift from a descriptive to a prescriptive tone both demand some sort of justification. In essence, he believes that statements of moral judgment cannot be deduced from initial statements of fact. He cautions philosophers not to fall prey to this kind of lapse, a warning that gives rise to the famous dictum "No 'ought' from 'is.'"

Since Hume's time, this dictum has been subjected to radically different interpretations. Some argue that it is nothing more than an object lesson in the technique of logical inference. According to Charles Pigden, in a syllogism

a conclusion containing 'ought' cannot (as a matter of logic) be derived from 'ought'-free premises. . . . the conclusions of a valid inference are contained within the premises. You don't get out what you haven't put in. Hence if 'ought' appears in the conclusion of an argument but not in the premises, the inference is not logically valid.[3]

According to this view, Hume believes that a moral argument is like any other philosophical argument in that it must satisfy logical standards. But there are others who disagree. These critics believe that Hume's dictum implies that moral judgments or opinions are not subject to the same kinds of rational justification as are other philosophical claims. If a moral judgment depends on an underlying moral value, and if a value cannot be justified by marshaling the appropriate facts, then values are beyond empirical confirmation. This leads to the conclusion that any value is purely arbitrary and must be accepted on faith. By positing an unbridgeable chasm between facts and values, the so-called fact-value gap, this line of reasoning culminates in moral skepticism.[4]

For our present purposes, it is less important to decide which interpretation of Hume is correct than to emphasize his belief in the sharp distinction between matters of fact and matters of moral value. One of the basic assumptions shared by most value theorists is that the "fact-value gap" is not as insurmountable as Hume claims, and that matters of value or "ought" are not necessarily incompatible with science. As we will see, Seeger, too, would later argue that the fundamental mission of musicology was to find a way of bridging the gap between the worlds of scientific fact and artistic value.

During the nineteenth century a new philosophical movement emerged that attempted to unify a broad range of disciplines, including aesthetics, ethics, economics, and political science, into a single, all-encompassing study. This approach was called "axiology," or the science of *axia* ("value" in Greek), and its pioneer was the German philosopher Rudolph H. Lotze (1817–1881). Lotze inherited many of the basic dichotomies of the German idealist philosophers such as science versus religion and reason versus emotion or intuition, but he also added his own twist. In order to reconcile his belief in divine experience with philosophical reflection, Lotze proposed the concept of value, by which he meant an extended form of ethical inquiry that embraced all human experience. In his philosophical scheme he posits three realms: the realm of fact; the realm of universal law, by which he means our experience of the divine; and the realm of human value, which mediates between the other two. The result is that, for Lotze, human values take on a transcendental character. Wilbur Urban, an early twentieth-century axiologist sympathetic with Lotze's approach, argues that the determination of value "is something independent of this world, and so little merely a part of it that it is rather the whole world seen from a special point of view. Over against a world of facts is set a world of values."[5]

Seeger's understanding of value differed dramatically from that of Lotze, for he never shared the German philosopher's idealist passion for trying to rationalize the supernatural. On the whole, Seeger was less interested in reconciling scientific logic with religious faith than with the creative impulse as expressed in composition, performance, and audition. The greatest point of resemblance between the two thinkers is the spirit of mediation that infuses their philosophical approaches.

Later in the century Franz Brentano, Alexius Meinong, and Christian von Ehrenfels, all from Vienna, fashioned their own approach to the problem, becoming known collectively as the Second Austrian School of Values.[6] As a point of departure, these Viennese philosophers all agreed that human beings, in essence, are hedonists in that all our actions are calculated to seek the greatest amount of pleasure or the least amount of pain. Where they differed was in the way each explained the psychological process by which one action was preferred over another. This technical dispute became a kind of chicken-and-egg paradox in which one group argued that we desire something because we value it and the other group insisted that we value something because we desire it. In their attempt to construct a philosophical system on a psychological base, the early axiologists became caught up in an "introspective bog."[7]

The first American to expound a philosophy of value and the axiologist who most influenced Seeger was Ralph Barton Perry. Compared

with the complexities of the Second Austrian School and the idealism
of Lotze, Perry's approach to value is refreshingly simple. In *General
Theory of Value* he proclaims that "interest" is the "original source and
constant feature of all value. Any object, whatever it be, acquires value
when any interest, whatever it be, is taken in it. . . . The view may otherwise be formulated in the equation: x is valuable = interest is taken in
x."[8] At first glance, this approach could easily be dismissed as a variation on the old adage "One man's meat is another man's poison." Yet
Perry approaches the question of human interest with the impartiality of a scientist. In chapter 1 of his principal work, he investigates the
broad category of actions he calls "criticism." "Critical" acts impute
some kind of emotion, either positive or negative, to an object; to love,
hate, deceive, envy, resent, idolize, are all treated as different species
of the same general family of actions.[9] Thus, the casual listener's taste
in music would fit Perry's definition just as much as the opinions published by a professional music critic. Rather than trying to summarize
his entire theory, I will focus on three of its essential principles and
then trace in what way they help shape Seeger's theory of knowledge
and its applications to the fields of music criticism and musicology.

   One area of ambiguity that the theories of Brentano, Meinong, von
Ehrenfels, and Perry all share is whether axiology was a science or
some form of metaphysics. This concern grows out of the "No 'ought'
from 'is'" controversy that Hume had raised about ethical inquiry over
one hundred years earlier. In a recent article comparing the attitudes
of various members of the Austrian Second School of Values, J. Prescott
Johnson argues that their general attitude toward science must be
seen as part of the legacy of Darwin's theory of evolution:

Value theory emerged as a philosophical discipline out of the tensions created by the application of the new genetic logic to man. The early value theorists believed that values were indeed bound up with organic and psychical
phenomena, yet they tried to find a place for value and the validity of value
as independent of its conditions in experience.[10]

In essence, Johnson argues that the present confusion about the scientific nature of values can be traced to different forces coming into
conflict within the field of philosophy during the late nineteenth century. The question boils down to this: If axiology were a science, then
individual values would be treated as empirical facts in the natural
world; if not, then values would possess a normative character that
transcends natural experience.

Perry argued that his broad-based study of human values was, indeed, a scientific affair, and that a given value could be tested with the usual methods of empirical confirmation. His conception of science is heavily indebted to the behavioralist school of psychology by which one could, in some sense, observe human values in action.[11] In Perry's version of the behavioralist creed, human motivation is a two-part process: a person is exposed to a given stimulus, and that person displays the same or similar actions repeatedly in response to the given stimulus.[12] A value thus was conceived as a "disposition" or expectation that could be deduced from a train of events, and, most important of all, the study of values could be considered "a scientific enterprise open to observation, hypothesis, and verification just like any other branch of science."[13]

The second basic characteristic of Perry's theory of value is his approach to the problem of subjectivism. As might be expected from his explanation of the "ego-centric predicament," he completely rejects the notion that a thing's existence is "idealist," that is, in any way contingent on our "idea" of it. Instead he appeals to a notion of common sense that was initially suggested by his philosophical mentor at Harvard, William James.

I can remember even the stage-setting . . . and the gestures with which James animatedly conveyed to us the intuition of common-sense realism. From that day I confess that I have never wavered in the belief that our perceptual experience disclosed a common world, inhabited by our perceiving bodies and our neighbours, and qualified by the evidence of our senses.[14]

This assumption of "common-sense realism" is what distinguishes Perry's conception of value from that of his idealist predecessors. For Perry, the problem is not in trying to establish whether the object of our sense-impressions exists, but in determining our relation to that object once it has been presented to us. Rather than being a property of the object, value is "a relation holding between an interest and an object."[15] This treatment of value as a relation between subject and object rather than a property of the object itself would reappear in Seeger's treatise.

The third important characteristic of Perry's theory concerns the objectivity of value. The following questions arise: How can anyone know for certain whether one individual's perception of value is shared by another? Does an interest-based approach lead automatically to a purely relative world of values where no objective or universal stan-

dards exist, or are there values we all share? Perry gave much thought
to the potential objection that his theory was relativistic and devised a
procedure for overcoming it. In short, his answer was that the question of value was ultimately inseparable from the questions of ethical
obligation and political responsibility. To find a method by which a
conflict between competing interests could be identified and resolved,
Perry turned to an ideal model of democracy in which the principle
of "harmonious integration of interests" could be carried out. First he
focused on the individual. He imagined that in an ideal world, each
person should try to develop a "hierarchical arrangement of interests,
such that an interest lower in the scale withdraws its claim at the point
where this conflicts with the claim of an interest higher in the scale." [16]
Having postulated this internal "harmony" of interests within a single
individual, Perry then generalizes it to an entire society. Two people's
competing interests could be adjudicated on the basis of whatever
maximizes the interest of the community as a whole. In his eyes, a
philosophical theory of human value was inextricably bound up with
his ideals of ethical conduct and social organization. [17]

Influence on Seeger

Throughout his life, Charles Seeger showed a passionate interest in
the concept of value, beginning with his two early essays on musicology in the 1920s, continuing in the treatise, and finally culminating in
his late philosophical musings on musicology. Yet of all the ideas
Seeger borrowed from contemporary developments in philosophy,
the theory of axiology was the one to which he was the least loyal.
Seeger focused more on the fundamental questions Perry posed rather
than on the specific, and at times complex, answers he offered—indeed, it was much easier to carry out the spirit of Perry's comprehensive enterprise than the letter.

   At this point it is helpful to use my three-part summary of Perry's
theory of value to measure the impact of his theories on Seeger's
thought. As will be recalled, Perry was preoccupied with the question
of whether the study of value was truly scientific, that is, carried out
using the traditional tools of empirical confirmation. Though Seeger
was certainly attracted to the rigors of logical analysis, he never relied
on science as the only authority for truth. His vision of musicology was

not that of a pure science but rather a blend of disciplines in which scientific and artistic impulses alternate and complement one another.

The first indication that Seeger was concerned with the study of value appears in the conclusion to his essay "Principles."[18] There he offers six recommendations, divided into two groups of three, which he believes will reshape the discipline of musicology. The first three address the relationship between the art of music and the art of language, and he refers to all three as a "postulation of fact." Juxtaposed against these, he presents three more postulates "of value," which include the inherent priority of language over music and his desire to compensate for this by emphasizing the "musical" point of view. In this context, "fact" means his empirical observations of the present state of musicology, and "value" refers to his proposals for change. While he never mentions the concept of value in the body of the essay, its presence in the conclusion shows the degree to which it helped organize his thoughts.[19]

Seeger also alludes to the same opposition in both the essay "Prolegomena" and the treatise. In the process of comparing music and language in his early essay, he discovers numerous parallels, which are summarized in figure 1. Throughout his analysis, Seeger applies the same dichotomy between science and criticism: the concepts of technique and skill are associated with the scientific understanding of music or language; style and taste, with the critical understanding of these two arts.[20]

At the end of the essay "Prolegomena" he introduces a new term. He emphasizes the necessity of preserving a balance between two arts, two forms of using language (mystical and logical), and finally "two methods—scientific and critical."[21] For Seeger the word "criticism" was far more than mere journalism, the business of writing reviews; rather, he translates Perry's meaning—the common basis for all evaluative actions—into musical terms. Seeger's brand of "criticism" encompasses a broad range of meanings, including the composer's inspiration and the performer's expressivity as much as the listener's rapture. In chapter 1 of the treatise he describes his ideal of balance in greater detail: "In any protracted study, scientific and critical procedure alternate and complement each other. We alternately emphasize facts and values, ever subjecting our facts to critical review and our values to scientific testing."[22] These passages reveal not only

Seeger's faith in a dualistic framework but also his reliance on an ideal of mediation. Seeger's overall purpose is twofold: to show the virtues of the intuitive, purely "musical" approach; and to sketch out a new philosophical ideal in which musical and scientific knowledge are balanced in equilibrium.

The approach Perry and Seeger take to the question of subjectivism provides another direct link between the two. In the treatise Seeger avoids any protracted discussion of whether the object of our perceptions actually exists. Instead he shares with Perry and William James a "common-sense realism," in which one begins by assuming that a relation between subject and object exists and then continues the process of self-reflection. (This point will be pursued in greater detail in my commentary on Seeger's theory of criticism in chapter 4).

The social dimension of Perry's theory, that is, the process through which differences among individuals' personal values are negotiated and resolved, is the aspect that influenced Seeger the least. What Seeger and Perry share is the ambition to move beyond internal questions, such as which mental faculties the individual perceiver employs, and instead generalize the notion of value so as to consider the perceptions and tastes of others. Where they differ is in the specific means by which this generalization is achieved. Though willing to borrow the rhetoric of Perry's overall paradigm, Seeger never embraced the procedures of behavioralist psychology.

Inspired by the breadth of Perry's study of value, Seeger undertook a comprehensive project of his own. He borrowed the all-encompassing view of human value, which he called "critical," and then narrowed its purview to include matters relating only to music. The greatest indication of Perry's influence on Seeger's thought is the latter's reliance on dualistic assumptions and philosophical models, first witnessed in the early philosophical essays, expanded in the treatise, and further refined in his later speculative essays. The opposition between science and criticism is one of a handful of dichotomies that together form the cornerstone of Seeger's approach to music-philosophical thought: fact versus value; reason versus intuition; speech versus music; and history versus system. Yet what is curious about Seeger's general approach is that his fascination for dualism led him to ignore Perry's overall goal of discovering a *single* source that unifies all matters of emotion, belief, and value. Instead, Seeger preferred a more loosely organized principle of balance, such as that advocated by Bertrand Russell, and a smaller field of inquiry: the art of music.

Perhaps Seeger's ultimate calling was that of a musical cartographer whose purpose was to reveal a new grand plan or map to guide others' musical explorations. He considered musicology a holistic and cooperative venture in which musicians and musicologists alike would work in concert within a larger artistic community. Like the Encyclopedists of the eighteenth century, Diderot and Rousseau, or their cartographic successors in the late nineteenth century, Guido Adler and Waldo Pratt, one of Seeger's principal philosophical aims was to organize and systematize the knowledge that others had already collected. His first attempt at mapping out a general philosophy of music appeared in his comprehensive treatise entitled *Tradition and Experiment in the New Music.*

Chapter Four

· · · ·

Seeger's Theory
of Music Criticism

The posthumous publication of *Tradition and Experiment in the New Music* in 1994 was the culmination of a long musical intellectual journey that Seeger had initially embarked upon while teaching at Berkeley during the teens, continued in his composition lessons with Ruth Crawford in New York during the late 1920s, and finally pursued intermittently throughout his later years. In many respects the treatise is a chronicle of that journey, a reflection of the many ideas and approaches drawn from different disciplines that Seeger assimilated in his ongoing passion for creating music, as well as for thinking about the process of creativity itself. In the introduction to the treatise, Seeger warns that a new style of music will never be attained unless composers reexamine all aspects of their craft:

If we are to hear a new music comparable to the music of Palestrina, Bach, and Beethoven, it will be less through a musical pre-Raphaelite movement or a timorous anti-intellectualism than through a systematic overhauling of all the elements in the situation—materials, methods, and values.[1]

To carry out his ambitious project of "overhauling," Seeger was compelled to adopt a variety of musical personae: at various junctures he speaks as a composition teacher, a critic, and finally a philosopher who investigates the nature of compositional theory and critical evaluation. What for others might have been a pure exercise in philosophical reflection was for Seeger integrally connected with the daily work of the musicologist and the practical world of the composer. The treatise as a whole reflects this ideal fusion of theoretical speculation and compositional practice; for him, philosophical exegesis went hand in hand with compositional genesis.

Before we can appreciate this interdependency of theory and practice, however, we must understand Seeger's philosophical speculations on their own terms. His ideas about musical knowledge are confined to the introduction and the opening two chapters of the treatise, entitled "Theory and Practice" and "Critique." In chapter 1 Seeger examines once again the relation between music and language, echoing many of the themes present in his earlier two essays "Principles" and "Prolegomena," such as the dichotomies between mysticism and logic, fact and value, and finally style and technique. He reserves his newest ideas for the following chapter, where he proposes a philosophical basis for a theory of criticism; as a result, I will concentrate on the material presented in chapter 2.

Seeger's exposition of the critical process has two dimensions. He proposes fourteen "principles" or "definitions" of criticism, which appear as a continuous narrative (these are summarized in figure 3). In addition, near the beginning of the chapter he includes an intricate diagram (reproduced in figure 4), which illustrates the same critical process but in greater detail than is found in the list of principles.[2] Apparently, Seeger found this combination of visual diagram plus running commentary highly congenial to his style of doing philosophy, for in his subsequent philosophical studies he employs the same dual format. Since the diagram is just as crucial as the original list of principles in Seeger's exposition of his theory of knowledge, my discussion is based on both.

Seeger's list can be divided into three types of statements, each coinciding with a different stage in the critical process: the initial intuition (principles 5–7); the mediation between that intuition and the critic's sense of reason (principles 1–4, 8–11), and, finally, a mix of historical and compositional claims (principles 12–14). The first type establishes that an individual's spontaneous intuition is the point of departure for criticism, the natural spring from which everything else in his approach flows. In these three principles Seeger shows a sympathy for mystical thinking that is an essential part of his unique point of view.

If the first group of principles constitutes Seeger's doctrine of aesthetic beauty, then the next group introduces a method of putting that doctrine into action. Principles 1–4 and 8–11 outline a process in which critics test their spontaneous intuitions about music with the

1. Music criticism assumes that musical value is relative.

2. The two mental faculties involved in music criticism, intuition and reason, not only complement each other, but one may actually influence how the other proceeds.

3. Music criticism aims at a relative balance between the faculties of intuition and reason and between the corresponding types of criticism, impressionistic and scientific.

4. A judgment of value has neither the objective neutrality of a scientist's observation, nor the subjective certainty of an aesthetic intuition. Instead it comes about when the relation between an aesthetically oriented subject and an aesthetic object is expressed in language.

   4(a) Corollary: In the eyes of the critic, three kinds of actions—the intuition of beauty, the statement of fact, and the eventual judgment of value—are all equally legitimate forms of knowledge.

5. The initial intuition of beauty, which forms the basis of impressionistic criticism, cannot be qualified or analyzed into parts. It is either present as a whole or it is not.

6. Beauty is a state of being between a subject and an object, and, accordingly, has no objective existence.

7. The experience of beauty is identical with the experience of love and of God. All three are different ways in which human beings experience value.

8. An individual's critical judgment is influenced by the broader social context in which it occurs, that is, others' artistic taste and their critical reports of it.

9. The final judgment of a musical experience must maintain a balance between any preliminary judgments that may have been made of various parts of the whole and the whole itself.

10. The judgment of beauty aims at a comparative balance between types of knowledge: for example, intuition and reason, phantasy and system, spirit and material.

11. The scientific critic should compensate for the impressionist critic's absolute standards, outlined in principle five, by employing a scale of values to measure relative degrees of beauty.

12. In the history of western music, value has usually been associated more with "style" than "manner" except during periods of radical change.

13. In the history of western music, value has been associated with a comparative balance between musical functions such as pitch or rhythm.

14. The greatest musical works in a given style are usually distinguished by a higher degree of workmanship or integrity than other works in the same style.

Figure 3. Seeger's fourteen principles of music criticism

tools of logical analysis. The general method outlined in these principles—the ideal of achieving a balance between opposing mental faculties—is the heart and soul of his philosophical approach. Here Seeger displays some interest in the practical challenges of negotiating between competing demands, imagining various hypothetical situations, and offering his solutions. By no means, however, are these

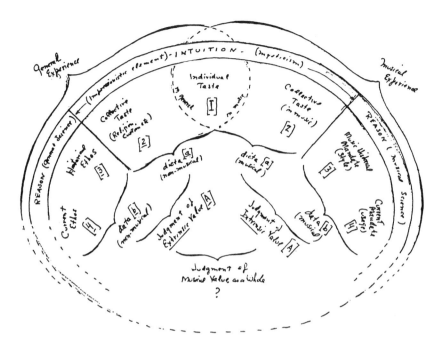

Figure 4. Process of musical judgment, *Tradition and Experiment in the New Music*

eight guidelines intended to be comprehensive. It goes without saying that more questions would arise if Seeger's method were applied in a variety of musical situations.

Finally, the last three principles are an eclectic mixture of Seeger's views on history and avant-garde composition. Here we see signs of his commitment to translate his abstract philosophical theories into specific musical proposals. In the accompanying commentary Seeger presents a theory of historical change that encompasses the development of Western music from monophonic chant to the rebellion against romanticism at the beginning of the twentieth century. Equipped with this theory, he then ventures a new stylistic ideal for contemporary composers that grows out of his view of history. Since these ideas are more concerned with the application of Seeger's theory of knowledge than the theory itself, a detailed study of his conception of history and his recommendations for composers must be postponed until part 2.

For some readers, Seeger's conception of music criticism as a set of fourteen principles might be a source of confusion. It is important to remember that the set is by no means comprehensive; Seeger himself

says, "One could have increased or decreased their number."[3] His remark confers a certain ad hoc character to the list, as if principles
could be freely added to or subtracted from the set without changing
the critical process he envisions. One reason for this is that the most
complete version of Seeger's musical-critical process is the diagram,
not the set of principles; the latter, by contrast, serve as a series of
afterthoughts, elaborations, and comments on the former. The strongest indication that the principles are incomplete is that Seeger himself
admits that one stage of the critical process described in the diagram,
the fusion of current and historical musical "ethos," is not yet possible:
"The formulation of critical principles based upon this confused field
is out of the question for some time to come."[4] Another reason for focusing more on the diagram than the list is that in the years following
1930 Seeger gradually increased the total number of principles from
eight to fourteen. Unfortunately, the list in figure 3 shows signs of this
process of accretion. For example, there are several instances of redundancy: principle 10 recalls 3; principle 6 echoes part of 4; and
principles 1–3 could be simplified into a single principle.

Hence, in the interest of clarity and economy, I have created a revised list of the three most essential principles of music criticism,
from which all else in Seeger's theory flows (reproduced in figure 5).
I will summarize these essential principles plus a handful of other
themes drawn from the diagram and Seeger's running commentary as
well as evaluate the theory's overall success.

Principle I

The first essential principle in my revised list establishes beyond all
doubt that the critical process begins with intuition. A brief comparison with Seeger's early essay "Principles" indicates that little has
changed in his formulation of intuition other than the way he refers
to it. The "musical" point of view has now been reincarnated as "impressionistic criticism" or the "spontaneous taste reaction." What has
changed is the way Seeger views language. Seeger provides a glimpse
of this dramatic shift while unveiling his diagram of the critical process. His scheme, he says, represents two things: "(1) the presentation
of musical value *in music* and (2) the constituting of the principles
upon which is based the process of presenting an account of musical
value *in language*."[5] At first, this opposition between music and lan-

I. The intuition of aesthetic value, which forms the basis of impressionistic criticism, cannot be qualified or analyzed into parts. It is either present as a whole or it is not.

II. Criticism aims at a relative balance between two opposing mental faculties, intuition and reason, and the corresponding types of criticism, impressionistic and scientific. These faculties not only complement each other, but one may actually influence how the other proceeds.

III. The process by which the critical mediation proposed in principle two comes about is itself a series of mediations between opposites: the individual's taste vs. society's taste; the historical study of musical style vs. the current development of composition; and the ethical conception of music, both past and present vs. the scientific analysis of musical phenomena. The final result of all these mediations is a judgment of musical value.

Figure 5. Three essential principles of Seeger's theory of music criticism

guage seems like the familiar jeremiad of skepticism that Seeger had previously dubbed the "linguo-centric predicament." In his early essays the discovery that language could never truly mirror musical experience was for musicology a confession of failure. To reject language as an imperfect medium for describing music amounted to a negation of music criticism. In the treatise, however, the same discovery serves as a professional statement of faith, a pledge that the critic's very reason for being is to master the art of expressing the inexpressible. The difference is that what was once the stigma of critical paralysis is now a slogan of critical practice. The "predicament" has now become a limit that can and must be transcended. By embracing language as the only possible medium other than music itself for conveying one's musical response, Seeger reaffirms the tradition of music criticism and gives it new life.

My first essential principle is also an eloquent testament to Seeger's success in adapting the ideas of Henri Bergson. What was originally the seed of a metaphysical theory is now firmly rooted in the soil of aesthetic speculation. For Bergson, philosophy was a vehicle for transcending our ordinary, commonsense view of time and space in order to enter a new world of intuition. Seeger's aim, by contrast, was not only to discover this new intuitive kingdom but also to somehow capture it in writing and transmit it to others. He was not content simply to reveal the wonder and mystery of musical immediacy; instead he focused on ways of cultivating and eventually transforming it into a judgment of musical value. In sum, the difference between the two thinkers is this: whereas Seeger was just as fascinated with mysticism as Bergson, he was more committed than his French counterpart to transforming mystical visions into specific musical judgments that could be of practical use to composers and critics alike.

Principle II

If intuition is the seed of Seeger's theory, then his ideal fusion of reason and intuition, as outlined in my second essential principle, is the philosophical fruit that it bears. Although the concept of fusion is certainly adumbrated in his early essays, it is not until the treatise that it reaches full maturity. The central doctrine of his aesthetic theory is the mediation between extremes; the intuition of beauty is balanced against the methods of scientific logic. Seeger envisions criticism as an ongoing dialogue between extremes.

Since criticism—regarded as the speech treatment of value in an art—music—is essentially concerned with the *relating* of Beauty and Truth, it can never have final results. The mystic may roar down his opposition, abash technical excellence and social usefulness with eloquence or silence it with enigmas. The scientist may bear it down with incontestable argument. But the critic can do none of these. Relativity is his subject matter and relative, his results—relatively beautiful, relatively true.[6]

The concept of mediation between extremes occupies a place of honor in Seeger's original set of principles (see principles 1–3 in figure 3), as well as in his diagram of the criteria involved in musical judgment (figure 4). The diagram serves as a map on which the various paths of critical mediation can be traced. The tree structure of this diagram begins with seven sources of musical knowledge and, through a series of negotiations between opposites or extremes, leads to a grand synthesis called the "judgment of value." Even though reason is technically not one of the original seven sources of value, to pass between any two levels in the hierarchy requires that we reflect on our basic habits, whether they be purely musical, social, or scientific. The diagram signals Seeger's faith in the ultimate power of mediation, or what he describes as "the balancing or equating of pairs of commensurable factors."[7]

The second essential principle also helps clarify the mosaic of philosophical ideas that helped shape Seeger's thinking. That he gives as much weight to reason as to intuition in his model of cognition shows how close an affinity he shared with Bertrand Russell. As will be recalled from chapter 2, Russell in his early writings proposes that neither the mystic's vision nor the scientist's precision is the "sole arbiter of metaphysical truth."[8] In a true philosophical theory each nourishes and depends on the other.

> But the greatest men who have been philosophers have felt the need both of science and of mysticism: the attempt to harmonize the two was what made their life, and what always must, for all its arduous uncertainty, make philosophy, to some minds, a greater thing than either science or religion.[9]

Seeger borrows this notion of mutual dependence between intuition and reason, and then applies it to art. To accommodate the study of music, Russell's aphorism must be slightly amended: in Seeger's mind, musicology is a greater thing than either science or musical intuition.

Seeger's reliance on the principle of mediation also serves as a reply to David Hume's skepticism regarding the contradictions inherent in ethical argument. As summarized in chapter 3, Hume's complaint was that if an ethical theory contains only statements of fact in its premises and those statements lead to ethical judgments in the conclusions, then the resulting logical contradiction renders the theory invalid. In Hume's experience all previous ethical theories had suffered from this contradiction: hence, the rule "No 'ought' from 'is.'" For music critics influenced by Seeger's theory, almost the reverse is true. In this case they begin with statements of taste, that is, musical intuitions, compare them to statements of fact, and then arrive at a determination of value. The goal is not to discover a permanent aesthetic value with universal applicability but rather something much more modest: to achieve a balanced aesthetic judgment.

Both Seeger and Russell preach a gospel of humanism in which the intellect is as important as artistic genius or religious faith. For Seeger, the musicologist is like an oracle unveiling the prophecy of musical revelation, a messenger who delivers the secret of musical intuition. Yet once the message was delivered, the secret revealed, Seeger also wanted to see that it came true, that it was realized in action. Like Prometheus, Seeger longed to bring the fire of intuition from heaven down to earth; yet after it was delivered, he was equally determined to keep the flame alive and pass it on to others. In short, the calling of the music critic was to record and transmit the mystery of music. To achieve that goal, musicologists had to become teachers as much as seers, dedicated not only to witnessing the unspeakable wonders of music but also to giving those wonders the power of language. Seeger's ideal music critic was part spiritualist, part activist, combining the tranquil wisdom of a musical visionary with the passion of a musical reformer bent on putting that vision into practice.

Principle III

This revised principle is the only one of the three that has no direct counterpart among Seeger's original fourteen. Instead it summarizes the diagram and explains the overall purpose for mediating between so many pairs of opposites. The immediate benefit of such a synopsis is that it shows Seeger's breadth of scope, an attribute that bears the unmistakable stamp of Ralph Perry. As discussed in chapter 3, Perry's broad conception of value provides a new philosophical framework in which the traditional questions of aesthetics are fundamentally connected to other disciplines. Had Seeger never been exposed to Perry's work, the first stage of the critical process schematized in figure 4 would have included only one source of value, intuition, instead of seven.

That said, the most significant difference between Seeger's scheme of musical judgment and Perry's monumental philosophical theory is the way each conceives of musical experience. For Perry, it is a point of departure, one manifestation of human volition among many, that all combine to serve as the empirical basis from which a general theory can be inferred. To the axiologist or philosopher of values, musical experience is significant only insofar as it demonstrates general properties of value that motivate a broad range of human actions. Seeger, however, is perfectly content to ignore Perry's broad spectrum of human preferences in order to focus on a single artistic medium: music. In Seeger's eyes, musical value is an end product, the culmination of a long critical process by which intuition is translated into judgment.

———————

At this stage it is useful to expand upon a handful of miscellaneous topics that are present in Seeger's diagram of aesthetic judgment and the original list of fourteen principles but were omitted from my three essential principles. A theme running through all of them is Seeger's desire to avoid complex and arcane philosophical debates. Always the skeptic, he relies on what he would later half jokingly describe as "uncommon common sense" to explain the nature of musical value.[10]

Subjectivity versus Objectivity

From Perry, Seeger learned a strategy for addressing a philosophical problem without the complex network of definitions and arguments that usually goes with it. A good example of this appears in principles 4 and 6, where Seeger discusses the objectivity of aesthetic perception. The question Seeger addresses could be rephrased as follows: How can we be sure that our perception of a musical performance corresponds to what is actually being performed? Seeger's answer to this perennial aesthetic puzzle is instructive, for it avoids any lengthy defense of his position. Instead, his strategy is to define value as what "inheres in relationships between the values and the thing valued."[11] In other words, "values" are created by a particular aesthetic attitude adopted by a listener toward a musical object: as to whether that object actually exists or is merely a hallucination, Seeger says nothing. Perry's own definition of the concept, first formulated in 1912 and elaborated in his monumental study of 1926, is quite similar: the relation between an "interest" and an object. Seeger wastes no time trying to prove that the object of our perceptions truly exists, for, as a believer in the doctrine of "common sense realism," he takes it for granted (for a summary of this doctrine, see chapter 3). Instead he and Perry devote most of their time to contemplating the various questions posed by the psychological world of the perceiving subject. Where the two differ most is in the complexity of their answers.

Another aspect of principles 4 and 6 is worth mentioning. By elaborating on a distinction implied in the diagram, Seeger borrows a page from the nineteenth-century axiologists' book. He emphasizes the difference between facts and values in his stipulation that *"facts* may be conceded to *exist* but *value* as some philosophers have it, *subsists.*"[12] By the word "subsist" Seeger means a form of existence that depends on some other medium or condition. Among the many definitions presented in the *Oxford English Dictionary,* the following comes closest to describing what Seeger intends. "To consist, lie, or reside in some specified thing, circumstance, fact, etc."[13] By insisting that a judgment of value "subsists" rather than merely "exists," Seeger is dramatizing the difference between a single stage in the music-critical process and the final outcome of value.

Yet this lesson in semantics raises even more questions. What word should be used to characterize the mystical intuition, the first step in

the long journey toward aesthetic judgment? Is there any real difference between intuiting and listening, or is an intuition merely a glori-
fied sensation? Since Seeger offered no opinion on these matters, he
leaves the field open for speculation. If, for the scientist, facts simply
"are," then from the mystic's point of view perhaps an intuition "must
be." The point of the terminological digression found in principle 4 is
that Seeger is differentiating the various stages of the critical process
and, in one case, he dramatizes that stage by using a special term.[14]

In the corollary to principle 4, Seeger states that the act of valuing
is "on a par" with the act of analyzing and intuiting. This claim comes
as no surprise, since it is implied by the dualistic nature of the critical
theory as a whole. As Bertrand Russell observes in his meditations on
religion, neither the mystic nor the rationalist has sole access to the
truth. The same can be said of music criticism. Musicologists who rely
on either spontaneous rhapsody or impartial analysis alone will never
achieve as honest an appraisal of value as when the two approaches
work together in concert.

Unfortunately, in his eagerness to equate the acts of intuiting, analyzing, and judging, Seeger confuses the issue somewhat. There must
be *some* difference between performing the preliminary stages of the
critical process and completing the final stage of aesthetic synthesis; if
not, there would be no philosophical incentive for the critic to move
beyond mystical silence or logical calculation. It must be preferable to
see the process through to the end rather than be waylaid indefinitely
in either preliminary stage.

Beauty, Love, and God

Principle 7 reveals another aspect of Seeger's thought that has evolved
since the early essays. What he initially described as an ineffable intuition of music he now compares to other profound human experiences
such as romantic love and religious faith. This comparison reveals two
things about Seeger's overall project: it amplifies the intuitionist approach to music, and it shows the residual influence of Perry's conception of value.

Having just defined the attitude of the impressionist critic, Seeger
then compares different types of musical experience. He mentions
three works that he believes demonstrate the highest degree of artistry:
the "credo" from Giovanni Palestrina's *Pope Marcellus Mass*, Ludwig

van Beethoven's "Moonlight" Piano Sonata in C# Minor, op. 27, no. 2 (presumably the first movement), and the "Liebestodt" from Richard Wagner's *Tristan und Isolde.* Each composition is associated with a sphere of human value: Palestrina with faith in the supernatural or the sublime, Beethoven with intellectual beauty, and Wagner with human love. Seeger then imagines that the titles and corresponding values have been rearranged, and he challenges the reader to distinguish one from the other. "Interchange the values and the titles. Is the association less apt? One may be sure that the true mystic will deny it. He may go farther and claim the three values are three names for one and the same experience, a reality beyond name." [15]

What is Seeger's underlying purpose in this section? Does he mean that all musical intuitions are exactly the same, and that as far as musical value is concerned, if you've heard it once, you've heard it all? This is surely a caricature of Seeger's view. The problem lies in the difference between experiencing musical value as an intuitionist and then trying to express one's intuition in words. It is safe to assume that Seeger believes our intuitive response to each piece is unique. If listeners who had never been exposed to these works heard all three in a single concert with their titles exchanged and the listeners were deeply moved by all three performances, their responses would *not* be identical. But if those same listeners tried to express their intuitions in words, the *verbal accounts* of their experiences would be equally superlative. The point is that the purely intuitive listener knows no shades of meaning, no gradations of value, no redeeming qualities of a slightly flawed performance. An intuition of beauty or, in Seeger's mind, of any other aesthetic value is all or nothing. In short, impressionist critics are not indiscriminate in their exercise of intuition; it is wrong to assume that they find love or beauty in everything they hear. Rather, they comprehend only two discriminations, all good or all bad, and, since intuition is absolute sovereign in their internal kingdoms, its edict is beyond dispute. Confined to an intuitive realm, these critics know only the aesthetic version of sheer pain or absolute pleasure.

Relative versus Absolute Value

In principle 11 the rationalist responds to the intuitionist's absolute standard of judgment just mentioned. Seeger describes the difference as follows: "It is the nature of the impressionistic criticism to run into a mystical monism. The obvious check on this tendency is the scientific pluralism of the present day. To the mystic statement that a work has the supreme value—beauty—or no value at all, the scientist opposes a whole scale of values."[16] Seeger reiterates the opposition between "monism" and "pluralism" that he used in his 1925 essay "Prolegomena" to characterize the difference between Eastern and Western culture. In this context, however, the opposition is stripped of its previous religious connotations and instead refers to the presence or absence of a scale of evaluation. By the notion of scale Seeger does not mean an exact numerical measure but a comparative valuation such as good, better, or best. Seeger's version of this tripartite scale is either interesting; worthwhile/important; or fine/great. In his rather crude hierarchy, whichever specific level one chooses is more important than which word within the level—particularly for evaluations other than "best." One of the scientific critic's greatest virtues is to defend works of art that come close to greatness but never quite reach it. In other words, one can assign genuine value to a composition and still have nagging reservations about it.

Principle 9 is a variation on the same theme of the refinement of critical valuation. Here Seeger emphasizes the difference between judging a performance on the basis of a single, salient part or on the basis of the whole. This problem comes about because of the critic's need for precision:

And in talking there is always the tendency to talk of parts rather than of wholes. It is easier to be logical about details. If a statement about a whole is challenged, we customarily start talking about the qualities of the parts. Thus we come to judge from the nature of the parts what is the nature of the whole.[17]

Seeger himself provides a compelling musical illustration of this principle in his essay "On Style and Manner in Modern Composition," published in 1923. In the course of his essay he outlines a three-step model of musical creativity in which logic and intuition each play a role. The first stage is "prevision," which involves a composer's preliminary knowledge of the necessary compositional techniques and their coordination with his or her musical taste. The second stage is the actual writing, what he calls "vision" or "inspiration." This leads to the third and final stage of "revision," in which the composer analyzes and usually modifies the product of his previous creative labors.[18]

Seeger then uses this model of creativity to evaluate the music of two contemporary composers: Arnold Schoenberg and Giacomo Puccini. Given Seeger's passion for the avant-garde, his choice of Puccini at first seems more like a straw man to knock down than a genuine critical comparison. Yet, surprisingly enough, he finds virtue in both men's work but for entirely different reasons. Although he admires Schoenberg's music because it "satisfies our curiosity and stimulates our intellectual life," unfortunately, it is incapable of moving the emotions. Puccini, by contrast, suffers from the other extreme. His music "stirs our vitals—we grow hot and cold, feel tears and choking sensations," yet afterwards Seeger despises himself "for having been moved so by what [I] cannot admire."[19] If we refer to Seeger's three-part model, Schoenberg indulges in the first and third stages, while Puccini never manages to transcend the second. The ultimate stylistic ideal, Seeger believes, should be a fusion of both extremes.

The most important conclusion to draw from this brief comparison of Schoenberg and Puccini is that, despite Seeger's grave reservations about each composer's music, he nevertheless finds value in them both. To have truly mixed emotions about a musical performance, while strictly anathema to the impressionist critic, is stock-in-trade for the style of balanced criticism that Seeger recommends.

Individual versus Social Taste

Principle 8 shows a practical streak in Seeger's approach that until now has been distinguished by its absence. He observes that, despite the mystical listener's noblest intentions, an intuition of value may be based as much on social factors as on a composition's intrinsic artistic worth. The process by which one develops taste is not a strictly introspective affair conducted in the privacy of one's own musical soul. The likes and dislikes of others, as well as the vagaries of commercial success, all can play a positive or negative role in shaping a critic's musical obiter dicta. It falls to the intellect to discover these social forces within one's spontaneous intuitions, to decide which are legitimate, and eventually to render a balanced judgment. Although Seeger supplies no specific examples to illustrate this principle, its mere presence in an otherwise ideal process shows the first signs of his later interest in the sociology of music.

History and Compositional Style

Principles 12–14 mark a dramatic departure from the previous eleven. Here we see Seeger merging two other subjects with his philosophical speculation: a new ideal of composition style accompanied by a theory of historical change. That he would try to link historical analysis with compositional instruction is a clear indication that, in his eyes, philosophical theory could not only foster musical practice but also directly shape it. In his view the history of Western music could be explained as a two-part cycle that alternates between "style," a musical aesthetic in which all resources are perfectly balanced, and "manner," the transition between "styles" during which one musical resource dominates all the others. Seeger's source for this model was Johann von Goethe, who envisioned it as an aesthetic ideal for all artistic media (In chapters 5 and 6 I examine more fully the consequences of this model for compositional technique.) Having posited this model of stylistic change, Seeger then applies it to the present. The last prevailing "style" had been nineteenth-century romanticism, and its decline during the first three decades of the twentieth century had coincided with what Seeger considered a series of "manners." Seeger hoped that the treatise as a whole—including the initial theory of criticism, and the general conception of neumatic form and regimen of dissonant counterpoint—would help usher in this new historical "style." Thus, principles 12–14 constitute a first glimpse of a practical application of his philosophical theories that would eventually occupy a lion's share of the treatise. Indeed, one of the aims of part 2 of this study is to examine how that application comes about and to evaluate its success.

Ethical Significance of Music

The most glaring discrepancy between Seeger's diagram and set of principles is that the latter never address one of the basic sources of value: the ethical significance of music. This subject leads us to reconsider the impact of Ralph Perry on Seeger's overall theory of criticism. Perry's and Seeger's approaches differ in the importance they assign to ethics. In Perry's eyes, the individual's interest in art, like other expressions of human value, must always be balanced against the interests of the community. Though he never offers an exact formula for calculating this balance, he believes that a harmony among interests not only can be achieved but also should reflect some sort of ethical ideal.

Seeger is equally committed to addressing the ethical significance of art, but he approaches the question more as an anthropologist than a philosopher. He uses the term "musical ethos" to refer to the various social beliefs and functions with which music is associated in modern culture. It would be a mistake, however, to assume that his reference to "ethos" is a means of reviving the ancient Greek doctrine that viewed music as a tool for ethical education or a means for instilling specific ethical values. As a point of comparison, next to Paul Hindemith's probing discussion of the subject in *A Composer's World,* Seeger's treatment seems rather naive.[20] Instead, Seeger hopes to explore what our current attitudes toward composition, performance, and audition may tell us about our culture as a whole. While he never goes into detail about the practical methods that are needed to acquire this knowledge, he does make a general suggestion regarding cultural comparisons: the ethical significance that Eastern cultures, such as those of China and India, attribute to music may illuminate the sorts of ethical values that are tacitly assumed in Western culture.[21]

Relativity

It would be a mistake to conclude from Seeger's diagram that the judgment of musical value, the pinnacle of this inverted pyramid, is final or that the process can lead to a single, inevitable result. Seeger provides several clues in his diagram and accompanying commentary that the notion of criticism by mediation is not a closed system. First, he places a question mark next to the hierarchy's final level, the "judgment of musical value as a whole?" This symbol is less an indication of uncertainty on Seeger's part than a reminder of his commitment to a process of mutual harmony and relativity, or, in his words, "relatively beautiful, relatively true." Second, in a telling footnote Seeger sketches two other possible diagrams that alter the critical hierarchy in significant ways. In one diagram he imagines a hypothetical world in which the process of criticism is reversed, beginning with a rational view of music and later balancing it with the individual's intuitive response. Seeger's reason for imagining such a reversal illustrates well his fasci-

nation with the method of fusing opposites. In the midst of constructing an elaborate model that outlines the music critical process, he
promptly turns the model on its head and invites the reader to compare this upside-down process with the original. He concludes by saying that the "final result" of this hypothetical model "would be just as
questionable" as that depicted in figure 4.

There is still another possible element of confusion in Seeger's exposition of the music-critical process, especially when presented in the
form of a list. The fact that the statements are numbered suggests that
they might be spelling out a logical argument—for instance, a set of
major and minor premises in a classical syllogism. It is no secret that
later in his life Seeger developed such a fascination for the writings of
the twentieth-century philosopher Ludwig Wittgenstein that he began to number the paragraphs in his prose like those of the latter's
Tractatus Logico-philosophicus.[22] But to interpret Seeger's style of
presentation in the treatise as an exercise in logic would be to mis-
judge the basic fabric of his entire approach to criticism. Contrary to
appearances, Seeger's theory of musical knowledge is neither a closed
system nor a comprehensive mathematical model of human judgment. Instead, he presents the mental faculties involved in musical
judgment and then imagines several hypothetical scenarios in which a
critic might determine musical value. The list is *not* an exhaustive
summary of all the possible ways in which our mental faculties inter-
act in the critical process, or of the wide spectrum of temperaments
that an individual critic may possess. Although Seeger himself refers
to his method of presentation as "scientific," he hardly means by this
comment that his conception is a genuine mathematical proof or scientific theory.[23] As he makes clear in his exposition, criticism is a rational process in that reason amends, tempers, and otherwise balances
the spontaneous taste reactions of the intuition.

Throughout my discussion of Seeger's treatise I have emphasized
that one of its essential characteristics is the ideal of fusing philosophical principles with practical proposals in such fields as composition,
history, and musicology. Yet this blend of theory and practice does not
come without a price. The question arises what kind of philosophical
theory his model of criticism truly is. If we borrow a comprehensive
ideal proposed by the distinguished aesthetician Monroe Beardsley, it
is possible to assess exactly what Seeger has achieved in the treatise.

According to Beardsley, a theory must belong to at least one of the following six categories in order to be considered a philosophy of music:

(1) an ontology of music: what kind of entity is a musical work of art, and how is it related to performances and scores? (2) a categorical scheme: what are the basic and universal elements or aspects of music? (3) foundations of a hermeneutics or semiotics of music (or a demonstration that these cannot be forthcoming): what, if anything, can music mean or refer to? (4) an epistemology of music: how are the objective properties (if any) of musical works known through our perceptions or experiences of them? (5) a theory of music criticism: what makes one musical work better than another (if that is possible)? (6) foundations of a social philosophy of music: what are the basic values and foundations of music in human life, individual and social?[24]

Seeger's work falls into several of these categories. The encyclopedic schemes of musicology that he devised in his later writings certainly belong to the second category. However, any detailed discussion of them must be reserved for part 2 of this study. If we study *Tradition and Experiment in the New Music* with this list in mind, Seeger's strongest contributions are in the fourth and fifth categories: an epistemological theory (or theory of knowledge) and a theory of music criticism. I shall consider each one in turn.

In chapters 1 and 2 Seeger presents an outline for a theory of knowledge in which he defines the basic faculties that constitute any type of human knowledge: intuition and reason. The fact that Seeger's typology of knowledge is so heavily indebted to the ideas of Henri Bergson leaves it open to some of the same criticisms that have been raised against the French philosopher. The most serious shortcoming is a general lack of clarity, particularly in the definition of terms. While the concept of intuition invented by Bergson, and later revived by Seeger, may be captivating (or even undeniable) for most musicians, its vagueness makes the delicate balance with logic that much harder to achieve. What is the difference between a commonplace sensation, such as the nocturnal wail of a train's horn, and an intuition of a French horn solo? Bergson believed that all artists are blessed with highly developed intuitive powers, more so than nonartists. Would Seeger agree? If so, does that mean there are two kinds of intuition, simple and artistic? What about the insights scientists make when they discover why newly collected empirical data do not fit an old, accepted theory? Does such an insight constitute a third type of intuition? The aspect of Seeger's theory of knowledge that is in greatest need of the discriminating power of logic is the concept of intuition itself.

When we turn to Seeger's proposals about music criticism, the problem of clarity still persists. While his aim is to develop a practical model of criticism, the final result is more of a general outline than a precise set of procedures. Questions abound. For instance, how does one settle differences between two music critics who have opposing intuitions? If one critic condemns a performance partly on the basis of what others have said about it and another critic praises the same performance partly because of its excellent reputation, how does one mediate? Although Seeger suggests solutions for some practical problems that might arise when applying his ideal of mediation—such as the confusion of the part for the whole in principle 9 and the difference between absolute and relative beauty stressed in principle 11— he does not foresee all of the potential problems.

The question comes down to how much we should expect a philosophical theory to explain. If we assume that a philosophical model of criticism should be able to account for every possible practical difficulty, then Seeger's model certainly falls short. But if we adopt more modest expectations, as I believe we should, and accept that a philosophy can be an outline or basic foundation of criticism, then the lack of precision in Seeger's theory is not necessarily a weakness. For a scheme of criticism, it can be an asset as much as a liability. In his primer on music criticism Michel-Dimitri Calvocoressi throws light on this question:

By seeking a compromise, we shall be following for a while the lead of the votaries of criticism by system; for every system is a compromise, an acknowledgement of the impossibility to judge except by reference to a system. . . . [But] we are in quest of a more satisfactory form of compromise, by virtue of which our course will follow a method and not a system, and which will include reference to no fixed . . . standard.[25]

Calvocoressi's distinction between "method" and "system" captures well the tension Seeger felt between a purely logical philosophical argument and a loosely designed "critical process."

To do justice to the infinite nuances of musical experience, Seeger, like Calvocoressi, can never embrace a systematic or a formal (in the mathematical sense) theory. Instead, each is satisfied with his own form of compromise: Calvocoressi calls it a "method," Seeger a "principle of mediation." To blame Seeger for not being precise enough when he explicitly designed his theory so as to avoid absolute precision is to misunderstand his entire venture. Ultimately, the best standard for evaluating Seeger's philosophical theories is the success of their musical applications, and this is the subject of part 2 of this study.

Conclusion

In the preface to his monumental work *General Theory of Value,* Ralph B. Perry invokes a metaphor from classical antiquity that may help illuminate the difference between his and Seeger's philosophical ambitions. There are two kinds of philosophy, Perry says, "that which cuts the Gordian knot and that which attempts to untie it. The present book aims to exemplify the latter."[26] This comment refers to a famous prophecy of Gordius, king of Phrygia, that whoever could loosen an impenetrable knot he had tied would rule all of Asia. That Perry would pledge to untangle the knot without cutting it shows his commitment to painstaking philosophical analysis, and, judging by the length and complexity of his principal work, he clearly lived up to his word.

It is significant that Seeger, too, invokes the challenge of the Gordian knot, but, unlike Perry, he vows to sever it. In this respect he follows in the footsteps of Alexander the Great, who, according to tradition, fulfilled Gordius's prophecy by splitting the knot with his sword. In the commentary to one of his principles Seeger announces: "The philosophic reader, will, if he has survived thus far, forgive the cutting of the Gordian knot. . . . It has to be cut somewhere if the present undertaking is to proceed as a treatise on musical composition rather than in philosophy."[27] To appreciate the full meaning of this remark, we must view it in the context of the treatise's design as a whole.

Seeger's flippant tone here misrepresents his underlying attitude toward philosophy. Even a quick glance at the table of contents reveals that *Tradition and Experiment in the New Music* is far more than a "treatise on musical composition." Were it simply a technical manual, Seeger certainly could have dispensed with his theory of musical criticism as presented in the opening two chapters. His search for a theory of musical knowledge not only promised its own intrinsic rewards but also was integrally linked to his life as a musician and musicologist. Despite his lifelong fascination with theory and abstract thought, Seeger always considered himself to be a professional musician with an amateur's love of philosophy. Although after his departure from Berkeley he stopped composing serious art music, he never lost the composer's practical orientation, particularly in his desire to find some way of applying philosophical theories to the critic's craft or the composer's art. When Seeger proposes to cut the Gordian knot, the empire he envisions would contain as many artists as philosophers of art.

Seeger's highly personal approach to philosophy was also in keeping with some of the most innovative thinkers of the early twentieth century. In an autobiographical sketch written in 1930, Ralph Perry portrays the unique character of this period in philosophy:

Idealists [of the nineteenth century] have been system-builders and have staked all on the monumental perfection of the whole. James, Bergson, Russell, and Whitehead, on the other hand, pay as they go. You do not have to be converted to their gospel in order to profit by them. They abound in suggestive hypothesis, shrewd observation, and delicate analysis which you can detach and build into your own thinking. The newer philosophy which has grown up in opposition to idealism, and which has set a fashion which even idealism is now adopting, has something of the fruitfulness of empirical science.[28]

According to Perry, what is remarkable about these four philosophers is that the very nature of their work lends itself to being split into parts—that is, "hypotheses," "observations," "analyses"—and used for some new purpose not envisioned by its author. In an economic image highly reminiscent of William James, Perry says that all four "pay as they go," that is, they provide explanations of their work at each step of the way, never assuming that readers will suspend their doubts and questions until the end. Since of the philosophers who helped shape Seeger's thought, two are on this list and the third is its author, any observation about them also throws light on Seeger's unusual philosophical temperament. Indeed, to appreciate fully the mosaic character of Seeger's philosophy, it will be useful to review the roles that Bergson, Perry, and Russell played in its development.

Of all the philosophers of the early twentieth century, Bergson was the most likely candidate to inspire a composer who was already suspicious of scientific abstraction. Bergson's principal message was that the intuition held inexpressible and inexhaustible wonders, and that those best suited to deliver that message were artists. While Seeger shared a like passion for the riches of intuition, he became more interested in its application to the art of music. Since he believed that composers, theorists, and musicologists had all lost sight of the intuitive and, thus, nonverbal nature of musical experience, Seeger saw his mission as that of a philosophical conscience, intent on restoring intuition to its rightful place of honor.

Perry's unique approach was to integrate different fields from the humanities and social sciences into a single philosophical venture. In his view, philosophy must be as inclusive as possible, and the philosopher "must run the risk of inaccuracy, or even court it, for the sake of that comprehensiveness of view, that tracing of connections and of contours, which is the only contribution to human wisdom which, as philosopher, he can hope to make."[29] Perry's vision of human value was philosophical speculation on a grand scale; in his view, the disciplines of ethics, political science, and aesthetics could all benefit from his integrative approach to philosophy. But Seeger was enthralled more by the spirit of Perry's study of human value than by his individual methods of argument. Seeger, too, had an expansive vision of musical knowledge, as if it were a vast body of water fed by the streams of various disciplines in the sciences and humanities. To guide musicologists on their critical voyages Seeger recommended that they rely on their experience as practicing musicians, like a personal compass amid an uncertain and unforgiving wind.

But the philosopher with whom Seeger shared the greatest affinity was Bertrand Russell. It was Russell's ideal of mediation, his conception of philosophy poised delicately between the fiery passions of the mystic and the levelheaded reflections of the scientist, that formed the centerpiece of Seeger's theory of criticism. In some respects, it is surprising that Seeger would have found inspiration for his concept of mediation in the writings of one of the greatest rationalist philosophers of the twentieth century. After all, the process of critical mediation that Seeger envisions has neither an exact procedure nor a definite end. Yet Russell's "Mysticism and Logic" was among his least precise and, at the same time, most provocative essays. That the concept of mediation is so flexible, so open to interpretation, is what must have attracted Seeger. The tension between logical and mystical thought that Russell embraces in his essay mirrors directly Seeger's simultaneous and sometimes contradictory attractions to composition and musicology. Perhaps it is best to regard Seeger's ideal of music criticism not as a method but rather as a marriage of conflicting temperaments: the creative with the analytical, the rhapsodic with the systematic, the experimental with the traditional. In part 2 we will discover the musical and musicological offspring to which this marriage eventually gave birth.

Part Two

Musical Applications

Chapter Five

. . . .

A Philosophy in Practice

Music Criticism

In a 1932 tribute to the American avant-garde composer Carl Ruggles (1876–1971), Charles Seeger makes a telling remark about his unusual approach to the discipline of criticism:

> A complete criticism (something this sketch cannot pretend to be) should have both its scientific-critical, or logical, section and its impressionistic, or rhapsodic, section. But in treating of Carl Ruggles, it is quite impossible to do justice by the former without writing a history of music and a manual of modern composition, not to mention a ponderous treatise upon musicological method.[1]

Notwithstanding his self-effacing tone, Seeger himself was in a good position to "do justice" to Ruggles's music, for he had just written a huge compendium that combined two of the three projects he mentions: a composition manual and a treatise on musicological method. He had not only the ambition to develop a "ponderous" theory of criticism but also the desire to put it into practice. One thing Seeger could never be accused of is philosophizing in a musical vacuum, and, for him, one way of bridging the gap between philosophical abstraction and compositional practice was criticism. In his mind, though music critics were free to exercise their musical taste, they were not free to ignore the music of the present; indeed, professional critics bore a special responsibility toward evaluating contemporary music.

After Seeger finished a major revision of the treatise in 1931, he soon began to practice what he preached, evaluating contemporary composers' work in occasional critical reviews. In five short essays he discussed the music of a handful of leading American experimental composers, including Ruggles, Henry Cowell (1897–1965), Ruth Crawford (1901–53), and Charles Ives (1874–1954). Seeger's personality as a music critic is ultimately inseparable from his aspirations as a composition teacher and a philosopher. On the whole, he was a highly selective critic: of the four composers he reviewed, two were former students—Cowell and Crawford—and another, Ruggles, was for many years a close friend and associate. Only Ives fell outside of this circle of personal and professional association. Indeed, Seeger never published his true opinion of Ives's music, which was, on the whole, rather negative. In a 1970 interview Seeger said

Well, shortly afterwards I was in touch with Ives, and—mostly through his wife. . . . I avoided meeting him because I couldn't feel that I could be honest with him. I couldn't stand for that man and say I admire your music but it doesn't move me.[2]

In some respects Seeger's view is understandable because the two composers had such different artistic personalities: whereas at this stage Seeger focused on experimental composition, Ives was a musical polyglot, integrating European art music with American popular, religious, and experimental traditions. Yet there were also striking similarities between them, especially in the degree to which philosophical ideas informed their aesthetic taste.[3]

It would be a mistake, however, to assume that Seeger's selectiveness as a critic translates into a strong predisposition or bias. On the contrary, Seeger directed his harshest criticism toward the composers he knew best. More important, the standards with which he judged them all were not some personal whim, but rather were the products of the theory of mediation he had proposed in the treatise. Thus, Seeger's criticism serves as a lens through which we can view his philosophical conception of musical knowledge and its relation to musical taste. Though few in number, these writings eloquently testify to what degree philosophy and criticism could be intimately connected to the daily work of the composer.

While teaching at the Institute of Musical Arts (the forerunner of the Juilliard School of Music), Seeger began writing articles for a small music journal known first as *Eolus* and then as the *Eolian Review*.[4] His attraction to the interdisciplinary study of music is nowhere more apparent than in his article "Reviewing a Review," which was conceived as a reply to Dane Rudhyar's critical review of the music of Carl Ruggles entitled "Carl Ruggles and the Future of Dissonant Counterpoint." Rudhyar's review and Seeger's reply appeared together under a single title, "Revolt of the Angels," which was a reference to one of Ruggles's most recent compositions, *Angels*.[5] Seeger's essay serves as an apt introduction to his critical writings as a whole during this period in that it (1) addresses the issue of a critic's objectivity, (2) justifies why a thorough knowledge of experimental techniques was particularly important for the evaluation of new music, and (3) provides a glimpse of his motivation for creating a philosophy of music. Each will be discussed in turn.

My point of departure is the issue of impartiality in music criticism. In his essay on Ruggles's music Seeger reveals that whereas an ideal critique would consider a given composer's life, music, and the latter's historical context all without any bias or prejudgment, in practice such an ideal is impossible to achieve. Instead, he concludes, "Next best is frank bias, clearly expressed and open to correction by any intelligent reader." In this connection it is interesting to see how Seeger characterized his *own* objectivity as a critic of Ruggles's music, especially considering their close association:

Therefore let it be understood that the present undertaking frankly admits a friendship of over ten years' standing, a quite unusual kinship of taste in artistic matters, and an almost blood-brotherhood—for without a doubt, common ancestors burned witches with uncommon fury.[6]

Despite Seeger's "unusual kinship" with Ruggles, he still felt he could pass honest judgment on his friend's music. In sum, it was better to acknowledge openly a personal or musical bias than to conceal it behind the guise of pseudoprofessional judgment.

Along with the responsibility of hearing new music, Seeger felt critics were also obliged to know something about what they were hearing. A professional hazard much more dangerous than partisanship was lack of proficiency with experimental techniques. It comes as no surprise that Seeger was utterly disgusted with the state of music criticism in New York at this time. Yet it was the *basis* for critics' musical judgments that disturbed him more than their judgments themselves.

The two most signal reviews that came to my notice last winter in New York were Mr. Krehbiel's on Schoenberg's *Pierrot Lunaire* and . . . Mr. Rudhyar's on Ruggles' *Angels*. The vituperative abuse of the one is as bad as the plausible intellectualizing of the other. I would beg musicians of earnest and active mind . . . not to attempt to legislate for new music until they have a firmer technical grasp of it.[7]

"Reviewing a Review" is a protest against the poverty and incompetence of most critics' technical knowledge of experimental idioms. By raising these objections, Seeger was less a critical purist, interested in art criticism for its own sake, than he was concerned about the effect that critic's judgments would have on the general public. Thus he would argue that Ruggles's music was maligned partly because it was misunderstood, that is, judged in relation to fixed formal models and obsolete aesthetic standards. Seeger became a self-appointed spokesman for the avant-garde, a teacher who believed his discourses on musical technique and critical theory might win over the taste of composers and critics alike.

The importance of criticism was also a direct result of the infrequency of avant-garde concerts. Since contemporary composers' works were seldom performed, a review of new music was often more accessible to the public than the music itself. Seeger muses: "In these days of the triumph of aestheticism over art, the literary reaction to a new piece of music is more readily current in our large public than the music itself. Thus, the music is known to most people not in its proper form but in the dress given it by its reviewers."[8] Under these circumstances it was all the more important that critics of new music like Rudhyar be well informed. If Seeger could not review contemporary music for the major newspapers or journals himself, the least he could do was to appraise other reviewers' knowledge of recent compositional techniques.

Finally, the essay reveals Seeger's fascination for the broader problems inherent in the criticism of any musical work. Its very title, "Reviewing a Review," retraces the process by which his interest in philosophy was awakened. Seeger believes that in Rudhyar's treatment of theoretical issues raised by *Angels* (mostly modality), he utterly neglects the music's intuitive aspect. In the final paragraph he warns his readers to beware of "the tendency, fostered by non-musical points of view, to regard the materials, effects, rules or contingent phenomena of music with such interest as to lose the music. To non-musicians, music is, justifiably, vibrations, reflexes, number-relations, beauty or what not: to the musician, equally justifiably, it should be always music—first and last."⁹ Already in this passing remark, we can see the seed of the intuitionist creed that in his later treatise would blossom into one of the fundamental principles of musical knowledge.¹⁰

In his critical writings during the 1930s, 1940s, and early 1970s, Seeger was simultaneously trying to put two different ideals into practice: a theory of balanced criticism and a compositional synthesis of tradition and experiment. Seeger sincerely believed that Ruggles, Crawford, and Cowell were on the verge of discovering a radically new style of composition, and that one way he could contribute to that discovery was to help articulate its aesthetic goals and technical principles. By submitting his colleagues' latest efforts to a sympathetic but honest critique, Seeger believed he could help inaugurate a new age of dissonant composition.

Carl Ruggles

There are three principal sources for Seeger's views on Ruggles: an article commissioned in 1932 by Carl Engel, the editor of *The Musical Quarterly,* which was reprinted in Cowell's anthology *American Composers on American Music;* an essay published in 1939 comparing Ruggles and Charles Ives; and a touching obituary following Ruggles's death in 1971.¹¹ Although Seeger wrote the obituary over thirty years after the other two essays, all three are cut from the same music-critical cloth. Each demonstrates exactly how Seeger put into practice the ideal of balanced criticism sketched out in *Tradition and Experiment in the New Music:* the mediation between intuition and scientific logic. My overview of Seeger's various commentaries focuses on three themes: (1) his intuition of Ruggles's mystical approach toward art, (2) his analytical reflections on Ruggles's musical technique, and (3) his attempt to reconcile the intuitive and technical views of Ruggles's music in a final judgment of value.

In his 1971 tribute to Ruggles, Seeger describes his colleague's unique approach to composition as a direct outcome of his highly personal spiritual beliefs. For Ruggles the art of composition must always be seen in relation to an abstract, metaphysical ideal. Since no musical experience ever reaches this ideal, the value of each musical work is measured by how close it comes to it. The motivation for the composer is that each compositional act promises a new opportunity to regain, if not exceed, the spiritual heights that previous works had attained.

But Ruggles's mystical conception of music is not without its paradoxes. One question raised by Seeger's critiques is whether Ruggles believed that musical experience was a spiritual end in itself or simply a means to a spiritual end. On the one hand, Seeger's comments suggest that Ruggles believed that the acoustical experience of music was subordinate to the discovery of a higher mystical or transcendent state. Inasmuch as all art has a spiritual motivation, the ultimate meaning of any single medium would be interchangeable with another. Thus the possibility of achieving spiritual transcendence was "independent of time, space, and 'art medium.'" [12] Seeger recalled that Ruggles would frequently either begin or end their musical discussions with the words: "The greatest painters, composers, poets all say the same thing." [13] In that respect music would be viewed strictly as a means to a spiritual end, a kind of high-powered aural incense, that was associated with but never truly belonged to the supernatural world itself.

On the other hand, if music were strictly a means to achieving a spiritual end, then the craft it displayed would be utterly irrelevant for its higher purpose. But this was not what Ruggles believed. An individual's success in achieving transcendence was also tied somehow to a composition's degree of technical perfection or refinement. Composing was analogous to improvising in that each participant was constantly in search of new sources of inspiration. Seeger compares the composer to a sitar player who, by performing a raga, tries to merge the musical act itself, that is, its sensual appearance, with a vision of the "eternal Sublime." [14] The greater the composer's technical mastery, the greater his or her chance for attaining spiritual fulfillment. In sum, Ruggles viewed music, according to Seeger, as some kind of middle ground between a means to a higher spiritual end and a spiritual end in itself.

When Seeger finally passes judgment on Ruggles's music, he lavishes it with extravagant praise. The mature compositions such as *Portals* or *Sun-Treader,* we are told, are the result of "pure intuition." Ruggles's music leaves listeners with the impression "of the clear unsullied crystal." If absolute beauty is the highest aim a composer can ever hope to achieve, in Seeger's mind Ruggles comes close to achieving it: "What is lacking in balance is there in conviction—sheer arrogant assertion—of value. . . . in hearing the work you have been in touch with or have had intimations of the sublime." [15]

As regards the technical refinement of Ruggles's compositional craft, Seeger was of two minds. Having witnessed the New Englander's approach to composition with his own eyes, Seeger knew that it was anything but systematic: "There was no method, nothing that could be called discipline in his compositional activity."[16] Although he was the first to indulge his intuitions as a critic, Seeger reserved his greatest respect for composers who could demonstrate a methodical approach toward their art. Hence, because Ruggles lacked a consistent and/or coherent technique, he did not live up to Seeger's ideal critical standard.

Yet, at the same time, Seeger goes out of his way in the 1932 essay to point out the innovative technical features that appear over and over again in Ruggles's mature works. Seeger focuses on one dimension: melody. Above all, Ruggles's music shows its author's mastery of the long melodic line:

> Sustained continuity of melodic line has been an outstanding characteristic of fine art composition in Europe for over four hundred years. It can be found in Josquin, Palestrina, Bach, Handel, Beethoven and all the greatest masters down to about 1900. Then, melodies began to grow halt and lame. They would break up into little, too obvious, sections; they would be short and repetitious; or they would spin round and round like a squirrel in a cage. . . . It is to Ruggles' honor and fame that he has succeeded beyond any other composer we know of in thus blending one of the oldest traditions in Occidental music with one of the newest.[17]

To demonstrate Ruggles's melodic control, Seeger describes a principle of nonrepetition at work in his music: once a pitch sounds in a melody, Ruggles does not use it or its octave equivalent again until a fixed number of other pitches have intervened. Regarding the actual number of pitches, Seeger is somewhat vague, vacillating between six and ten. Immediately after unveiling this rule for melodic construction, however, Seeger mentions excerpts from one of Ruggles's most recent works, *Portals* (1925, revised 1929), that do not conform to it.[18] Thus, what Seeger initially presents as a strict rule for composing melody is now shown to be closer to a rough guideline or rule of thumb.

It is telling that Ruggles had no interest in the recent discoveries of the Viennese experimental composers. He felt no compulsion to follow Schoenberg's approach to serialism, that is, to employ collections either vertically or horizontally that contained all twelve pitch classes. Instead, he tried to develop a dissonant idiom that employed a constant variety of pitch material but did not rely on any principle for determining the ordering of the pitch classes themselves. Other aspects of Ruggles's melodic practice that Seeger praises include a preference for lines with an instrumental rather than a vocal character, the avoidance of dancelike or regular phrasing, which reflects the composer's general desire to emulate principles of prose rather than poetic construction, and a fascination for contrapuntal rather than homophonic textures.[19]

At last we arrive at the goal of Seeger's critical journey: the judgment of value. Faced with synthesizing the "critical" and "technical" aspects of Ruggles's oeuvre, Seeger concludes that it falls short of greatness. Listeners are "in touch with" or have an intimation of what Seeger calls "the Sublime," but they never truly reach it. Like an exquisite jewel with a single flaw in it, *the beauty is there* or *is near.* The point is that, despite Seeger's sympathy for Ruggles's spiritual cast of mind, the music never quite attains the mystical transformation that, according to Seeger, its author intends. Seeger's technical qualms and logical reservations loom like large shadows, dulling the intense glow of Ruggles's elusive, mystical imaginings. In the end, Seeger cannot reconcile Ruggles's enlightened aesthetic aspirations with the music's technical shortcomings, in particular, with the absence of any rational or consistent principles. "The technique as a whole shows a curious ratio between organization and fantasy. Assuming . . . that a work of art should present an approximate balance . . . between the two—organism and fantasy—it would appear that in Ruggles' work there is a vast preponderance of fantasy. . . . As to Ruggles' critique as a whole, here again is unbalance, where a theoretical balance should be."[20] By the word "unbalance," Seeger means that, despite the critic's best intentions, the music resists any final synthesis.

Let us draw several conclusions about Seeger's critical reflections on Ruggles. First and foremost, Seeger portrays him as a pure intuitionist, a visionary who never escapes the opening stage of musical knowledge. It is as if Ruggles were single-handedly reviving Henri Bergson's theory of art, intent on lifting the "veil of appearance" but only partway. Though Seeger never explicitly compares Ruggles and Bergson in his critical writings or in the treatise itself, it is clear that in his mind the two are kindred spirits. Second, despite Seeger's deep empathy with this aesthetic posture, pure intuitionism does not satisfy the ideal balance of knowledge presented in the treatise's fourteen principles of criticism. In this connection, it is significant that Seeger even bothers to present a technical summary of music that relies so heavily on its author's native intuition. If his ultimate purpose had been to promote Ruggles's music, he would surely have ignored its shortcomings. That Seeger refuses to do so testifies to his commitment to fulfilling the ideal of balanced and comprehensive criticism.

Henry Cowell

Seeger's critical assessment of Henry Cowell must be understood in the context of the latter's first exposure to formal music training, which occurred under Seeger's supervision between 1914 and 1917 at the University of California, Berkeley.[21] Because the precocious seventeen-year-old had already completed over a hundred compositions, together they agreed on a balanced program of study that bore Seeger's pedagogical stamp. Cowell would study the traditional disciplines of harmony and counterpoint with Edward Stricklen, one of Seeger's colleagues at Berkeley, leaving Seeger free to guide Cowell's own compositional development in the context of recent avant-garde music. In fact, it was in conjunction with Cowell's private composition lessons that Seeger first devised his regimen of dissonant counterpoint.[22] In the late teens Cowell organized some of his new approaches toward composition in the form of a treatise called *New Musical Resources,* which he later revised and published in 1930.[23] Although only two pieces, the *Quartet Romantic* (1917) and the *Quartet Euphometric* (1919), can be singled out as direct outcomes of the "new resources" Cowell describes, other piano works from Cowell's early period (1912–30) can also be traced to the treatise.

Seeger's critique of Cowell was addressed to a general audience, appearing in the *Magazine of Art* in 1940.[24] As in his review of Ruggles, Seeger places his evaluation of Cowell's music in the context of a psychological portrait of the composer. Above all, Cowell possessed a "prodigious naivete" and a childlike simplicity.[25] Seeger describes Cowell as the exact emotional antipode of his parents: his father, we are told, was a member of a San Francisco "literary set" that counted among its members Jack London and Ambrose Bierce; his mother was an author and poet. Ironically, as Seeger notes, "In this extremely romantic and sentimental literary atmosphere, Cowell grew up to be the most unregenerately unromantic and anti-sentimental musician of our times."[26]

Other significant factors in Cowell's development as a composer were his limited access to music and his haphazard education in general. Following his parents' divorce in 1903, he spent most of his time by himself or caring for his sick mother and, as a result, had little exposure to traditional musical culture. Since he was completely unaware of the significant role that tradition played in the history of western European music, he could hardly respect what he did not know. Seeger regarded Cowell's sensitivity toward art as truly ahistorical: "To him, music is not to any extent (so far as I know) a means of communication between people—a means moulded and handed down to him by generations of musical ancestors. Rather, it is a field, a *tabula rasa,* in which there are infinite possibilities of combination—so why not try them?"[27] This unusual combination of high intelligence and meager education was corroborated by Lewis Terman, a professor of psychology at Stanford. Terman was quite impressed by young Cowell, speculating that his gift in science, specifically botany, was almost as prodigious as that in music.[28]

Seeger then uses his analysis of Cowell's unusual creative gifts as a means of assessing the expressive and spiritual range of his music. For Seeger, the fact that no single characteristic unified Cowell's wide-ranging experiments in composition was a symptom of either an inability or an unwillingness to express his intuitive or emotional life in his music. Seeger was utterly dumbfounded by how little personal emotion Cowell invested in his work:

In a period in which music has been valued above all for "depth," "sincerity," high emotions, and lofty thought, Cowell sardonically or perversely avoids all four. The music is almost without "content." It seems calculatedly shallow. One often suspects the tongue in the cheek; but I doubt it is there. Many pieces are tremendously exciting; but there is no ascertainable emotional coefficient—one cannot sense what the emotion is about. . . . [His music] seems to exist in a universe of its own.[29]

Because Cowell was just as likely to treat the same work with reverence as with frivolity, the emotional impact of his music was usually achieved by accident. For him, composition became a purely intellectual activity, an arbitrary process of choosing among "objective" designs that bore little, if any, connection to an audience's collective emotional response. Seeger regarded this "objectivist" aesthetic as fundamentally incomplete, as engaging only half of the artist's creative potential. He continues: "On the whole he has come unusually close to ignoring the subjective element, both in the field he has examined and in handling the materials of his craft."[30] By the expression "ignoring the subjective element," Seeger means that Cowell's aesthetic approach suppresses the emotional aspect of his mental life in favor of pure rationality. It is not a question of an absence of integrity on Cowell's part as much as a difference in aesthetic orientation. For Seeger, Cowell's compositional approach threatens to become an exercise in sonorous self-indulgence.

Seeger's judgment of Cowell in the article is by no means entirely negative, for he also underlines the redeeming features of such an "objectivist" sensibility. One consequence of Cowell's logical extrapolations of the overtone series, for instance, was to explore new compositional resources for their own sake. Considering Seeger's own commitment in his treatise to uncovering new approaches to composition, his sympathy with Cowell in this regard is not surprising. In Seeger's view, although Cowell's fascination with logic and system directly influenced few composers, it contributed to the general trend toward experiment and innovation witnessed during the early and middle twentieth century in America.[31]

Seeger's evaluation of Cowell, though eight years later than his essay on Ruggles, still shows signs of the same ideal model of criticism. By this time his fascination with Ruggles's search for attaining spiritual transcendence had receded in favor of a balance between the "known" and the "unknown":

Are not the emotional and intellectual "fevers" inescapable correlates of the handling of this field in a reasonably complete manner? After all, is the known, in respect to which we may be objective, any weightier in the whole picture than the unknown, in respect to which another approach is necessary? . . . Do we not, by adopting either a purely objective or subjective attitude, merely avoid not only half our difficulties but half our opportunities? I believe this to be a fact.[32]

While some of the vocabulary may have changed—the dichotomy between mystical and logical had now been replaced by an opposition between subjectivity and objectivity—Seeger's commitment in 1939 to the ultimate goal of achieving a synthesis of opposites was stronger than ever.

Another curious twist in Seeger's article grows out of his close association with Cowell during the teens. Seeger's misgivings about Cowell's "objectivity" might be interpreted as a teacher's chastising a former student after the fact for having followed his own advice. According to that conjecture, Cowell's desire to systematize the analogies between the overtone series and other musical parameters could be considered an attempt to satisfy the theoretical expectations of his mentor. In Seeger's defense, we might note that there is a difference between a pedagogical strategy developed for one highly gifted student and the philosophical basis of a general theory of criticism. Furthermore, Seeger's attitude toward systems of composition changed dramatically between his Berkeley days and the early 1930s. Although throughout his life Seeger was strongly attracted to scientific rigor for its own sake, the ideals he articulated in his critical and theoretical writings were anything but purely logical.

Ruth Crawford

The only critique of Ruth Crawford's music Seeger ever published also appeared in 1932 in Cowell's anthology, *American Composers on American Music*.[33] Viewed as a whole, Seeger's critical review focuses more on technique and less on critical judgment than all those considered thus far. Nowhere do we find any detailed psychological portrait, and, as for her creative temperament, he provides only a brief, if provocative, sketch. Most of the essay is devoted to a technical survey of her latest works—a kind of insider's guide to her compositional workshop. He outlines such things as intricate schemes of polyrhythm, pitch rotational procedures, and plans of irregular phrase groupings. Considering that most of the music he describes was written after Crawford began studying with him in 1929, it is not surprising that a certain affinity exists between the procedures employed in her music and the theories expounded in his writings. (A more detailed exposition of Seeger's theories of composition appears in chapter 6.)[34]

Following his catalogue of technical resources, Seeger makes several general remarks concerning Crawford's style as a whole. Crawford, he says, is to be commended for her music's economy and precision, and for her preference for small ensembles. Even though her compositions show a refreshing "absence of pretense," they still manage to be "uncompromisingly and successfully radical." Among her other virtues are a "resourceful" treatment of form and a variety of rhythmic invention. Her only shortcoming is her failure to write any music for large orchestra; he even suggests that making a "bid for orchestral laurels" might raise her overall stature as a composer.[35]

While discussing his wife's "lack of pretension," Seeger makes a short but telling digression. In the process of exploring whether showmanship is essential to great art, Seeger revives an eighteenth-century approach to aesthetics that sheds considerable light on the relation between his philosophical ideals outlined in the treatise and their application in the form of critical judgment. To guide him in his aesthetic meditations he relies on the great German poet, critic, and philosopher Johann Wolfgang von Goethe. Seeger invokes a distinction between "style" and "manner" that Goethe initially developed in an essay written in 1799 entitled "The Collector and His Circle," which outlines his aesthetic ideals.[36] According to Goethe, most artists and art lovers possess one of two contrasting manners: the "serious" or the "playful." In the course of the essay he presents three examples of "seriousness," each of which can be opposed to a form of "playfulness," for a total of six manners. The "serious" manners—"imitators," "characterizers," and "miniaturists"—are juxtaposed against the "playful" manners—"phantomists," "undulators," and "sketchers"—to create three pairs of opposites. Having inaugurated this "mannered" catalogue, Goethe then unveils an aesthetic principle whereby opposite manners are combined. The highest ideal comes about only when all three pairs of opposites are fully synthesized in a single style.[37]

In his article on Crawford, Seeger draws an analogy between Goethe's synthesis of literary "manners" and a musical fusion of seriousness and showmanship. These abstract categories also have their counterparts in his theory of musical knowledge: the critical synthesis of intuition and reason outlined in the treatise. Seeger asserts that great music "may be play but . . . one is deeply moved, as well to thought as to feeling."[38]

It is not entirely clear whether Crawford's music realizes the ideal of "style" that Goethe proposes. On one hand, Seeger's comment that her music lacks "pretension" suggests that it may be missing a certain theatrical flourish, a display of showmanship required for achieving the ideal fusion of "manners." On the other hand, he also says outright that her music can be appreciated both for its purely "impressionistic" effects and for the meticulous logical foundation on which, in some sections, every note depends. It is characterized by a "joyous play of the intellect."[39]

Seeger's critique of Crawford raises several questions. One wonders, for instance, why he was so reticent about passing judgment on her music. One contributing factor might be the difference between her rate of musical development and that of Ruggles and Cowell. Since by 1932 she was not as accomplished a composer as the other two under consideration, Seeger's essay was designed more as an introduction of a young composer to the musical community at large than as a judgment of a mature artist's works. The promotional character of the essay is especially evident in the fact that Seeger provides a brief sketch of a work in progress, an orchestral piece that Crawford never completed.[40] The other likely reason for Seeger's hesitation about passing judgment on Crawford is the obvious conflict of interest. Not only was this promising American composer his wife, but the techniques displayed in her music reflect some of the fruits of his own teaching. Thus what may appear as pure discretion on his part may well contain an element of self-promotion.

Finally, it is curious that Seeger never tried to locate Crawford's creative temperament between the extremes of Ruggles's ineffable mysticism and Cowell's cool rationality. There is evidence to suggest that, beginning with her years in Chicago, Crawford not only had an abundant spiritual life but also tried to express that life in her music. In a fascinating study, Judith Tick explores the relationship between Crawford's musical style and her burgeoning spirituality formed by a confluence of influences including theosophy, Eastern religion, nineteenth-century American transcendentalism, and the imaginative tradition of Walt Whitman. Tick argues that in her compositions between 1926 and 1930 Crawford "was drawing on an eclectic legacy of ideas and values that had been linked in American intellectual life since the turn of the century."[41] The presence of Crawford's spiritual leanings and her fascination for logical calculation, as outlined in Seeger's review, suggest that, of the three composers, she may well have come the closest to realizing in musical terms Seeger's lofty critical ideals.

Seeger's Ideal of "Style"

It is impossible to assess Seeger's ambitions as a music critic without taking into account his vision of a new style of composition. For him, critical judgment and musical creativity grew from the same aesthetic roots: a modern adaptation of Goethe's ideal of "style." To understand this parallel, it is useful to review his judgment of the contemporary composers in Europe.

Like virtually all of his formulations, Seeger's view of the musical climate in Europe is conceived in dualistic terms: one idea is juxtaposed against a contrasting idea and, out of this juxtaposition, a new synthesis emerges. What initially sparked his imagination was a trio of compositional approaches that prevailed in Europe between 1900 and the mid-1920s: neoromanticism, neoclassicism, and an experimental approach characterized by Schoenberg's "atonal" music as well as his early serial compositions. Seeger regarded all three as mere "manners" in that they exaggerated some technical aspect at the expense of the perfectly balanced aesthetic that Goethe and, in turn, Seeger had idealized. Composers of neoromantic persuasion, such as Scriabin, regarded the creative process as mystical and, as a result, rejected all attempts to systematize musical technique. Of all the species of "manners," Seeger had the least to say about this one. The neoclassical school, epitomized initially by Erik Satie and later by Igor Stravinsky, either rejected new approaches to composition or parodied them in impersonal, "historical similitudes." Since Satie tried to simplify the diffuse and overcomplicated character of late romanticism, his music "gave the appearance of a kind of musical pre-Raphaelitism."[42] Although Seeger was less explicit in the treatise about the third "radical" manner, saying only that it focuses on a "further development of innovations already established,"[43] it is clear that the prototype he had in mind was Schoenberg. As early as his critique of Rudhyar in 1923, Seeger discussed the music of Scriabin, Stravinsky, and Schoenberg, whom he referred to as "the three S's."[44] Seeger was clearly of two minds about this controversial Viennese composer. On the one hand, he did not approve of Schoenberg's propensity for logical calculation. Although Schoenberg's music certainly stimulated the intellect, the results of his ratiocination usually failed to touch the emotions. On the other hand, Seeger held some aspects of Schoenberg's music in high esteem, such as the intricate phrase organization and rich contrapuntal texture displayed in the music between opp. 23 and 30.[45] In the treatise Seeger even compares Schoenberg to Ruggles in the degree to which he "comes nearer than any living composer to attaining the sublime in music."[46] Thus, of the three manners, the third was the most promising as a basis for realizing Seeger's grand vision of a new "style."

Seeger's assessment of the state of contemporary music in Europe between the wars is particularly significant when compared with his critical evaluation of Ruggles, Cowell, and Crawford. There is a certain parallel between Seeger's judgment of the three American experimentalists and of the leading contemporary composers in Europe. In both contexts his theory of knowledge serves as a philosophical prism that transforms musical phenomena into a spectrum of highly contrasting aesthetic principles and stylistic types. Yet it would be a mistake to assume that a one-to-one correspondence exists between the two trios of musical styles. By underlining the similarities as well as the differences between Seeger's opinions of contemporary American and European composers, one can understand in what way his philosophical model informs his critical analysis.

In some respects there is a strong sympathy between Seeger's view of European modern music leading up to World War I and the American experimental tradition that followed it. Composers like Scriabin and Ruggles share the same spiritual legacy. The resemblance owes its origin to a common conception of human creativity in that the compositional process is strongly linked to the search for emotional rapture and spiritual fulfillment. Likewise, there is a unifying thread between such composers as Stravinsky, Satie, and Cowell by virtue of their mutual rejection of the very aesthetic attitude that Scriabin and Ruggles embrace. Instead of worshiping at the romantic (or neo-romantic) altar of spirituality, they adopt a more detached and objective approach. In their view, reason plays a much larger role than spirit or emotion in human creativity. Finally, Schoenberg and Crawford can be grouped in the same aesthetic category because of their mutual desire to avoid the extremes of pure emotion or reason. Motivated by neither pure emotion nor cold calculation, they stand the greatest chance of realizing Seeger's lofty aesthetic ideals.

However, Seeger's critical judgment is by no means restricted to a comparison of various composers' creative temperaments: he is equally interested in matters of musical technique. The categories he borrows to characterize the leading European composers are based on specific technical criteria as much as broad aesthetic principles. For this reason it would be a grave mistake to draw too strong a parallel between Scriabin, Stravinsky, and Schoenberg and the three American "ultramodernists." While Ruggles and Scriabin share a similar conception of human creativity, for example, their musical languages are worlds apart. Despite the objections Seeger raises about Ruggles's technical failings, he nevertheless considers his innovations with melodic line and counterpoint to be a vast improvement over Scriabin's continuing obsession with harmonic color in his final compositions. Likewise, even though both Cowell and Stravinsky rebelled against the nineteenth-century tradition of heightened emotion, the two differed dramatically in the nature of the musical solution they offered to take its place: whereas Cowell, in Seeger's view, tried to cultivate new musical resources, Stravinsky contented himself with parodying old ones.[47] Finally, notwithstanding the fact that by 1932 Crawford's musical development had not reached the same stage of maturity as Schoenberg's, she showed a greater potential for achieving the ideal fusion of intuition and logic that would help usher in the new "style" of balanced composition. On the whole, although none of the American composers that Seeger reviews had realized the stylistic ideal he envisioned, all were closer to achieving it than were their counterparts in Europe.

Conclusion

The 1920s and early 1930s marked a crucial stage in the development of Seeger's ideas. Not only was he intent on developing a philosophical theory of musical knowledge; he was equally committed to applying it in the fields of criticism, compositional theory, and musicology. Though Seeger's writings in music criticism are limited in number, they highlight three of the most radical experimental composers in America during this period: Carl Ruggles, Henry Cowell, and Ruth Crawford. Despite his personal ties to all three artists, his assessment of each is discriminating: he praises some aspects of their work and rejects others. Not surprisingly, Seeger puts into practice the critical ideals he had developed in the treatise: the balance between intuitive and logical dimensions of musical experience. Yet it is ironic that while Seeger is eager to condemn European composers for renewing nineteenth-century approaches to composition, so-called neoromanticism, the ideal he ends up championing is itself a revival of a German aesthetic model from the early nineteenth century.

When Seeger's critical commentaries are viewed as a whole, one discovers two different aims. Sometimes Seeger assigns value by the degree to which a given composer's temperament realizes his own ideal synthesis of mystical faith and rational thought. Here the focus is on the *composer's* subjective process of creativity. Since Seeger had a strong personal tie with each of the three composers he reviewed, his comments about each one's artistic personality and its relation to their broader constellation of values and beliefs carries considerable authority. At other times, however, Seeger assigns value by the degree to which his perception of the music itself realizes the ideal aesthetic synthesis. Now the focus shifts to the *critic's* subjective process—the exercise of taste. In Seeger's view, these two aims ultimately must converge: the judgment of individual musical works becomes inseparable from the judgment of the subjective process by which they were created. These aims not only overlap in Seeger's writings as a critic but also are intertwined in the fourteen principles, as presented in chapter 2 of *Tradition and Experiment in the New Music*.

Chapter Six

. . . .

A Philosophy in Practice

Compositional Theory

Introduction

In the introduction to *Tradition and Experiment in the New Music,* Seeger warns that a new style of music will never be attained unless composers reexamine all aspects of their craft:

If we are to hear a new music comparable to the music of Palestrina, Bach and Beethoven, it will be less through a musical pre-Raphaelite movement or a timorous anti-intellectualism than through a systematic overhauling of all the elements in the situation — materials, methods, and values.[1]

To carry out his ambitious project of "overhauling," Seeger adopted a variety of musical personae: at various junctures he speaks as a philosopher, as a critic, and finally as a compositional theorist. Thus far, our study has focused almost exclusively on the first two personae, exploring Seeger's philosophical ideals and their realization as a standard for music criticism. The present chapter remedies this imbalance by addressing his work as a compositional theorist.

In the opening chapter of the treatise, Seeger boldly asserts that in part 1 he intends to "deal with composition in general."[2] Since he never specifies exactly what he means by such an assertion, it is worth exploring Seeger's underlying motivation for writing the treatise as a whole. An important clue appears in the unpublished foreword for his collection of essays entitled *Principia Musicologica*, where Seeger explains that the word "*Principia* names a concept that is to be understood in two senses: of beginnings or foundations: of Principles and criteria."[3] Despite the fact that Seeger wrote these words nearly forty-five years after he had completed a revised draft of the treatise, and that he was in the process of explaining his approach to the discipline of musicology, not composition, nevertheless, they reflect his aims in the 1930s. When he refers to "composition in general," he means the "first principles" in the Aristotelian sense, that is, the foundation on which any composer relies, regardless of historical period. In the context of the treatise, this "foundation" is a philosophical theory of knowledge, which Seeger presents in the opening two chapters. Seeger even presents his philosophical ideas as a set of fourteen "principles."

However, the relationship of the remaining seven chapters in part 1 to the eight chapters of part 2 is somewhat more complex. On the whole, the two-part plan of the work reflects a progression from general to particular, as if Seeger wanted to reveal the general structure of musical language itself before considering an individual, if somewhat experimental, idiom. For instance, in part 1 he establishes his conception of form as a hierarchy among the basic unit of melody, the phrase, and the whole before explaining in part 2 what specific intervals and rhythms are required to make a "dissonant" phrase.

Yet, when one examines closely the approach Seeger adopts in his study of "composition in general," several questions arise. First of all, while the topics covered in part 1 suggest a broad-based survey—intervals, scales, modes, harmony, and form—in fact there is a strong bias in the way he explores some of them. A general theory of composition that devotes merely eight pages to harmony and never mentions the seventh chord has a curious view of what constitutes "general." And that is just the point. Seeger's neglect of harmony reflects his own bias against the nineteenth-century fascination with chromaticism. Since one of his most serious complaints about contemporary composition was the decline of melodic line and counterpoint, his version of a theoretical foundation of composition would enable composers to focus more on line than on chord. In addition, his tendency in part 1 to devote as much time to matters of rhythm and meter as to pitch indicates a prescriptive desire to instill a new sensitivity to musical time.

The second question about Seeger's general theory of composition is that the chronological order of topics in the treatise does not always reflect their logical relationship with each other. For instance, since Seeger most likely experimented with consonance and dissonance as intervals (the subject of chapter 10, part 2) *before* he began extrapolating these concepts to the nonpitch functions (the subject of chapters 4 and 6, part 1), his study of the general properties of dissonance presupposes an interest in a specific experimental technique. In sum, while the treatise's overall scheme moves from general to particular, his conception of a general foundation is at times influenced by the specific experimental idiom he unveils in part 2.

There is also the question of whether Seeger believed his general principles would explain the music of non-Western cultures. In the introduction he reveals:

It is to be hoped that eventually, with a more adequate knowledge of the various non-European musics, no very extensive alteration would be necessary to bring it to the point of being useful in connection with revolutionary composition in any music—Chinese, Japanese, or Indian, as well as European—that employs an *articulated* technique.[4]

At this stage in Seeger's life he believed that if he could develop a theory of one musical tradition, then, with a few appropriate modifications, that theory could be applied to any musical tradition. Although he would later marvel at the naïveté of the preceding remark,[5] in fact he devoted much of his life to trying to perfect analytical tools of universal scope—that is, tools that could describe any musical experience.[6]

This chapter focuses on chapters 3 through 9 in the treatise, in which Seeger addresses a broad range of questions involved in composition and analysis. Instead of undertaking a comprehensive survey of all seven chapters, I will explore how Seeger's theories of human knowledge and criticism serve as a basis for his general theory of composition. Toward this end, I have selected three representative questions: (1) Seeger's reappraisal of the traditional distinction between consonance and dissonance and his attempt to adapt it in order to better understand the nonpitch functions; (2) his revival and adaptation of the nineteenth-century theory of harmonic dualism; and (3) his revival of the romantic ideal of "organic" unity and the neumatic theory of form he develops to realize it. Viewed together, these investigations also reveal the degree to which the various sources of Seeger's philosophical ideals—from Henri Bergson's intuitionism to Bertrand Russell's ideal of mediation—helped shape his music-theoretical speculation. Whether it be an expanded conception of dissonance, a new theory of melody as gesture, or a different basis for reckoning chords,

Seeger's aim was to try to reconcile traditions of the past and experiments of the present.

Reappraisal of Materials

Throughout chapters 3 through 6 of the treatise Seeger pursues two aims: to use theoretical speculation as a means of uncovering new musical possibilities that composers could exploit; and to develop a comprehensive taxonomic method for describing any musical experience, whether old or new. What is unique about Seeger's project is that he was convinced the two aims were fundamentally connected:

> It is of prime importance that the craftsmen have practically automatic control of this manipulation so that the elements of composition are not the qualities of the raw but of the manipulated materials. In other words, the experimenting with the *materials* must be practically completed before the experimenting with the *forms* can progress beyond an elementary stage.[7]

A new, more refined method of description not only would clarify our theoretical knowledge of musical phenomena but also might eventually lead composers to new creative ideas. Indeed, in Seeger's thought as a whole, there is an ongoing process of mediation between these two extremes: the prescriptive aim of stimulating composition and the descriptive aim of refining analysis. At different stages in the treatise, the two aims shift in their order of priority.

Seeger begins his musical meditations by drawing a sharp distinction between two conceptions of musical sound: the "raw," physical approach in which music, like any other sound, serves as the data for scientific measurement; and the "manipulated" approach, which treats music as a "product of culture." He goes to great lengths to distinguish the scientist's from the artist's perspective of musical experience, contrasting the understanding that each has of the basic materials of the medium. In his words, the manipulated forms of musical sound "resemble the *physical forms* . . . as much as the forms of baskets and vases resemble the forms of willow trees and clay in pits."[8] He even invents new terms in order to refer to the basic materials of music from either point of view: "function" implies an analytic, and hence more scientific, orientation, whereas "resource" implies a more creative or artistic orientation. Whereas the six "functions" of music can be conceived of and measured independently, the six "resources" are inseparable and must be conceived as a single gestalt.[9]

INFLECTIONS

	Tense	Poised	Relaxed
Pitch	higher	same	lower
Dynamics	louder	same	softer
Timbre	"warmer"	same	"cooler"
Proportion	divided	same	prolonged
Accent	stronger	same	weaker
Tempo	faster	same	slower

FUNCTIONS

Figure 6. Matrix comparing inflections with musical functions

Yet Seeger was as eager to measure sound as he was to "manipu-late" it. In chapter 3 he begins his investigation of the "raw" materials by proposing that musical sound consists of tone and rhythm. Each of these broad categories, in turn, can be divided into three functions: tone is made up of pitch, dynamics, and timbre; rhythm consists of proportion (or subdivision), accent, and tempo. To indicate the change, or what Seeger calls "inflection," of any function, he coins the terms "tension" (an increase), "poise" (no change), and "relaxation" (a de-crease). The resulting classification scheme can measure three values for each musical function, yielding a total of eighteen possible values (this scheme is shown in figure 6). The concept of inflection is crucial for Seeger's overall project in that it becomes the basis for his study of the similarities and differences between the six functions.

Seeger then considers the traditional distinction between conso-nance and dissonance from both a scientist's and an artist's point of view. This distinction is problematic, he argues, because of a general misunderstanding of the boundaries between science and art. More precisely, composers, performers, and musicologists falsely believed that the relationship between principles of acoustics and judgments of aesthetic quality was one of cause and effect. Seeger had no desire to question the accepted principles of acoustics; rather, he objected to the tradition of relying on the physical properties of sound as the only justification of musical practice. To appreciate his critique, we must summarize briefly his understanding of acoustical science.

According to Seeger, the harmonic series has traditionally been the starting point for determining intervallic quality. The interval between the fundamental and a given upper partial can be represented as a specific numerical ratio: the octave, $2:1$, the fifth, $3:2$, and so on. Thus the implicit rule for assigning consonance or dissonance to an interval usually depends on how "close" the upper partial forming the interval's upper pitch is to the fundamental. The lower a ratio is in the series, the more consonant the interval: conversely, the higher a ratio is in the series, the more dissonant the interval.

In Seeger's view the problem arose when this acoustical theory became the sole basis upon which an interval's consonant or dissonant quality and, by extension, the pain or pleasure associated with this quality, were determined. To assume that a one-to-one correspondence existed between acoustical theory and musical taste was, for him, preposterous. Nothing could convince him that an interval between two partials that were low in the series, such as the perfect fifth $(3:2)$, should have a preferred musical status over another interval between two partials higher in the series, such as the major third $(5:4)$. In his mind the perception of intervallic quality was primarily a question of musical custom. He believed that the association of consonance with beauty and pleasure, on the one hand, and of dissonance with ugliness and pain, on the other, was acquired by cultural tradition, not by nature. Seeger concludes in no uncertain terms: "No one, musician or nonmusician, can maintain that any interval, tuned or untuned, is more pleasant or unpleasant than any other, except on the basis of tradition and habit. And habit can be changed—even reversed."[10] A good example of this is the changing fortunes of the perfect fourth $(4:3)$, which over the course of time has been perceived as dissonant as well as consonant.

While Seeger rejects acoustical theory as the absolute basis for determining intervallic quality, he avoids going to the other relativistic extreme—denying any standards whatsoever and endowing each listener with sovereign authority to distinguish consonance from dissonance. Instead, he arrives at a compromise in which he mixes the traditional scientific view with a more open-ended approach based on

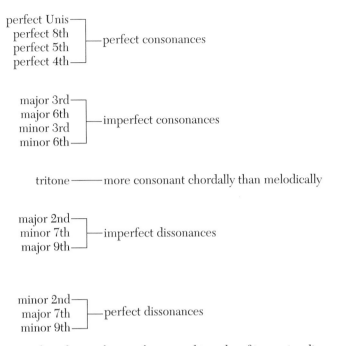

perfect Unis ⎤
perfect 8th ⎥
perfect 5th ⎥— perfect consonances
perfect 4th ⎦

major 3rd ⎤
major 6th ⎥
minor 3rd ⎥— imperfect consonances
minor 6th ⎦

tritone ——— more consonant chordally than melodically

major 2nd ⎤
minor 7th ⎥— imperfect dissonances
major 9th ⎦

minor 2nd ⎤
major 7th ⎥— perfect dissonances
minor 9th ⎦

Figure 7. Quality of vertical intervals arranged in order of increasing dissonance

context. The final judgment of intervallic quality depends as much on an interval's immediate musical context as it does on its acoustical properties. This mixture of scientific theory and artistic adjustment is clearly illustrated in Seeger's distinction between the harmonic (or simultaneous) and melodic (or successive) presentation of intervals. Figure 7 correlates numerical size with quality for harmonic intervals. The only place where Seeger's list departs from the prevailing nineteenth-century approach to interval quality is the tritone, which he categorizes as a neutral diatonic interval—equally consonant and dissonant—rather than as some form of dissonance.

It is in Seeger's understanding of melodic intervals that his contextual approach shows its true colors. When viewed in isolation, melodic intervals have the same consonant and dissonant qualities as their harmonic counterparts, as displayed in figure 7. However, other factors, such as overall melodic or tonal context and register, can radically influence the listener's perception of a melodic interval. The tritone and perfect fifth serve as contrasting illustrations of the first factor. As shown in example 1(a) and (b), a single melodic tritone sounds disso-

Example 1. Illustrations of the relative nature of dissonance at (a) and (c); and of consonance at (b) and (d)

nant; yet, because two tritones in succession outline an octave span, they sound consonant. By contrast, by itself a perfect fifth is consonant, yet a succession of two perfect fifths sounds dissonant. Seeger also believes that any dissonant diatonic interval can sound consonant if the broader melodic context is sufficiently tonal; conversely, any diatonic consonant interval can sound dissonant if the context is sufficiently nontonal. Example 1 illustrates both possibilities. At (c) the "neutral" interval, the tritone, marked by a bracket, sounds more consonant than when played alone; likewise at (d) the perfect fifth sounds more dissonant than when played by itself.

The last stage in Seeger's critique of the traditional conception of interval quality is a new model for classifying harmonic intervals. Like Schoenberg and Cowell before him, Seeger believed that, as history progressed, composers employed intervals higher and higher in the harmonic series. This expanded palette for intervals corresponded to changes in the general perception of what constituted consonance and dissonance; as a result, certain intervals could no longer be categorized according to the old bipartite system. In its place, he proposes a tripartite system in which consonant intervals remain the same and dissonant intervals are further divided into two new subcategories. Seeger's approach grows out of his concept of inflection: whereas a consonance would always be "relaxed," a dissonance could be either "tense" or "poised." The most practical consequence of this new concept is that dissonances would no longer need to resolve if they were perceived as "poised" inflections.

Examples of these new successions of intervals can be found in part 2 of Seeger's treatise within the context of a discussion of types of "dissonant" contrapuntal textures. While his primary focus is on the horizontal succession of intervals and rhythms within a given line, he enumerates various harmonic possibilities within a two-part texture, as shown in example 2. In both measures four vertical intervals occur, which are listed below the staff. Of particular interest is the succession

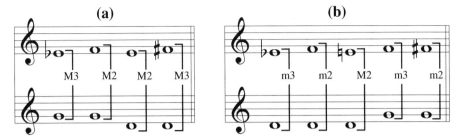

Example 2. Illustrations of tripartite models of consonance and dissonance

minor second, minor third, major second. Using the system of interval classification prevalent during the nineteenth century, this would be labeled as dissonance/consonance/dissonance; however, if Seeger's new concept of inflection is employed, the same succession could be interpreted as "tense"/"relaxed"/"poised." In this contrived example the "poised" interval, the major second, would not need to be resolved.

Crawford relies on a similar succession of vertical intervals in the closing measures of the second movement from her *Diaphonic Suite no. 3* (1930), which are summarized in example 3. Written for two Bb clarinets, this work is characterized by great rhythmic contrast between the two voices. In the opening measures a three-note melodic motive appears in Clarinet II, Bb3—C4—B4. When this same motive reappears at m. 35 in Clarinet I (here transposed by T8), it forms a succession of vertical intervals against the F3 in the other clarinet part. What is striking about this excerpt is that Crawford employs two series of inflections in which dissonances prepare and resolve consonances: "tense"/"relaxed"/"poised" (minor second/minor third/major ninth); and, assuming that two consonances can take the place of one, "poised"/"relaxed"/"tense" (major second/perfect fourth/major third/minor second). For Crawford, the minor second was not only an appropriate way to "resolve" a consonance but also a good way to end the movement.

When evaluating Seeger's investigations of intervals as a whole, it is tempting to view them strictly as an attempt to lay a theoretical foundation for all musical experience. If this indeed was Seeger's primary goal, then surely he failed to achieve it. His study covers no new ground; instead, he assembles a patchwork of old theories and definitions inherited from theoretical treatises of the past and applies it to the present compositional climate. In a meticulous historical overview

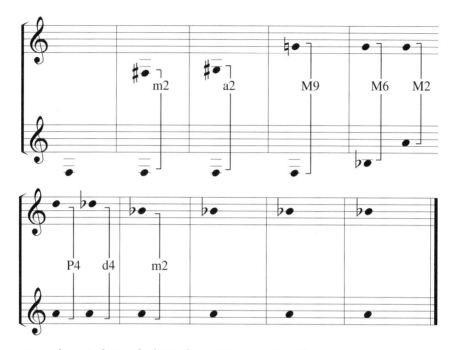

Example 3. Ruth Crawford, *Diaphonic Suite* no. 3: II, pitch summary of mm. 34–43

of the distinction between consonance and dissonance, James Tenney offers a convenient method for assessing Seeger's thought.[11] Beginning with the teachings of Pythagoras and ending with the empirical studies of Helmholtz, Tenney identifies five conceptions of consonance and dissonance that have appeared in the history of music theory. In his treatise, Seeger manages to revive aspects of two of them: Renaissance contrapuntal theory, as seen in the writings of Zarlino, as well as some ideas of the Enlightenment composer and theorist Jean-Philippe Rameau.[12] In short, Tenney's study reveals that Seeger's conception of interval quality was anything but new.

While Seeger's discussion of intervals has shortcomings as a comprehensive theoretical system, its greatest redeeming value is the new resources and possibilities it offers for avant-garde composers. In compiling his digest of past acoustical theories of pitch relations, Seeger was less interested in history per se than in using these older theories as a means of generating new ideas for composers. Ultimately, the significance of Seeger's meditations on intervals lies in his desire to combine creative speculation with theoretical investigation.

At this point it is useful to consider how the ideas of Bergson and

Russell—philosophers who played such an important role in shaping the theory of criticism—affected Seeger's discussion of intervals. The distinction between "function" and "resource" illustrates how deeply Bergson's intuitionist assumptions influenced Seeger's thinking. For instance, the term "resource" is less an analytical category than a symbolic protest against scientific analysis altogether. Indeed, to insist that no musical parameter can be separated from any other is a clear affirmation of the intuitionist creed. Yet, in part 1 of the treatise Seeger lavishes more attention on the consequences of separating the six musical parameters than he does on treating them as a single intuitive whole. In fact, his desire to use theoretical investigation as a means of generating new ideas for composition shows the degree to which Bertrand Russell's ideal of mediation inspired Seeger's unusual approach toward basic musical materials. This will become even more clear in Seeger's exploration of other musical parameters.

Extensions of Dissonance

Any discussion of Seeger's extensions of the traditional categories for describing pitch must begin with Johann J. Fux's celebrated treatise *Steps to Parnassus* (*Gradus ad Parnassum*). Seeger's opinion of this eighteenth-century pedagogical regimen was integrally connected with his critique of contemporary composition. On the one hand, Seeger shared Fux's cultivation of line, which he believed was noticeably absent from the music of recent experimental composers such as Scriabin and Stravinsky. On the other hand, Seeger was also discontent with the gap between the scholastic rules about dissonance treatment and contemporary composers' taste in intervals; in his view, Schoenberg's fascination with dissonance was matched only by his fear of consonance.[13] Seeger's solution was to propose a new approach he called "dissonant counterpoint" in which the traditional definitions were reversed: a consonance must be prepared by and resolved to a dissonance. The motivation for this anti-Fuxian plan was twofold: to rebel against the received tradition through an exercise in pure negation (Seeger waggishly called it a "school-room discipline");[14] and to discover a new intervallic sensibility. Most of part 2 of the treatise is devoted to developing this new contrapuntal regimen in two- and three-part textures.

Next Seeger tries to generalize this process of negation to the other five functions. He was acutely aware that, despite the apparent neutrality of his classification system, the six functions that it describes traditionally have not enjoyed equal status among composers. Pitch has been endowed with a certain priority over the other five for two basic reasons, one natural, the other historical. First, pitch has a higher priority simply because it lends itself to being measured and characterized in words.[15] The second reason reflects Seeger's strong reaction against the music of his immediate past, because most late nineteenth-century composers had aimed at developing a highly refined and personal harmonic language. This priority given to pitch was worrisome for Seeger, for if a hidden bias existed in the very nomenclature of musical description, then it could conceivably influence the course that modern composition would eventually take.

Seeger's solution for remedying this imbalance was to model the organization of the underdeveloped functions after that of the pitch function. In his words, his goal was not "to transfer tonal practice bodily into the other functions, but rather taking the *method* of pitch organization, insofar as we can understand it musically," and seeing if it yields "musical results" when applied to other parameters.[16] He devises an experiment in which the terminology traditionally used to describe matters of pitch is reinterpreted as a means of measuring the nonpitch functions. He unveils the following list of terms:

1. gamut, both articulated and unarticulated
2. interval
3. scale
4. mode
5. chord
6. consonance and dissonance
7. tonality

Much of chapter 4 is organized as though Seeger were carrying out some kind of public demonstration, putting old musical "wine" in new dissonant bottles. Since it is not possible here to review all of the results of Seeger's terminological experiments, I will focus on the hypothetical analogues for the concepts of "gamut" and "consonance vs. dissonance." For convenience, the information concerning consonance and dissonance is summarized in figure 8.

According to Seeger, the functions of dynamics and timbre were so

	Consonance	Dissonance
Dynamics	a) no change in loudness in all parts b) consonant change in loudness in all parts	a) frequent and sudden shifts in dynamics b) simultaneous increase and decrease in loudness within different parts
Timbre		
Proportion	durations which form a ratio between 1 and a whole number > 1	durations which form any other ratio
Accent	regular accentual pattern	irregular accentual pattern either in one part or between multiple parts
Tempo	gradual change in tempo	sudden change in tempo

Figure 8. Analogues of "consonance" and "dissonance" for the nonpitch functions

poorly understood that the terms borrowed from pitch nomenclature were of limited use in describing them. The chief problem was that there existed no universally accepted unit for measuring differences in gamut for either function and, therefore, no concept of scale. In spite of this shortcoming, Seeger proposes provisional definitions of the consonant and dissonant use of dynamics.[17]

Seeger begins with some preliminary definitions. Changes in dynamics are articulated, as in *fortissimo, forte, mezzo forte,* and so forth, or unarticulated, as in the terms *crescendo* and *diminuendo.* Seeger's way of adapting the distinction between consonance and dissonance for this function is to determine initially the traditional use of each type of change and then imagine its opposite. Hence, "consonant" dynamics indicates either no change or a constant change in loudness, both of which during the past two centuries have become the norm. By contrast, the concept of "dissonant" dynamics denotes either a sudden alternation between loud and soft in a musical texture or a simultaneous increase and decrease in dynamics within different parts of a texture. As will be shown later, this distinction helped inspire one of the most powerful works Ruth Crawford would ever compose: the third movement of the String Quartet.

On the whole, Seeger's investigation of rhythm is somewhat sketchy and uneven. Of the five functions considered, proportion is the most conducive to pitch nomenclature. By proportion, Seeger means the relationship between two groups of durations, either successive or simultaneous, assuming the two share a common beat or pulse. Seeger's strategy is to borrow the acoustical model traditionally used to explain intervals and then adapt it to rhythm. In his adapted model a proportion between two durations, like that between two frequencies, may be expressed as the ratio of two whole numbers. Seeger then takes the pitch/proportion analogy one step further by proposing a "harmonic series" of durations as a basis for distinguishing between proportional "consonance" and "dissonance." Figure 9 displays proportional "intervals" both in their melodic (successive) and chordal (simultaneous) forms.[18] "Consonant" proportions occur between each pair of measures at (a) and within each measure at (b). Each ratio consists of one and a whole number greater than one (e.g., 2 : 1, 3 : 1, 4 : 1), and can be likened to a fundamental measured against one of its upper partials. "Dissonant" proportions are ratios of whole numbers that cannot be reduced to a consonant proportion, as shown in figure 9(c) and (d).

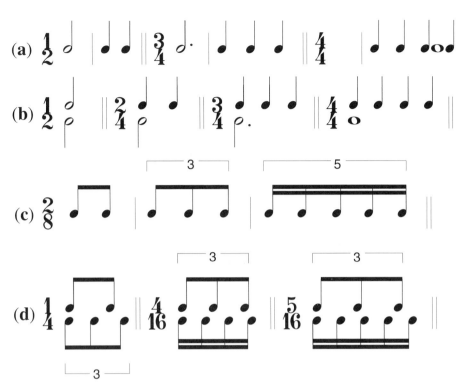

Figure 9. Examples of "consonant" proportions: (a) and (b); and "dissonant" proportions: (c) and (d)

They correspond to the relation between two upper partials (e.g., 3:2 and 5:3). Throughout this section of the treatise, Seeger's ideas about proportion bear a strong kinship with those of Henry Cowell, as presented in his book *New Musical Resources,* which will be discussed in greater detail below.[19]

Seeger's explanation, like those of Cowell and Arnold Schoenberg,[20] belongs to a long theoretical tradition stretching back to the ancient Greeks, which relies on mathematical ratios to account for musical practice. His failure to acknowledge any previous voice within that tradition suggests that his "dissonant" speculations were conducted in somewhat of a historical vacuum. Even more important, however, is the fact that his model contains no detailed study of previous rhythmic practices. If he wants to reverse the well-worn formulas of nineteenth-century composers, he must first explain exactly what those formulas were. He seems more interested here in generating new patterns of durations and new ways of organizing traditional patterns than in developing comprehensive descriptive tools.

The two remaining aspects of rhythm, accent and tempo, are intimately linked with proportion. Accent consists of two elements: the relative amount of stress a given beat receives in relation to the beats preceding and succeeding it; and the interval of time between beats that receive the greatest stress.[21] Since of all the functions, accent is the least likely to be perceived as a gamut, much less an interval or scale, Seeger focuses on the pattern created by a succession of accents. "Consonant" accent is a regular pattern in either a single voice or multiple voices; "dissonant" accent, by contrast, refers to irregular accentuation in one part or cross-accenting between two or more parts.

As regards tempo, Seeger observes that in our musical culture sensitivity to differences in tempo is not as highly cultivated as sensitivity to differences in pitch. Although objective measures of tempo do exist, such as the metronome, most musicians ignore them in favor of a relative and, therefore, less exact approach. Directions such as *piu mosso* or *meno mosso,* for example, indicate neither exact tempi nor exact changes of tempo. As a result, Seeger is content to focus on the rate of tempo change. Gradual changes, either increasing or decreasing, are classified as consonant; extreme changes in tempo as dissonant. He also compares the ratios between two tempi using the same definitions of consonance and dissonance as he did for proportion. For example, if a slow introduction is followed by an allegro movement two or four times as fast, the change is consonant. If the ratio is closer to 2:3 or 2:5, the spans of time are in a dissonant relationship.

Seeger's ultimate goal in this section of the treatise was to find a comprehensive framework for comparing a broad range of musical materials. As it turns out, one of the problems he encounters when hypothesizing such things as an "interval" of dynamics or a "scale" of tempi is the absence of a viable unit of measure within each function. Indeed, this absence is what fuels his attempt in later chapters to discover a musical calculus for all six functions. Furthermore, his terminological experiments also led him to discover the degree to which different musical dimensions depend on one another: a dramatic change in one function often entails a corresponding change in another. Thus, a truly comprehensive system of description would need to take these interrelationships into account.

Style as Synthesis

In addition to investigating the behavior of individual functions, Seeger is equally interested in a developing a new relationship *among* functions, which he calls "style." The source for his aesthetic inspiration here is the eighteenth-century poet, critic, and philosopher Johann Wolfgang von Goethe. Seeger revives a distinction between "style" and "manner" that Goethe had initially proposed for all the arts in a 1799 essay entitled "The Collector and His Circle."[22] According to Goethe, most artists and art lovers exhibit one of two ways of thinking, which he calls manners: "serious" or "playful." In the course of the essay he enumerates three "serious" manners, which are then juxtaposed against three "playful" manners to create three pairs of opposites, or six in all.[23] The highest aesthetic ideal comes about only if all three pairs of opposites become fused to create a grand synthesis known as "style."

In his early writings Seeger revives Goethe's aesthetic ideal, yet he also adapts it to suit his own musical ends.[24] He introduces the dichotomy between "style" and "manner" in his set of fourteen principles of chapter 2 of the treatise and then elaborates on it in his classification of the elements of musical experience.[25] For Goethe's rather abstract notions of "serious" and "playful" Seeger substitutes something purely medium-based: the six functions of musical experience, three tonal and three rhythmic. However, the most significant difference between Seeger's and Goethe's models is in the nature of their ultimate aesthetic goal. Whereas Goethe imagines a harmonious and well-balanced synthesis of all six manners, Seeger's end product is less extreme. Given the prioritized ranking that composers have traditionally assigned to pitch, dynamics, timbre, proportion, tempo, and accent, Seeger's aim is for composers to arrive at a "new comparative balance" among these six functions.[26] Thus, Seeger's notion of "style" is a balance born of negotiation and experiment, not a preexisting equilibrium.

Crawford's Quartet

One of the shortcomings of Seeger's treatise is that he does not consistently provide musical examples to illustrate the new terminology he envisions. The third movement of Ruth Crawford's String Quartet is useful in this connection, for, according to Seeger, its genesis can be traced to a composition exercise he assigned to her sometime between 1929 and 1930.[27] While continuing work on the quartet in Europe during the following year, Crawford was as well versed in the theory of "dissonation" as anyone. Not only had she been studying privately with Seeger in New York City for the previous year, but during the summer of 1930 they worked on the treatise as a team; he dictated while she typed and edited the text.[28] This movement has received more scrutiny in the analytical literature than any other work by Crawford. Whereas previous studies have explored such topics as pitch, rhythm, climax, and registral structure over the entire movement,[29] the purpose of my analysis is to show in what ways Crawford brings to life the aesthetic vision that Seeger outlines in the treatise. Indeed, the movement is a record not only of Crawford's experiments with Seeger's extended forms of dissonance but also of her ability to transform these experiments into a polished work of art.

The movement is an essay in "dynamic" counterpoint, in which the independence of the parts is determined more by the treatment of volume than of pitch or rhythm. There is a constant ebb and flow of dynamics in all the parts such that, for most of the movement, while one is climaxing, the other(s) are either advancing toward or receding from a climax. Crawford creates this "wavelike" effect through a traditional imitative device: the canon. Instead of using a melody as imitative material, Crawford uses a succession of high and low points of volume, which is then echoed by all the voices in the texture, usually at intervals of one or two quarter notes. An example of this appears in mm. 39–40, where all four instruments present the same pattern of decrescendo and crescendo within a five-beat span and the interval between entries is a quarter note (see the excerpt in example 4). Thus, the "subject" of imitation is not only the designated loud and soft points but also the *progress* between them. Such a juxtaposition of independent crescendi or decrescendi in multiple voices is a clear example of Seeger's extended "dissonance" applied to dynamics.[30]

The continuous canons in dynamics also create "consonant" yet surprisingly subtle patterns of rhythm and instrumentation. In order to study the interaction of these three factors, it is useful to simplify the contrapuntal texture so that a climax in dynamics coincides with a single attack point. This approach assumes that, in a four-part texture, listeners can focus more easily on a climax than on a gradual change in volume. Measure 39, for example, contains four climaxes within five

Example 4. Ruth Crawford, String Quartet: III, mm. 39–58

beats, creating a rhythmic pattern of a half note followed by three quarter notes, a pattern that continues until m. 42 (see figure 10). This four-measure excerpt is representative of the whole movement, for when the meter changes, the rhythmic pattern created by the succession of climaxes usually shifts as well. Within this passage the ordering of instruments also reflects the rhythm formed by the climaxes: violin I, violin II, viola, and cello, which I have indicated on figure 10 using the integers 4, 3, 2, and 1.[31] Since Crawford often uses tessitura ranges in this movement, her choice of instrument does not necessarily indicate the conventional register within the string family, as demonstrated in m. 39, where the cello plays above the viola, and m. 40, where it leaps above all three other instruments. Nevertheless, while the pattern of instrumental rotation may not be reflected in pitch space, it is reflected in what might be called "performance space," that is, the physical location of an instrument within the ensemble.[32]

By creating fixed patterns of instrumental ordering and rhythm and then later displacing them, Crawford also creates an effect of "phase" shift, a phenomenon that can be divided into three stages: (1) the establishment of a pattern of rhythm and instrumental rotation; (2) a disruption of the pattern; and (3) the resumption of the original pattern but now displaced by one or two beats. There are two instances of "phase shift" in the movement. The first appears in mm. 39–43, where an initial pattern of rhythm and instrumental ordering is established, as described in figure 10. At m. 43 the climax in volume echoed by all four instruments increases from *mezzo forte* to *forte*. This change in volume also coincides with an interruption of the previous four measures—in this measure five peaks occur, including two in violin I. At the pickup to m. 44, however, the original rhythmic pattern (half note followed by three quarters) and ordering of instruments (4–3–2–1) both reappear, but now delayed by one beat. The second example of this displacement occurs in mm. 50–58, where an initial pattern of four quarter notes and instrumental ordering, 2–3–1–4, first appears on an upbeat (mm. 50–52), then shifts ahead by one quarter note to the downbeat (mm. 54–56), and finally returns to its initial upbeat setting (mm. 56–58). Figure 10 uses brackets to highlight this recurring pattern of ordering.

The question arises how are we to judge Crawford's treatment of dynamics and rhythm in this movement from the perspective of Seeger's

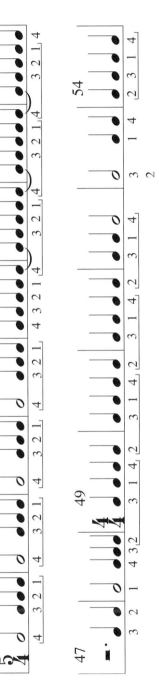

Figure 10. Ruth Crawford, String Quartet: III, mm. 39–58: Patterns of rhythm and instrumental ordering created by succession of climaxes (1 = cello; 2 = viola; 3 = violin II; and 4 = violin I)

compositional theories. On the one hand, the canonic interplay of crescendi and decrescendi is a tour de force in "dissonant" dynamics.
Crawford appears to have taken to heart Seeger's exhortations in the
treatise to explore the neglected resources. On the other hand, the
subtle displacement in rhythmic patterns and in the corresponding instrumental rotation, plus the continuous quarter-note pulse until m. 75
clearly fall within the broad category of "consonant" proportion.

Is such a mixture of old and new approaches to these two musical
functions some kind of aesthetic flaw—a sign that Crawford failed to
embrace fully the underlying intent of extended "dissonance"? On the
contrary, it is a strong testament to how much faith she had in Seeger's
ideal of synthesis. In the end, the concept of "dissonation" is a specific
and limited technique to be used in concert with other techniques or
principles. Crawford, herself, underlines this point in a letter written
to Edgard Varèse in which she outlines the elements of her aesthetic
"credo" during the period of the quartet:

1. Clarity of melodic line
2. Avoidance of rhythmic stickiness
3. Rhythmic independence between parts
4. Feeling of tonal and rhythmic center
5. Experiment with various means of obtaining at the same time organic unity and various sorts of dissonance[33]

Her juxtaposition of new kinds of "dissonance" and "organic unity" in
the same breath is a condensation of a number of ideas propounded
in the treatise. Ultimately, what is striking about the third movement
is the overall effect of *balance,* in which the "dissonance" in one musical function—in this case, dynamics—is compensated for by "consonance" in the remaining five functions. Instead of exploiting the
technique of "dissonance" for its own sake, Crawford aims for an equilibrium among different musical dimensions. Such a sensitivity to balance shows her desire to realize the spirit, if not the letter, of Seeger's
aesthetic ideal of synthesis as presented in *Tradition and Experiment
in the New Music.*

In exploring the practical application of Seeger's theories, one more
issue remains to be settled: the interdependence of the notion of extended "dissonance" and his ideal of a balanced style. The motivations
behind Seeger's extended "dissonance" can be explained as a two-step

process that parallels the initial two principles of musical understanding outlined earlier. First, Seeger felt an intuition to reject the musical traditions inherited from the nineteenth century. The next step was a rational and more specific means of achieving this intuition; after determining what treatment of a given function was commonplace, he tried to formulate its opposite. If we take this process of "dissonance" to its logical extreme and negate the customary usage of every musical function, then we arrive at "heterophony," a new brand of polyphony in which each individual melodic line or, by extension, each musical function achieves the maximum possible independence. In the essay "On Dissonant Counterpoint" Seeger describes this model as follows: "So it becomes necessary to cultivate 'sounding apart' rather than 'sounding together'—diaphony rather than symphony."[34]

But when this model of "diaphony" is compared with the balanced ideal of style, there appears to be a glaring contradiction. How can a composer write music that "sounds apart" or that explicitly avoids any feeling of unity and at the same time creates a unified and well-balanced whole?

As it turns out, this contradiction can be reconciled if we consider Seeger's discontent with nineteenth-century mannerisms. His search for pitch analogies reveals that he was reacting against the past as much as he was trying to initiate a modern-day "music of the future." Seeger believed that if composers were ever to escape the influence of the nineteenth century, they must try to cultivate those musical elements that their late-romantic predecessors had neglected. The various terminological experiments he proposes in the treatise were merely one part of a larger group of "disciplines," which he describes in a previous essay:

Such a set of disciplines would serve, in a way, as a temporary substitute for the unattainable style they aim eventually to establish and at the same time would serve as a corrective for the mannerisms against which they revolt. Work in them would, indeed, be half stylistic and half manneristic.[35]

This brief remark speaks volumes about Seeger's overall motivation in writing the treatise. On the one hand, he felt that before the foundation for a new compositional practice could be established, he must overcome the "malpractice" of the past. The spirit behind Seeger's idea of dissonant dynamics is to "correct" the inferior manners inherited from the late nineteenth and early twentieth centuries. This, no doubt, is what Seeger means when he predicts that composers who experiment with his regimen of dissonant counterpoint will experience an effect of "purification."[36]

But, on the other hand, as much as Seeger rebelled against some aspects of late-nineteenth-century music, such as the general fascination for chromatic harmony, he never abandoned one of the period's most essential aesthetic principles: organic unity. The "disciplines" Seeger imagines must not only compensate for the musical extravagance of the past but also extract something from it that will help initiate a new musical tradition. In this respect, one part of Seeger's aesthetic temperament always remained conservative—something he and his wife shared. During the late 1920s and early 1930s, Seeger and Crawford achieved an unusual symbiosis in which his theoretical and philosophical speculations helped shape her compositional creativity.[37] In sum, when conceived as an isolated technique, the idea of dissonant dynamics is "corrective"; yet when introduced in an undulating "sea" of independent musical functions, as Crawford did in her String Quartet, Seeger's goal of a balanced style seems well within reach.

Revival of Dualism

The second question that Seeger considers in part 1 of the treatise is the principle of harmonic dualism. In reviving this principle, Seeger was joining an international theoretical debate that had been raging for over 350 years. After all, to propound in 1930 an idea whose history could be traced to the writings of sixteenth-century Renaissance theorists was an anachronism of enormous proportions. The fact that Seeger was attracted to such an old idea illustrates two characteristic themes that appear throughout *Tradition and Experiment in the New Music:* the conflict he felt between trying to reconcile current experiments in composition with the musical traditions of the past; and the significance he attached to the philosophical ideal of mediation.

To appreciate the historical context of Seeger's revival of dualism, let us briefly review the development of this idea within the history of music-theoretical speculation. The theory first appeared during the late sixteenth century, when the older system of pitch organization— the church modes—were gradually supplanted by a new system in which two modes, major and minor, played coequal roles. Focusing on the most basic unit of harmony, the triad, Giuseppe Zarlino reasoned that, since major and minor triads produced opposite effects on listeners, they must depend on opposite principles. These two principles, he believed, were fundamentally linked to the very definitions of musical intervals. He began with the most consonant intervals, the perfect octave and fifth, and then segmented them in two opposite ways called harmonic and arithmetic division. Harmonic division was conceived as an ascending arrangement of simple ratios, 4:5:6; in arithmetic division the same ratios were arranged in descending order. The result was a unified system in which major and minor triads arose out of opposite yet symmetrical principles.

The next chapter in this ongoing debate appeared in the writings of the eighteenth-century French theorist and composer Jean-Philippe Rameau. In his work *Génération harmonique* (1737), Rameau, too, proposed that major and minor triads were generated from two opposite and symmetrical principles, but he justified his claim with a new form of evidence: empirical observation. Using the theory of resonance proposed in 1700 by the French physicist Joseph Sauveur, Rameau argued that the notes of the major triad were present in the overtone series. Thus, the fundamental and second upper partial form the interval of a twelfth (compound version of a fifth), and the fundamental and fourth upper partial form a seventeenth (compound version of a major third). Emboldened by this physical confirmation of one type of triad, Rameau tried to extrapolate it to the other. He speculated that a second series of sounds, what has come to be known as "undertones," must exist *under* the fundamental, and that these sounds were the mirror image of the overtone series. In order to generate the minor triad, he hypothesized that the same intervals of a twelfth and seventeenth spanned below a given fundamental rather than above it. The physical evidence for this alternate series was that the F and Ab, the longer string lengths corresponding to notes a twelfth and seventeenth below the C, vibrated sympathetically when the C was plucked; however, Rameau mistakenly assumed that these lower strings were vibrating in their entirety when, in fact, they were vibrating in parts. A further flaw in his hypothesis was that, although the intervals necessary for the minor triad do appear in his descending series, they cannot be arranged in root position, a fact that mars the otherwise perfect symmetry of the system.

In the nineteenth century there followed a host of German theorists, including Arthur von Oettingen, Moritz Hauptmann, and Hugo

Riemann, who placed the notion of dualism at the heart of their harmonic theories. Whether the primary justification lay in a natural *Gegensatz,* or opposing principle, or in a dialectical theory of human knowledge, as propounded by Hegel, all of these theorists placed great stock in the symmetrical derivation of the major and minor triads. It is interesting, however, that after initially claiming that empirical observation supported the theory of dualism, both Rameau and Riemann subsequently retracted this claim, conceding that no such proof existed.

In Seeger's early treatise the concept of dualism initially appears in the context of his overview of several traditional topics of harmonic theory in chapters 5 and 6. There he claims that when a given sounding body is divided into halves, thirds, fourths, and so on, the intervals formed between them and the original body create a collection of simple intervals: for example, 3:2 a perfect fifth. Likewise, the same process of division may be reversed, yielding the same sounds, but by means of multiplication. He calls these two processes "the harmonic series in superior and inferior resonance."[38] He then juxtaposes two scales using the same series of whole and half steps, one ascending from C and the other descending from G: the result is the major and natural minor scales, the latter of which begins on its fifth degree (see example 5). In arranging the major and minor scales in this symmetrical fashion, Seeger was borrowing a page from the *Cours de composition musicale* of the French composer Vincent d'Indy, who at the turn of the century also revived the theory of harmonic dualism. In a slightly different formulation d'Indy describes the relation between ascending and descending scales which share the same pattern of steps as "relative."[39]

Then, like some of his French and German predecessors, Seeger asserts that these abstract theories have been confirmed by empirical observation: "The above conclusions of a purely musical nature are supported by acoustical research into the nature of a sounding body, into resonance, and into the sensation of tone generally." Later, he concludes that it "has recently been proved that a similar inferior series can be characteristic of the resonating body."[40] As to who performed this "acoustical research" or, more important, who "proved" the existence of an inferior series, Seeger is silent.

The most likely source for this spurious acoustical view is Henry Cowell, who, during a visit to Moscow in 1929, discussed the theory

Example 5. Major and minor modes, *Tradition and Experiment in the New Music*

in question with the Russian theorist Nikolai Alexandrovitch Garbusov (1880–1955). Apparently, Cowell witnessed an acoustic demonstration that, he believed, provided new evidence to support the long-discredited theory of undertones. Joscelyn Godwin speculates as to what sort of phenomenon Cowell observed.

A large body, stimulated by a vibration faster than its own fundamental one, will either not react at all, or will vibrate in its nearest overtones to the stimulating vibrations. Perhaps the ear would be deceived into hearing a non-existent fundamental . . . , but this is not an undertone. It is possible that Garbusov's instrument was connected in some way with "difference tones," and that it was insufficiently explained to Cowell in Russia.[41]

If Cowell did indeed misunderstand the phenomena he witnessed in Garbusov's laboratory, he also must have passed on that misunderstanding to his former mentor. In a revised draft of the treatise dated 1931, Seeger wrote "cite Garbusov" in the margin next to his remark that the theory of superior and inferior resonance had "recently been proved."[42] The comment is striking considering that Seeger had never met the Russian theorist and most likely had never read any of Garbusov's writings, none of which by that time had been translated into English.

There is also evidence that Seeger had been convinced of the theory of undertones as early as 1916. In the harmony textbook on which he collaborated with Edward Stricklen, the authors employ this theory as a way of explaining the minor scale.[43] Furthermore, Seeger's close association with Crawford during the genesis of the treatise might have reinforced his dualistic convictions, since during her years in Chicago she had studied with one of the foremost American advocates of Riemannian harmony, Adolf Weidig.[44]

In sum, Seeger most likely based his dualistic view of harmony on the writings of nineteenth-century German theorists such as Hugo Riemann; furthermore, Seeger believed that recent experiments by a respected Russian theorist had breathed life back into a once extinct acoustical theory.[45]

But Seeger's most radical use of the theory of harmonic dualism appears in the midst of his regimen of dissonant counterpoint. In the history of tonality, he observes, theorists have tried to explain the nature of chords in one of two ways: either by the superposition of a fixed interval, usually thirds, or by the harmonic generation of superior and inferior resonance. In order to accommodate the experimentation of recent twentieth-century composers, Seeger suggests a third alternative: to combine the two previous methods, that is, to mix superposition of a fixed interval with the two-dimensional model of harmonic generation.[46] To generate chords found in contemporary music, Seeger is not content to select various partials from either above or below a given fundamental. Instead, he chooses the first five partials from both the overtone and the so-called undertone series, then constructs a five-note chord, or "pentad," which is reproduced in example 6(a). While the final product appears to be a chord composed of stacked thirds, Seeger cites two musical examples in which the original intervals have been inverted and rearranged in various ways: the opening chord in Schoenberg's Five Pieces for Orchestra, op. 16, movement 3, and the final chord in Ruggles's *Angels.* Both are reproduced as examples 6(c) and (d).

Finally, Seeger imagines a situation in which both methods of chord construction, harmonic generation and superposition by a fixed interval, are used simultaneously. He postulates a seven-note chord by adding a major third above and below the previous pentad. His justification for adding these notes is that they can be generated by superimposing a fixed interval above and below a given note, in this case, the major seventh. He calls the three-note chord displayed in example 6(b) the "*trias perfecta* of dissonant composition," a name that most likely reflects the predominance of "tense" inflections or "perfect dissonances." As for musical examples of this rather dense "septad," Seeger offers none.

Seeger's fascination for dualism is significant in that it corresponds so closely with his underlying philosophical aims. In the introduction Seeger declares that he hoped to develop a broad-based theory for all musical styles, that is, "composition in general." However, when one examines the content of chapters 3–6 of the treatise, it quickly becomes clear that in many respects his notion of "general" was limited

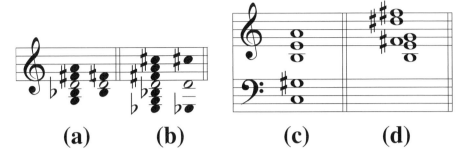

Example 6. (a, b) Chord generation using a mixture of "inferior" and "superior" resonance; (c) example of new "pentad" in Schoenberg, Five Pieces for Orchestra, op. 16: III; (d) example of new "pentad" in Ruggles, *Angels*

to eighteenth- and nineteenth-century art music. For instance, while no one can dispute that Seeger's six functions are fundamental to any musical style, surely the number of modes available to composers is greater than two (major or minor). A more realistic interpretation is that Seeger was attracted to properties and characteristics of tonal harmony whose structure conformed to that of his philosophical ideals. It goes without saying that the symmetry of a dualistic model of harmony was highly sympathetic to the aesthetic of balance that he espoused in the early chapters of the treatise. Thus, his motivation for including a discussion of the minor mode immediately after decrying theorists' overemphasis of pitch relations may be as much philosophical as musical.

His discussion of nontonal chords also reflects the importance he ascribed to the method of mediating between extremes. This is apparent in two ways. First, rather than account for new chords by selecting partials further and further away from the fundamental in either the overtone or the so-called undertone series, he insists on choosing partials from *both* series. Second, in chapter 16, after introducing two separate procedures for explaining chords, harmonic generation by the theory of resonance and superposition by a fixed interval, he fuses them. Throughout this discussion Seeger focuses more on the kind of explanation he is employing to generate new chords rather than an exhaustive inventory of nontonal chords for its own sake. In short, at times he speaks more like a philosopher than a compositional theorist, seemingly fascinated more by the aesthetic principle itself than by the practical ideas it can yield for composers.

Another curious aspect of Seeger's summary of harmonic dualism is his paradoxical attitude toward science. On the one hand, in the early chapters he calls into question the use of scientific theory as a means of justifying musical practice, in particular, the acoustic principles that serve as a basis for determining consonance and dissonance. He gives the impression that it was anathema for composers to rely on the assumptions and methods of science. On the other hand, he is perfectly content to use what he understands as acoustical science, the theory of harmonic dualism, as a basis for distinguishing between major and minor triads.

The explanation for this seeming paradox lies in Seeger's view of the relation between art and science, for the two fields are not as independent and autonomous as the impassioned rhetoric found in chapter 4 of the treatise might suggest. In short, there are occasions when scientific principles could clarify the theoretical organization of music: an example of such a relationship, he believed, was the symmetrical balance between major and minor triads. Seeger had inherited the dualistic explanation of tonality from previous generations of theorists and had never subjected it to empirical confirmation. There are other occasions, however, when musicians' dependence on scientific knowledge should be questioned. While such changes in attitude might be interpreted as inconsistent or hypocritical, they grew out of a realistic, more flexible view of the relation between science and composition.

Ultimately, Seeger's changes of heart about the uses of science underline a more profound theme that permeates the composition treatise: his desire to reconcile his understanding of eighteenth- and nineteenth-century theoretical traditions with current compositional practice. Had Seeger chosen to write strictly as an experimental composer, that is, exploring new sounds for their own sake, then controversies over the validity of dualism would surely never have arisen. That he insisted on integrating a regimen of dissonant counterpoint with his theories of taxonomic description, general melodic form, and music criticism shows the breadth of his intellectual aspirations.

Neumatic Theory of Melody

One of the distinctive characteristics of *Tradition and Experiment in the New Music* is Seeger's propensity to fuse the interpretive aims of analysis with the creative aims of composition. This is nowhere more apparent than in the final three chapters of part 1. As will be recalled, Seeger's first step in developing a general approach to composition is self-reflexive; by reevaluating the materials of music themselves, he hopes to generate new ideas for composition. In chapters 7–9 of the treatise, however, his ambitions are more systematic. Here he presents a theory of form based on two distinct approaches to melody: contour and motivic transformation. While the principal audience for this theory is contemporary composers, it is also intended for those who analyze and interpret music of the past two hundred years. In sum, Seeger's discussion of melodic form is truly interdisciplinary, showing yet another way in which his ambitions as theorist, composer, and philosopher converged in a single project.

In his initial remarks Seeger establishes a basic framework that bears the philosophical stamp of his meditations on music criticism. He believes that form arises out of the interaction between two opposite activities: synthesis and analysis. Synthesis is the process by which a collection of individual parts are joined together and eventually coalesce into a whole; analysis is the reverse process by which the whole is divided into its constituent parts. Whereas synthesizing is inherent in the very act of music-making, analysis, as Seeger understands it, lies outside of purely musical experience, resulting from either a dramatic "plot, idea, emotion, or other 'program'"; a mathematical or philosophical idea; or some combination thereof.[47]

Having presented this rather traditional dichotomy, Seeger takes it one step further by considering these two processes from an intuitionist as well as a scientific point of view. According to the former, synthesis and analysis are complementary, and thus occur simultaneously in any musical activity: "In actual composing, playing, and listening, these two methods are inextricably interwoven. Indeed, *form* in music *is* in its essence *the interplay of the two.*"[48] By contrast, the scientific point of view separates these two processes and chooses one over the other. The origin of their separation lies in the act of speech: "It is only in talking about music and in studying it that either method is used singly. And on such occasions we *must* use them singly."[49] As in his investigation of musical materials, Seeger is content to adopt a scientific persona, while occasionally showing strong intuitionist sympathies. What is more, the initial definitions for Seeger's conception of melody reflect the very essence of Bergson's theory of human knowledge: the strict separation of intuitive immediacy and rational thought.

In the three chapters devoted to form, Seeger declares that he will confine most of his attention to the synthetic realm. There are two reasons for this choice: one historical, one pedagogical. He believes that throughout the history of musical speculation theorists have devoted most of their attention to the analysis of preexisting works and, consequently, have neglected the art of constructing the whole from the part. In comments like these, Seeger reveals how much he himself had neglected the history of eighteenth- and nineteenth-century theories of melodic form.

The second reason for Seeger's preference appears in a handwritten addendum to chapter 7 that was not included in the 1994 edition of the treatise: "It is very difficult to treat of 'wholes' logically and that against the somewhat mystical handling of this aspect of the situation it is desirable to balance a more logical treatment, thus ensuring a complete encircling of the 'inner sanctum' of musical thought."[50] To begin with the parts and from them construct the whole is not only logical but also more promising as a method for teaching composition. While Seeger continues to emphasize his intuitionist sympathies, he ultimately hopes to blend musical logic and intuition, thus "encircling" the musical work with the complementary approaches of synthesis and analysis.

In chapters 7–9 the seeds of two different but interrelated approaches to melody can be perceived: a theory of form based on contour or gesture, and a theory of motivic transformation. Sometimes it appears that Seeger envisions them as two aspects of a single, vast theoretical system: one aspect explicitly avoids mention of specific intervals in favor of a melody's general contour; the other focuses on intervallic properties of melodic cells and the transformations necessary to generate one from another. Yet at other times the two seem autonomous, each designed to achieve different aims. In the remarks that follow, each theory will be summarized and assessed on its own, while emphasizing what points the two share in common.

Theory of Gesture

The point of departure for Seeger's theory of gesture is to assume that musical space and time are united, and to treat the two functions as a single entity. While at this point he had no specific term for this spatial-temporal fusion, he did invent a unit of measure, the "tone-beat," which is either a tone that occurs on a beat or a beat that coincides with a tone. By measuring melody in terms of "tone-beats," Seeger hoped to overcome the inevitable separation of pitch and rhythm found in most musical discourses, and treat them as a mutually dependent pair of dimensions. The union of musical space and time was a recurring leitmotif throughout Seeger's writings, and it gave birth to a variety of neologisms such as "timespace" and "spacetime."[51] Though, in general, Seeger discusses musical parameters in this chapter with a decidedly scientific tone, he still includes an occasional intuitive aside—as if to remind the reader that the separate "functions" of musical space and time ultimately belong to an indivisible whole.

For the fundamental increment of melody, Seeger turns to medieval chant notation. He revives the term "neume" as a means of indicating pure melodic direction, but he avoids specifying a melody's intervallic span or durational length. Neumes are defined by the melodic direction between tone-beats: two melodic gestures in the same direction constitute a "line"; two gestures in opposite directions, a "twist" (English equivalents of the Latin terms *scandicus* and *torculus*).[52] Neumes are also categorized according to the number of melodic gestures they contain, either binary (three tone-beats) or ternary (four tone-beats). In all, there are six possible combinations of "lines" and "twists," as shown in the first column of the diagram reproduced in figure 11. The remaining columns in this diagram are evidence of Seeger's desire to generalize the concept of neume to other musical parameters. Thus, he postulates similar units of measure, or what I call "neume-analogues," for dynamics, proportion, accent, and tempo, examples of which are provided in the appropriate columns in figure 11.[53] He omits only timbre, which, he concedes, cannot be classified with his newfound neumatic method.

In many respects Seeger's taxonomy of neumes and neume-analogues is a microcosm of his entire project. This "periodic chart" of musical "elements" shows the degree to which descriptive and creative aspirations are inseparably linked. The assumption is that any composer who hopes to develop the "dissonant" approach to dynamics that Seeger sketches out in chapter 4 must have a precise analytical language with which to describe it. In this respect, the diagram in figure 11 is a natural outgrowth of his "dissonant" speculations in chapters 3–4. Although he does not succeed in establishing a common unit of articulation for all six functions, his attempt to extrapolate

			TONAL			RHYTHMIC		
			Pitch	Dynamics	Timbre	Tempo	Accent	Proportion
BINARY	LINE	1a				acc-acc	/ /	— —
		b				rall-rall	∪ ∪	∪ ∪
	TWIST	2a				acc-rall	/ ∪	— ∪
		b				rall-acc	∪ /	∪ —
TERNARY	LINE - LINE	3a				acc-acc-acc	/ / /	— — —
		b				rall-rall-rall	∪ ∪ ∪	∪ ∪ ∪
	LINE - TWIST	4a				acc-acc-rall	/ / ∪	— — ∪
		b				rall-rall-acc	∪ ∪ /	∪ ∪ —
	TWIST - LINE	5a				acc-rall-rall	/ ∪ ∪	— ∪ ∪
		b				rall-acc-acc	∪ / /	∪ — —
	TWIST - TWIST	6a				acc-rall-acc	/ ∪ /	— ∪ —
		b				rall-acc-rall	∪ / ∪	∪ — ∪

Figure 11. Chart of neumes and neume-analogues ("acc" = accelerando; "rall" = rallentando)

his contour-based approach to melody is an eloquent testament to the degree of his taxonomic ambitions.

Seeger then goes into greater depth regarding the pitch structure of melody, illustrating his neume typology with composers from the eighteenth and nineteenth centuries. Example 7(a) presents the opening gesture of the first movement of Brahms's Symphony no. 2, which Seeger would regard as a ternary neume and specifically a "double twist." Then he explores ways in which these gestures may evolve within a work. For example, in example 7(a), the horn's arpeggiation figure, which appears in m. 2 of the same movement—F#4–A4–A3–D4— is a gestural inversion of the original "double twist."

Seeger then proceeds to higher levels in his formal hierarchy, namely, the "phrase" and the "whole." To characterize his notion of

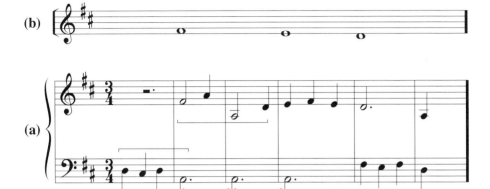

Example 7. Johannes Brahms, Symphony no. 2: I: (a) Piano reduction of mm. 1–6; bass's ternary neume, mm. 1–2, inverted in treble, mm. 2–3 (both marked in brackets); (b) phrase-neume of horn part, mm. 2–5

phrase, Seeger exploits a parallel between music and language, paraphrasing the theories of the great Roman orator Cicero, who defined the "period" as that which takes less than two full breaths to say.[54] In adapting this definition to music, Seeger describes the phrase as "one emission of the breath, one stroke of the bow, or one descent of the wrist," whether or not there are any divisions in the music.[55] Thus it may contain from three to seven neumes and may span from one to twelve measures. The bulk of chapter 8 in the treatise is devoted to a catalogue of the various operations by which neumes can be assembled into phrases, a topic that will be pursued at greater length below.

The next stage in Seeger's exposition of his gestural theory of melody is perhaps the most telling, for he reveals that intuition plays a greater role in the synthesis of neumatic melody than might be expected. He introduces a concept called the "phrase-neume," which can be defined as a gestural summary of a phrase that both encapsulates its principal tones and gestures and measures its overall unity. An illustration from the opening material of Brahms's Second Symphony is shown in example 7(b). The horn's material in mm. 2–5 is simplified to a phrase-neume of two descending steps, F#4–E4–D4, or a "double line." However, any reader interested in applying this basic definition to either analytical or creative situations is bound to be frustrated by Seeger's meager commentary; he never spells out what criteria are necessary either to reduce a phrase to its skeletal phrase-neume or, conversely, to expand a phrase-neume into a full-bodied phrase. He also intro-

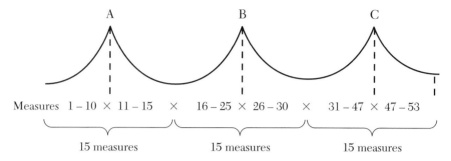

Figure 12. Seeger's form-neume analysis of Richard Wagner's *Tristan und Isolde*, act 3, mm. 1–53

duces an analogous concept to characterize the ideal relation between the phrase and the whole which he calls "form-neume." This term indicates "the rise and fall of pitch, dynamics (climax and anti-climax), tempos, etc." over an entire movement or piece.[56] As in his discussion of the term "phrase-neume," Seeger provides no specific procedure regarding the application of this concept, instead relying on musical illustrations to explain his ideas. He provides two analytical sketches of the beginning of act 3 of Wagner's *Tristan*, one of which is reproduced in figure 12. While one appears to be a concatenation of individual neumes arranged in an overall ascending or descending pattern, the other contains an intermediate level of detail, postulating three sections within the opening fifty-three measures.

Seeger's discussion of phrase-neumes and form-neumes is somewhat controversial. First, these two concepts emphasize the parallels between different levels in his hierarchy; the relation between neume and phrase strongly resembles that between phrase and whole. This parallelism shows that Seeger aimed for a certain balance and consistency in his conception of melody. But, by the same token, he was less than forthcoming about the ways in which phrase-neumes and form-neumes should be applied as analytical tools. His basic definitions raise a number of questions. For example, is there any consistent pattern between a phrase-neume and its underlying harmonic support? What is the method for calculating the general direction of a long series of individual neumes or phrase-neumes?

Indeed, taken by themselves, these two concepts constitute a *framework* of a theory of melody rather than a full-fledged theory itself. The crucial missing ingredient is the intuition that composers or analysts must supply themselves in order to put this abstract framework into practice. Thus, Seeger leaves it for the reader to decide which notes of a given neume complex constitute the underlying phrase-neume and, likewise, which phrases in a work belong to the overarching form-neume. Viewed in the context of Seeger's overall approach, this rather open-ended summary of the theory of melodic contour appears to be by design, not by accident. To conceive of melody as merely the mechanical application of a set of logical rules would have been anathema to his underlying philosophical beliefs.

In sum, Seeger's theory of gesture combines a balanced structural hierarchy that serves as the basis for comprehensive taxonomic description. Yet there are aspects of this conception of melody that are more open-ended and that require the individual musician's own intuition before they can be fully exploited as analytical or compositional tools. Evidently, Seeger himself was not entirely satisfied with these chapters in the treatise, because he continued refining the typology of neumes and neume-analogues during the 1960s as a descriptive method for ethnomusicologists.[57] Indeed, in recent years there have been signs that his interest in melodic contour and in extending the notion of contour to other musical dimensions has left a vital legacy in music-theoretical circles.[58]

Theory of Motivic Unity

The second theoretical approach that Seeger presents in chapters 7 through 9 of the treatise is a theory of motivic unity. Seeger's reliance on such an approach shows his true debt to the nineteenth century, for the guiding principle behind the notion of motivic unity is "organicism." An organically conceived melody possesses an underlying unity in that a single musical idea is suffused over the whole. It is characterized by an economy of means whereby a "minimum of initial material constitutes or conditions most of what follows." Seeger contrasts this ideal of "organic" melody with something called "diffuse" melody, in which "the initial material often does not appear again, nor does it lead logically to what follows."[59]

Seeger never explicitly identifies a specific individual or national style as the model for his ideal of melodic organicism, instead saying that examples of this approach "abound in the music of the last four centuries."[60] Indeed, he implies that, since "organic" melody has guided the development of composition since the Renaissance, it must transcend historical periods. Yet if one studies his musical examples closely, there is a marked preference for late eighteenth- and nineteenth-century German composers such as Mozart, Beethoven, Schubert, and Brahms. For instance, he contrasts the "organic" character of the opening movement from Beethoven's Symphony no. 5 with the "diffuse" initial material from Bruckner's Symphony no. 9.[61] Moreover, in another essay, he identifies the music of J. S. Bach—in particular, the textures found in ricercares or fugues—as the inspiration for a new contrapuntal style of composition.[62] Thus, while he claims that the principle of "organicism" has guided composers for over four centuries, the evidence he marshals in the treatise suggests that it is an idea rooted in the eighteenth and nineteenth centuries.

The organic ideal is a crucial ingredient in Seeger's formal hierarchy, for it is the glue that holds his theory of melody together. Of the three levels of melodic activity, the phrase is where the organic criterion takes on the most significance. The phrase is the cornerstone of his pedagogical approach to composition, the point at which analysis and synthesis meet. Seeger believes that the greatest challenge for composers is not to learn how to write neumes but rather, given an initial neume, how to transform it into a unified phrase. At the end of chapter 8 Seeger waxes eloquent about the subject:

The phrase is the normal breath, stride or span of musical thought. Indeed, a composer may gauge his power in no more positive way than by the length of phrase in which he can think and feel. The young composer especially should practice in thinking as much by the phrase as he can, and not run aground on the shoals of detail or become lost in the too large open spaces of form analysis and its facile generalizations.[63]

Seeger's explanation of organically conceived phrases and wholes is the most practical section of the treatise's entire first half. In fact, most of the final three chapters in part 1 are devoted to a meticulous catalogue of various operations that may be applied to a given "neume." In the course of his exposition, Seeger classifies these operations into three groups: (1) "conversions," which include transposition, inversion, retrogression, and retrograde inversion; (2) phrase-building operations; and (3) "modifications."

Example 8 illustrates the four "conversions" using excerpts from the first movement of Ruth Crawford's *Diaphonic Suite* no. 1. The neume appearing in the opening measures shown at the top is related to the transformed neumes by means of the operation indicated on each line. To anyone familiar with early twentieth-century compositional techniques, these four "conversions" are usually regarded as the cornerstones of twelve-tone serialism as practiced by the Viennese trio of Schoenberg, Webern, and Berg. Seeger, too, confers special status on these operations in that he believes a neume which has been "converted" by one of these four operations never loses what he calls its "fundamental logical identity."[64] Apparently, he intends to distinguish these operations from others in his catalogue by virtue of their near-mathematical precision—hence the term "logical identity." Seeger also identifies seven separate phrase-building operations in the treatise, though there is considerable redundancy in his list.[65] They include repetition, opposition, sequence, continuity, extension, intension, and ellipsis; the last five are demonstrated in example 8. (Incidentally, the format for illustrating "extension," "intension," and "ellipsis" differs from the other operations in that the original and transformed neumes are both presented on a single staff instead of merely the transformed neume.)

Finally, Seeger's third type of operation, "modification," is defined far more broadly than the other two types. It may take either of two forms: tonal, that is, an alteration of a neume's intervallic contour, or rhythmic. In short, modification is a catchall category that embraces a mixed assortment of transformations. Examples include "progression by complement" or "addition of a fixed interval."[66] Though the former modification may take many forms, including combining with other operations (such as inversion), Seeger's example is complementation by the octave, which involves introducing the same pitch of a given neume but at a different register.

In example 9(a), the initial descending minor second, B—Bb, is rewritten as an ascending major seventh. The "fixed interval" type is shown at (b), where the intervals between the first and second pitches, A—B, and first and third pitches, A—G#, are expanded by a perfect fourth (or five half steps), while still maintaining the neume's original contour. Furthermore, a modification may also be carried out after any of the six "phrase-building" operations, thus creating a larger process of neumatic change. Seeger illustrates this more elaborate form of modification using the opening theme from Schubert's Symphony

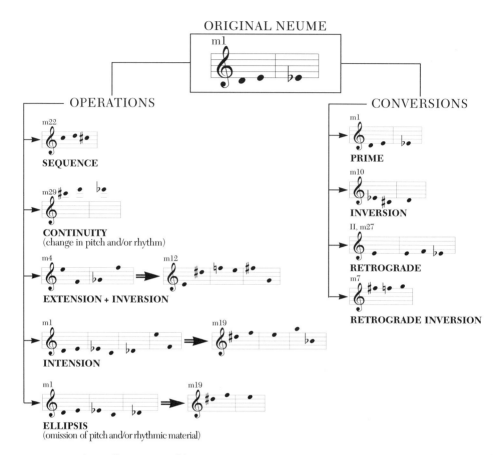

Example 8. Illustrations of four "conversions" and five other phrase-building operations using excerpts of Ruth Crawford's *Diaphonic Suite* no. 1: I and II

in C Major, as shown in example 10. The opening binary "line" neume, C—D—E, undergoes a modified repetition in m. 4 in which the G substitutes for the C (the rhythm does not change). A similar modification occurs between mm. 2 and 3, where the ascending major second in the original binary "line," A—B, is replaced by a descending minor third, D—B, and then the whole neume is transposed up two degrees in the C major scale.

On close inspection, Seeger's concept of "modification" is less an operation per se than a license to experiment with a neume's intervals and/or durations while preserving the original gestural shape. According to Seeger's definition, a neume's melodic or rhythmic identity can be altered so radically that the transformed neume loses almost all

Example 9. Illustrations of two tonal "modifications": (a) by octave complement; (b) by fixed interval: perfect fourth

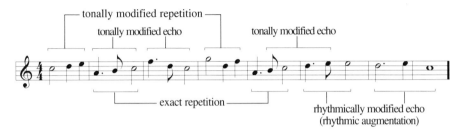

Example 10. Illustrations of various types of modification in Schubert's Symphony in C Major: I

resemblance to the original. Indeed, he even goes to the trouble of creating a special operation called "continuity" (which might be more aptly named the "anything goes" operation) in order to emphasize that a given neume may be transformed into any other neume, provided the process is gradual enough. He demonstrates this "operation" by slowly altering the pitches and rhythms of the opening theme from Schubert's Symphony in C Major until he arrives at the theme of Strauss's tone poem, *'Till Eulenspiegels lustige Streiche* (see example 11). Unlike conversions or operations, then, modifications are truly gestural in that attention is focused primarily on melodic contour rather than an exact series of intervals.

Finally, Seeger's exposition of melody would not be complete if he did not counterbalance his theoretical catalogue with some invocation of intuition. Having enumerated a panoply of logical principles with which neumes can be transformed, he argues at the end of chapter 7 that any good composer must possess a certain "sense" or "feeling" for neume conversion. He declares, "Tradition, in our art, has approved for a thousand years the reliance upon sense rather than upon calculation in this direction."[67] To demonstrate this notion of "sense," he then offers two highly contrasting models: an anonymous French folk

Example 11. "Continuity" modification: opening theme from Schubert's Symphony in C modified in six stages into theme from Strauss's *'Till Eulenspiegels lustige Streiche*

song and the opening of the Prelude from Arnold Schoenberg's Piano Suite, op. 25. Though the two differ enormously in the sophistication of their craft, each shows an intuitive "sense" for what form of repetition or inversion is appropriate. Despite his penchant for classification, Seeger ultimately believed that the artful combination of neumes and phrases resisted any definitive logical explanation.

The best way to understand the organizing potential of the various definitions in Seeger's conception of neumatic melody is to apply them in a brief analysis of a specific work. The first movement of Crawford's *Diaphonic Suite* no. 1, a pitch summary of which is reproduced in example 12, is highly conducive to this type of analysis.[68] This entire movement is based upon the principle of contrast, which is evident in the opening measures. The initial dotted rhythms in mm. 1–3 are answered by the reverse dotted pattern in mm. 4–5. Crawford's selection of intervals also reinforces this sense of contrast: the opening conjunct line gives way to a pair of major seventh leaps. The material in this opening phrase is developed subsequently by means of inversion, sequence, and retrograde inversion. The opening five pitches, D—E—Eb—C—Db, are inverted and transposed up a half step in mm. 10–12 (Eb—C#—D—F—E). In addition, the opening gesture (a "binary twist") recurs throughout the work, for example in mm. 19–22, and in retrograde inversion in m. 7.

Example 12. Ruth Crawford, *Diaphonic Suite* no. 1: I, pitch summary

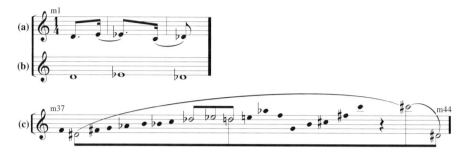

Example 13. Ruth Crawford, *Diaphonic Suite* no. 1: I: (a) mm. 1–3; (b) phrase-neume of mm. 1–3; (c) development of same phrase-neume in mm. 37–44

The oboe's final ascent beginning at m. 37 is a particularly apt illustration of the concept of phrase-neume.[69] To begin with, the rhythmic values accelerate as the melody progresses, instead of decelerating, as in the second and fourth phrases. Within this sinuous ascent, several statements of the opening binary neume occur, one of which is marked by beams on the score. The concept of phrase-neume comes into play as two of the three essential pitches classes from the opening melodic idea reappear as the boundary pitches of the final rising gesture (see example 13). The pitches, D, Eb, Db, were selected as the phrase-neume for mm. 1–3 because of two factors: greater metric accent and longer rhythmic duration. In the final ascent Crawford highlights Eb and Db (here spelled as D# and C#) in several ways: by contour (they are the highest and lowest pitches of the gesture); by rhythmic treatment (their duration is extended, and the final leap is delayed with a rest in m. 36); and by reiteration (the D# appears twice in mm. 37 and 44).

When viewed as a whole, Seeger's conception of melody reflects his commitment to the philosophical principle of mediation between opposites. At first glance, it is tempting to assume that Seeger's two theories of melody—one focusing on gesture and the other on motivic unity—create a perfect opposition and that it is up to composers and theorists to negotiate a compromise between the two. However, as different as these theories are, they are not, strictly speaking, opposites. Instead, the opposition exists between the activities of analysis and synthesis within both theories or, more precisely, between Seeger's motivations as a composer and a theorist. It is worthwhile to consider how this opposition manifests itself within each theory.

If nothing else, Seeger's catalogue of neumes and neume-analogues reveals the temperament of a taxonomist par excellence. One of Seeger's underlying motives for reexamining the basic functions of music is to discover a simple but comprehensive method of description that can be applied to any musical style. Beginning with a highly atomistic approach to melody and a simple unit of measure, the neume, Seeger then tries to generalize this approach to four of the other five musical functions. Although he freely admits that changes in some functions, such as dynamics or timbre, may never be as amenable to classification as are changes in pitch, his goal of developing a comprehensive taxonomic tool remains the same.

By the same token, at times Seeger also speaks like a highly intuitive composer in his protest against any approach to melody that tries to separate pitch and rhythm. Seeger's concept of melodic "progression," the ideal union of time and space, is more of a poetic metaphor or intuition than a rational method of composition. There is an unmistakable *incongruity* in his desire to combine this intuitive approach to melodic contour with his comprehensive method of neumatic description. This tension between reason and intuition is also evident in the hierarchical apparatus Seeger chooses to discuss melody. The specificity required to divide a melody into incremental units or, conversely, to add those units together to create a whole melody, is at odds with Seeger's definition of gesture, which explicitly avoids dividing pitch space into smaller units. Indeed, his concept of gesture can be interpreted as a *reaction against* the very scientific spirit that is one of the fundamental premises of his chart of neumes.

The conflict between the analytical and creative impulses is even more dramatic in Seeger's theory of motivic unity. His discussion of this approach consists of an inventory of operations or transformations by which a neume's intervals or rhythms can be altered and yet retain some kind of familial relationship with the original. If an entire work is suffused by a single cell and its various transformations, that work is considered "organic." Among the various operations listed, Seeger highlights four, called "conversions," which are distinguished from the others by their mathematical precision.

Yet Seeger supplements this quartet of "conversions" with another type of operation called "modification," which is anything but precise. If a neume's intervals and/or rhythms are sufficiently "modified," as in

Seeger's example of a Schubertian theme being transformed into a Straussian theme (see example 11), the resulting melody bears almost no resemblance with its neumatic progenitor. If "modification" creates a relationship between any two neumes, regardless of their differences in intervallic and/or rhythmic content, then the distinction between "organic" and "diffuse" becomes meaningless. A clever analyst could discover organic unity in virtually every composition and every musical style. The point is not that "modification" is useless as a compositional procedure; on the contrary, it may provide the creative spark for some composers to write good melodies. Rather, by listing procedures such as "modifications" alongside "conversions," Seeger endows what is essentially a spontaneous, creative act with a pretense of scientific rigor.

In sum, although Seeger's desire to develop a systematic model of melody may seem at odds sometimes with his vision of intuitive creativity, in his mind the two projects were mutually dependent. In the three chapters in the treatise devoted to his theory of form, Seeger strikes a balance between two sets of conflicting impulses: the clash between the legacy of eighteenth- and nineteenth-century art music and the latest experiments of avant-garde composition; and the opposite but complementary processes of descriptive analysis and creative synthesis. As a whole, these chapters illustrate well how his philosophical ideal of mediation could be brought to musical fruition.

Historical Influence

With this overview and critique of Seeger's theory complete, it is appropriate to consider the historical sources that influenced his theory of melodic form. It is difficult to identify exactly what sources influenced Seeger's theory of motivic unity because, despite his formal training at Harvard between 1904 and 1908, his musical education was essentially autodidactic. His unorthodox theoretical views can be traced to the years between 1912 and 1917 when, as a fledgling music professor at the University of California, Berkeley, he devised a regimen of critical readings in music, as well as in a broad spectrum of disciplines such as philosophy, history, anthropology, psychology, and the history of science. The difficulty is also compounded by Seeger's failure to document sources in the treatise. Nevertheless, it is possible to identify three theorists who exercised some degree of influence on

Seeger's thought: Jules Combarieu, a French theorist writing at the turn of the century; Vincent d'Indy, a prominent French composer and theorist during the same period; and Arnold Schoenberg, as represented by one of his former students, Adolph Weiss.

Jules Combarieu

If Seeger's notion of melodic gesture was inspired by medieval chant notation, the original source for his formal hierarchy was an even older theoretical tradition: the ancient Greek theory of poetic meter. The most likely source for this poetic borrowing is Jules Combarieu, whose treatise Seeger cites in his exposition of musical form.[70] Since this is one of a handful of theoretical treatises to which Seeger refers in his entire work, and since the two theories have so much in common, we may safely conclude that Combarieu guided Seeger's thinking. Combarieu himself draws freely upon the ideas of the well-respected German classicist Rudolf Westphal, who devoted his life to translating and interpreting the works of Aristoxenus and, then, applying Greek theories of poetic meter to eighteenth- and nineteenth-century music. A direct correspondence exists between Seeger's system of melodic organization and Aristoxenus's system of poetic verse as reconstructed by Combarieu from the extant portions of the treatise *Elements of Music*. The parallel terms are displayed in figure 13.

The correspondences between Seeger's and Combarieu's theories of musical form are striking. Both construct a rhythmic hierarchy in which shorter melodic segments are combined to form longer segments until the whole is reached. Like his French counterpart, Seeger wanted to establish a system of nomenclature that could describe any musical event—hence the one-to-one correspondence in figure 13 between unity-syllable-foot in the right-hand column and tone beat–progression–neume in the left-hand column. Furthermore, both had a predilection for units of measure that were in twos and threes; indeed, binary and ternary neumes correspond directly to poetic feet of two- and three-syllables, respectively. For Seeger as well as Combarieu, melody could be parsed like a line of verse.

Despite these similarities, fundamental differences exist between the two schemes. Above all, Combarieu believes that the rhythmic aspect of music is primary, and he makes no attempt to take into account a melody's contour. For Seeger, just the opposite is true; melody

Melody	Poetry
tone beat	
progression	syllable
neume – binary – ternary	foot – iambic/trochaic – anapestic/dactylic
phrase	member of phrase (kôlon)
	period
	strophe
whole	poem

Figure 13. Comparison of Combarieu's theory of poetic
meter (based on Aristoxenus) and Seeger's theory of melody

is perceived initially as pitch contour and then as rhythmic shape. The
second difference is in the relation between different levels in each
one's formal hierarchy. By omitting some levels of Combarieu's metric hierarchy in his own musical scheme, Seeger ensures that there is
considerable freedom in the ways by which a neume can be expanded
into a larger segment of melody. Seeger invested as much importance
in precise operations such as inversion as in the less strict procedures
known as "modifications." Finally, Combarieu's model does not establish precise rules by which different levels within a musical hierarchy
can be related. One wonders whether Combarieu's only criterion
for combining musical syllables to make neumes is mere adjacency.
Seeger, by contrast, attributes great importance to the varied or exact
repetition of an initial neume. In sum, Seeger's ideal of employing rhapsody and reason in equal proportions was at odds with the purely logical foundation of Combarieu's model of rhythm.

Vincent d'Indy

Vincent d'Indy, another French theorist writing at the turn of the century, also helped shape Charles Seeger's theories of melodic form.

The evidence supporting d'Indy's influence on Seeger is very much like that in the case of Combarieu. First of all, there are resemblances in substance. Numerous parallels exist between specific terms, as well as between the internal structure of Seeger's and d'Indy's approaches to melody. Furthermore, Seeger also makes a passing reference to d'Indy's principal theoretical work, but not where one would expect it: in the treatise's introduction rather than in the chapters concerning the theory of melodic form. Considering that other theoretical works that he documents in the treatise have much in common with his own ideas, it is highly likely that d'Indy's writings played some part in the formation of Seeger's thought.

D'Indy's principal theoretical work, *Cours de composition musicale,* grew out of his teaching at the Schola Cantorum, one of the two principal conservatories in France at the turn of the century. Though d'Indy was the school's director, he still found time to teach an intensive course combining composition and history that usually took students from seven to ten years to complete. Two of d'Indy's former students, August Sérieuyx and Guy de Lioncourt, used their notes as a basis for assembling the final text of this four-volume compendium. The only volume that has any direct bearing on Seeger's treatise is the first, which consists of an investigation of the fundamental materials of music, followed by a highly personal survey of historical styles, genres, and theories of pitch organization.

The point of departure for d'Indy's conception of melody is the analogy between music and language:

Musical language and spoken language are, in effect, ruled in the same way by the laws of accent. The rhythmic groups we have described are the musical image of syllables, the succession of which engenders words and phrases.[71]

D'Indy modeled his theory of melody loosely after a theory of grammar, drawing parallels between parts of speech and theoretical concepts wherever possible. His approach includes three basic elements of music: rhythm, melody, and harmony. Of the three, rhythm is the most central to musical experience, and it ultimately depends on the phenomenon of accent. To demonstrate this assumption, he imagines a stream of pulses that are equal in duration and accent yet devoid of aesthetic character. In order for such a neutral pattern to acquire any artistic attributes, it must possess "a true inequality in the duration, in the intensity, or in the acuity of the sounds."[72] D'Indy's inspiration for this primordial opposition between strong and weak accent is the German theorist Hugo Riemann, who presents his own theory of melody in the early work *Musikalische Katechismen.*[73]

In the second chapter of his treatise d'Indy unveils another hierarchy of melodic structure, which combines pitch and rhythm. He develops pairs of principles, such as movement and repose, which are opposing but at the same time mutually dependent. D'Indy eventually amasses a catalogue of such things as incises, periods, phrases, and cadences, as well as the procedures necessary for applying them to a single line of melody.[74]

In comparing Seeger's and d'Indy's approaches to melody, one discovers similarities as well as differences. The greatest resemblance is in the terminology each uses to describe melody. As his most basic unit, d'Indy chooses the "incise," which he defines as an indivisible fragment, monad, or cell of melody. He then arrives at the concept of "neume," which he defines "as a sort of musical syllable, serving to establish the musical discourse by means of melodic groups and periods."[75] Hence, while both theorists resurrect the same medieval term as a fundamental increment of melody, they use it in different ways: d'Indy defines it strictly as a pattern of accentuation; Seeger, by contrast, treats it as a unit of melodic gesture. In addition, both employ units of measure that are either binary or ternary, though not in the same way. For d'Indy a binary "rhythm" is an alternating pattern of accents within a stream of equal durations—weak followed by strong; a ternary rhythm is the same pattern of accents, but the strong accent is twice as long as the weak.[76] For Seeger the two terms refer to kinds of melodic gestures, not patterns of accent.

Finally, the most significant point of resemblance between the two theories is their similarity in methodology. Both were strongly attracted to theoretical models in which pairs of opposites were balanced in equilibrium: for d'Indy the principal oppositions were between strong and weak accent and between movement and repose; for Seeger it is a matter of balancing opposing mental faculties: reason and intuition.

Arnold Schoenberg

Assessing the degree of influence that Schoenberg exercised on Seeger's theory of form is more problematic than in the case of Combarieu and d'Indy. The issue of influence hinges on two questions:

(1) how much access did Seeger have to Schoenberg's music itself and his many writings about music? and (2) what did Seeger learn about Schoenberg's theories of composition and aesthetics through Schoenberg's students or various other proponents of his ideas? By answering these questions, we can begin to assess the Viennese composer's influence on Seeger's neumatic theory of form.

Regarding Seeger's exposure to Schoenberg's creative output, it is important to separate the music from the theoretical writings. Seeger was certainly aware of at least some of Schoenberg's so-called atonal and early serial compositions, for at various points in the treatise he refers to specific compositional techniques displayed in opp. 16, 19, and 25.[77] Judging from his comments, it appears that Seeger must have had access to the scores of these works.

However, it is unlikely that Seeger read much of Schoenberg's own writings on compositional technique. This conclusion is based on two factors: Seeger's limited fluency in German, and the meager number of Schoenberg's works available in English translation during the 1920s. It is not entirely clear how well Seeger read German. On the one hand, since he lived and worked in Cologne for one year and traveled between Berlin and Paris for another, he must have acquired basic fluency in the language. On the other hand, in a series of interviews taped in 1966 and 1971, Seeger admitted that his reading skills during the teens were no match for Immanuel Kant's metaphysical tomes.[78] Also, most of the references and all the philosophical writings that Seeger cites in the treatise are in English.[79]

Considering the difficulty of Schoenberg's prose style, it seems reasonable to conclude that Seeger could have had access to the Viennese composer's writings only in translation. By 1931 Schoenberg had published very few of his ideas concerning thematic unity and developing variation—only three articles—and only one was available in English translation.[80] The latter, "Tonality and Form," though provocative, is too short to do justice to Schoenberg's rich complex of compositional and aesthetic ideas. Another essay, "Problems of Harmony," while more representative of Schoenberg's views, appeared in translation three years after Seeger had finished his revised draft of the treatise.[81] Since the definitive statement of Schoenberg's compositional theories, entitled *The Musical Idea and the Logic, Technique, and Art of Its Presentation*, appeared after both composers had died, Seeger would have had no knowledge of it.[82]

Judging by the number of articles about Schoenberg in such music journals as *Modern Music* and *The Musical Quarterly* during the late 1920s and 1930s, the curiosity among American composers about his innovations must have been keen.[83] Seeger's most likely source for Schoenberg's ideas was Adolph Weiss (1891–1971), the first American student to work directly with the Austrian master. In 1925 Weiss traveled to Mödling, Austria, to study privately with Schoenberg, and one year later he followed the Viennese composer to Berlin to continue his composition lessons. Upon Weiss's return to America, he settled in New York and occasionally attended the salons of Blanche Walton, where he came in contact with other avant-garde composers such as Seeger, Henry Cowell, Ruth Crawford, and Dane Rudhyar. Seeger must have attended Weiss's lecture entitled "A Comprehensive View of the Schoenbergian Technic" on April 27, 1931, at the New York Musicological Society, since, as secretary of the organization, Seeger provided summaries of all meetings for the bulletin.[84] Finally, Seeger more than likely read Weiss's article "The Lyceum of Schoenberg," which appeared in *Modern Music,* since Seeger himself occasionally contributed to the periodical. It will be useful to describe this essay in some detail.

Weiss's essay is a highly condensed pastiche based on his experiences as a student and his study of Schoenberg's writings. It includes a redaction of Schoenberg's general theories of form, melody, and aesthetics, as well as brief summaries of parts of the treatise *Theory of Harmony* and his twelve-tone serial procedures. Weiss enumerates five basic principles or laws that form the foundation of Schoenberg's approach to composition, several of which are relevant to our comparison with Seeger. First, the most essential attribute of a work of art is form; it is what distinguishes an artwork from any other experience, whether natural or man-made. Weiss proposes that in any artwork form depends on contour, which, when translated into musical terms, means melody. Second, the attributes of balance and symmetry are as vital for a work of art as for a living thing. The means by which this balance can be achieved in music is "the recurrence of themes or phrases either in their original form or in variation." Since Schoenberg rejects sheer repetition as a legitimate compositional procedure, the emphasis is on techniques of variation—what Weiss calls the "continuous subdivision of the original germ-cell" or motive.[85] In all, Weiss lists the following nine methods:

1. fixed rhythms, varied intervals;
2. fixed intervals, varied rhythms;
3. varied intervals *and* rhythms;
4. inversion;
5. elongation;
6. contraction;
7. elision;
8. interpolation;
9. *motus cancrizans* (retrogression).

Finally, Weiss proposes a principle of contrast, which is necessary as a means of differentiating parts within the whole. But he also cautions that this principle must never be taken to extremes, for too much contrast would threaten the unity achieved through variation.

At this point it is helpful to augment Weiss's summary in order to convey the considerable degree of overlap between Seeger's and Schoenberg's theories of composition when viewed as a whole. The principles of continuous subdivision and contrast that Weiss mentions together constitute one of the linchpins of Schoenberg's aesthetic approach: "developing variation." In his textbook *Fundamentals of Musical Composition,* Schoenberg would later characterize this concept as follows:

Homophonic music can be called the style of "developing variation." This means that in the succession of motive-forms produced through variation of the basic motive, there is something which can be compared to development, to growth.[86]

For some readers, Schoenberg's terminology can be misleading, for his concept in no way refers to the "development" section of a sonata movement (the material immediately following the exposition) or to a set of discrete variations. Instead it is a broad principle of organic unity.

Another central principle of Schoenberg's thought is the concept of dualism, which is present in a variety of ways. The first is in the dichotomy between science and art. While science must proceed by the use of logic and empirical evidence, art can present "only a certain number of *interesting* cases and strives for perfection by the manner of presentation."[87] Though Schoenberg willingly borrows the methods of science for the purposes of teaching, the musical work must ultimately be understood as a single totality. Another example of dualism is Schoenberg's reliance on an opposition between balance and unrest. According to Patricia Carpenter and Severine Neff, Schoenberg conceives of a musical whole as a "balance of forces." A preliminary state of rest leads to the introduction of an "idea," which creates imbalance by means of the unrest inherent in the musical material itself; eventually, the "idea," in the course of its development, restores the initial state of balance.[88] Finally, it is possible to view Schoenberg's tendency toward dualism as a reflection of his evolving spiritual life, in particular, his intermittent but impassioned faith in Jewish mysticism.[89]

When placed side by side, Schoenberg's and Seeger's approaches to composition reveal similarities as well as differences. Both theorists place a premium on melody. For Schoenberg, the inherent priority of melody over all other musical dimensions becomes a universal aesthetic law. For Seeger, the emphasis on line is a means of compensating for the harmonic excesses of nineteenth-century composers. While both shared a similar interest in the craft of writing good melody, only Seeger tried to locate his technical principles within a broader historical context.

Second, both theorists emphasize the importance of organic unity, enumerating a profusion of operations by which a motivic cell can be transformed yet still preserve a sense of overall coherence. In fact, the two lists of operations overlap to a great degree. The only differences are that Seeger regards "repetition" and "sequence" as legitimate operations, whereas Weiss's version of Schoenberg does not; and Seeger simplifies the quartet of "elongation," "contraction," "elision," and "interpolation" into two more general categories: "extension" and "intension."

Seeger's and Schoenberg's interest in the anatomy of melody falls within a long tradition in the history of music theory inaugurated in the late eighteenth century by Joseph Riepel, Heinrich Koch, and Johann Kirnberger, and continued in the nineteenth century by Hugo Riemann. All these theories begin with the smallest units of melody and then combine them to form larger units, finally culminating in the whole. When compiling his list of operations, Seeger could easily have been influenced by any theory from this melodic tradition, especially that of Schoenberg as seen through the eyes of one of his students. But, in the long run, the likeness among lists is less important than the value that both Seeger and Schoenberg give to the principle of organic unity as measured by the varied repetition of an initial melodic idea. In this respect both drew inspiration from the romantic fascination with organicism that was manifested in all the arts during the nineteenth century.

The third similarity is that both Seeger and Schoenberg placed the principle of balance at the heart of their theories. In Seeger's case, this principle can be traced to his philosophical theory of musical knowledge as presented in the opening two chapters of the treatise, a theory that grew out of Seeger's own synthesis of such early-twentieth-century philosophers as Henri Bergson and Bertrand Russell. Weiss does not try to characterize the philosophical soil in which his mentor's aesthetic ideas took root, though it is safe to conclude that Schoenberg's aesthetic sensibility grew to maturity in the crucible of Viennese culture at the turn of the century.[90]

In sum, Seeger's theories bear a number of resemblances with those of Combarieu, d'Indy, and Schoenberg. The influence of the writings of Combarieu and d'Indy on Seeger's theory of form is, on the whole, less significant than that of Schoenberg. D'Indy was more of an encyclopedist, organizing and assimilating a wide range of historical styles and theories of musical structure. The greatest resemblance between d'Indy's and Seeger's approaches to melody is their common reliance on equal but opposing principles. Combarieu, by contrast, was in essence an analyst, intent on applying an ancient theory of poetic meter to the European masterpieces of the eighteenth and nineteenth centuries. The strongest resemblance between the theories of Seeger and Combarieu is their mutual attraction to a formal hierarchy, though Seeger reduced the total number of levels from seven to five. Finally, Seeger shares with Schoenberg an atomistic approach to melody in which a single idea is subjected to endless variation and transformation. Both tried to renew modern composition by reviving older approaches to melody and form.

In a highly opinionated and entertaining collection of essays, Camille Saint-Saëns derides two French theorists for their reliance on ideas of German vintage:

Here we have an instance of the practice so often indulged in before the war . . . of *crossing the Rhine in our search after truth.* Thus also Combarieu endeavoured to instil[l] into our minds the wild and senseless ideas of Westphal. . . . M. D'Indy gives us elaborate notes on Riemann, Hauptmann, Helmholtz, von O[e]ttingen (emphasis added).[91]

If we judge Seeger's work according to Saint-Saëns's standard, it suffers on two counts, for in his search for "musical truth," Seeger not only crosses the Rhine but, before even setting foot in it, must cross the Atlantic Ocean, too. In other words, he relies not only on German theories of musical form but also on French interpretations of German theories.

Aside from Saint-Saëns's anti-German bias, his chief criticism is that d'Indy relies too much on other theorists' ideas. Likewise, given the number of sources from whom Seeger probably borrowed ideas, some might conclude that he was a theoretical epigone, with few original ideas of his own. However, this would not give Seeger the credit he is due. While both Seeger and Schoenberg may have recommended that composers vary an initial melodic idea by inversion, for Seeger a new technique of variation was only one part of his enormous project for renewing modern composition and musicology. In the end, none of these theorists placed as much importance on philosophical reflection and pure speculation with new resources as does Seeger. Though he may borrow bits and pieces of others' theories, the framework in which he blends these pieces is a music-intellectual synthesis all his own.

Historical Context

In order to understand the broader historical context of Seeger's approach to composition, it is useful to sketch out the landscape of music-theoretical speculation during the late 1920s in America, especially New York, and ten years later in Germany. There are two ways of interpreting the historical significance of Seeger's thought. The first is within the immediate context of the music-intellectual environment in which he conceived the treatise. Since Seeger was in close contact with such speculative theorists as Joseph Yasser, Joseph Schillinger (both Russian émigrés), and Henry Cowell while he was developing the ideas that would later be recorded in the treatise, it is only natural to compare their highly diverse approaches to musical explanation. Such a comparison is but an initial step in a broad-based investigation of the development of avant-garde music in New York between the wars.[92] The second way of interpreting Seeger's work is within the broader sweep of early-twentieth-century music-theoretical speculation. Six years after Seeger completed a revised draft of the treatise,

Paul Hindemith published the first of a series of theoretical studies, which bears a remarkable resemblance to Seeger's work. Although the two authors ask some of the same basic questions about composition, each arrives at a different set of answers. While this is not the place to pursue a detailed comparison of the two thinkers, it is appropriate to draw some initial conclusions regarding their approach to compositional theory.

Seeger was among a handful of early-twentieth-century American theorists, including Yasser, Schillinger, and Cowell, who rejected the theoretical legacy they had inherited from Europe and, in its place, tried to establish a new theoretical basis for composition. Seeger must have conversed often with them, since in January 1930 these four, along with Otto Kinkeldey, founded the New York Musicological Society, the forerunner of the American Musicological Society. Yasser, Schillinger, and Cowell all wrote technical treatises that form a backdrop against which Seeger's more philosophically oriented theories stand out in relief.

In his book *A Theory of Evolving Tonality,* Yasser unveils a new "supra-diatonic" scale, which he believed would provide a theoretical basis for the music of the future. For him, the history of music is best understood as a gradual evolution of the tonal materials that composers have employed, progressing from simple to more complex. He identifies three distinct scales: (1) the pentatonic, which consists of five principal and two auxiliary tones; (2) the diatonic, which consists of seven principal and five auxiliary tones; and (3) for the future stage of musical evolution, an equal tempered, nineteen-note "supra-diatonic" scale, which can be divided into twelve principal and seven auxiliary tones. When these three scales and their internal subgroups are expressed numerically ($5 + 2 = 7$; $7 + 5 = 12$; $12 + 7 = 19$), they create a series ($2, 5, 7, 12, 19 \ldots$), which holds the secret for musical development over thousands of years. As evidence of this nineteen-note scale, Yasser cited excerpts from a broad spectrum of early-twentieth-century composers, including Scriabin, Debussy, Schoenberg, and Stravinsky.

In his own treatise Joseph Schillinger sets his theoretical sights even higher than those of Yasser. Originally a ten-volume correspondence course, Schillinger's massive compendium, *The Schillinger System of Musical Composition,* includes chapters on such topics as rhythm, pitch-scales, variations by "geometrical projection," melody, harmony, counterpoint, form, "strata" harmony, composition, and orchestration. The author's aims are ambitious: to discover the general laws of all tonal phenomena; to classify all available resources of the tonal system; and to present a computational method of composition that enables "all reasonably intelligent people to master the art of composition."

Henry Cowell's treatise *New Musical Resources* has much in common with Seeger's treatise, yet there are also substantial differences between the two. He employs the same modus operandi as does Seeger—to adapt pitch nomenclature to explore nonpitch functions—but he takes it to much greater extremes. Cowell proposes a correlation between the acoustical phenomenon of the harmonic series and the other elements of music (synonymous with Seeger's "functions"). Focusing particularly on rhythm, he translates ratios of frequency into ratios of duration, meter, and tempo. His goal is to create temporal "harmony," that is, multiple durations, meters, and tempi sounding simultaneously: such "harmonies" could range from the rhythmic counterpart of the triad (2:3:4) to the infamous "tone cluster" of seconds.

Based on this brief overview, the above three works have many characteristics in common with Seeger's treatise. Yasser shared with Seeger a desire to explain contemporary music as a logical development from previous musical traditions, integrating the entire history of Western music by means of a progression among increasingly complex scales. The final stage in this progression is a new way of dividing the octave. Cowell, too, hoped to expand the resources available for modern composers, but he did not limit himself to pitch. His correlations from pitch to nonpitch functions bear a strong affinity with Seeger's neumatic explorations; Cowell, however, goes to further extremes—as though he were writing a set of compositional variations on an acoustical theme. Schillinger's approach was the most far-reaching; he postulated that a wide range of phenomena in music (and, for that matter, in other artistic media) were the product of simple mathematical formulas.

Despite these similarities, Seeger's thought differs dramatically from that of the other three theorists in that he relies on a principle of mediation in which logical and intuitive impulses are poised in equilibrium. He emphasizes this difference in the following comment: "The fault of Schillinger's work is one into which many men have fallen who have fought too hard against mysticism, emotionalism, and aestheticism. It is to over-do the logical and rational."[93] As fascinated as Seeger was with the rigors of scientific analysis, he always tried to balance it with his intuitions—whether compositional or critical.

Unlike Seeger, Paul Hindemith devoted his life to composition and, in his early years, to performance. He also wrote a number of books, including six theoretical texts and a set of philosophical and critical essays about music. The work that bears the greatest resemblance to Seeger's treatise is *The Craft of Musical Composition* (*Unterweisung im Tonsatz*), numbering four volumes in all: volumes 1 and 2 appeared in Hindemith's lifetime (1937, 1939), volume 3 was published posthumously (1970), and volume 4 was neither completed nor published. In this work his goal is to develop a new, broader framework that would redefine composers' approach toward all musical materials; in volume 1 he concentrates on pitch. This framework has a creative and, to a lesser degree, an analytical purpose. He hopes to open up new possibilities for composers and, at the same time, try to account for musical styles of all historical periods.

His point of departure is a close study of the science of acoustics, including the overtone series and the phenomenon of "combination" tones.[94] Building on this physical theory of sound, he proposes two ordered "series," one of pitches, the other of intervals, which he believes can explain the harmonic and melodic practice of any musical style. According to a recent study by David Neumeyer, Hindemith tried "to reverse the priorities of traditional theories of harmony and melody; where chromatic tones and chords had been understood as special cases . . . which could be referred or reduced to underlying diatonic patterns, he understood the diatonic as a special case of the fully chromatic."[95] Hindemith argued that composers should aim for a new kind of balance in which the primary musical elements, that is, melody, harmony, and rhythm, are interdependent, and elements such as dynamics and tone-color are secondary. "The musical structure is, thus, dynamic but proportioned; a balance of forces but hierarchic."[96]

The second volume of *The Craft of Musical Composition* consists of a regimen of two-part exercises that fall in the pedagogical tradition of counterpoint initiated by Johann J. Fux in the early eighteenth century. As in Fux's treatise *Steps to Parnassus*, Hindemith begins with simple rhythmic values: whole notes in one voice and later a one-to-one ratio between two voices. Likewise, at the outset he places sharp limits on the student's choice of melodic intervals, as well as a melody's overall shape and length; eventually, he lifts those limits and introduces various melodic formulas such as passing tones, neighbor tones, suspensions, and anticipations. Perhaps the biggest difference between Hindemith's and Fux's approaches is that the former does not link the introduction of certain dissonant intervals with a specific rhythmic texture, instead allowing a much broader palette of dissonance from the very beginning.

Considering that in 1937 Hindemith could have had no knowledge of *Tradition and Experiment in the New Music,* the similarity in the overall scope of the two treatises is striking. Both authors present an approach in which creative and analytical aims are fused. Seeger's belief that the scientific and artistic points of view are inseparable is a direct consequence of his ideal of mediation between opposing mental faculties: reason and intuition. In his mind, not only should music critics balance two different perspectives (the "scientific" and the "impressionistic") in judging musical value, but composers as well should try to integrate a more reflective or philosophical approach within their overall creative process. Hindemith, too, tries to merge synthesis and analysis into a single approach, but his exposition in volume 1 emphasizes more of the latter. Indeed, he makes a better case for the analytical power of his explanatory model than does Seeger by offering works from a greater range of historical periods, including a Gregorian chant and works by Machaut, Wagner, Stravinsky, Schoenberg, and himself. The degree to which Hindemith's ideas provide guidance for composers is less clear. There has been some controversy regarding the success with which Hindemith's theory of composition explains his own music, a claim he never actually makes in the work.[97]

In the end, the differences between Hindemith's and Seeger's theoretical works outweigh the similarities. Both attempt to develop a general basis for composition, yet, for different reasons, both fall short of their goal. Seeger's bid for "generality" depends entirely on his philosophical analysis of human knowledge. When viewed by themselves, his proposals for a "general" theory of composition are a curious historical hybrid: those of a twentieth-century experimental radical with an abiding faith in the nineteenth-century principles of counterpoint and organic unity. By contrast, Hindemith's conception of "general" grows out of his reliance on an acoustical model of musical experience. He underscores his belief in the unlimited application of his ideas when he says that his two-part exercises give the composition student "complete freedom in the forming of an independent style of writing."[98] Yet most critics categorically reject his naturalistic assumptions—Seeger would have regarded them as overly scientific, focusing more on the "raw" than the "manipulated" materials of sound. The question is not whether the theory of "resultant" tones is true— few would doubt their existence—but whether this physical theory should serve as the sole basis for justifying musical practice.

Hindemith's and Seeger's approaches also differ in the way they approach counterpoint. Hindemith is more of a true pedagogue, devising a lengthy and intricate regimen of two-part exercises in the second volume of *The Craft of Musical Composition,* in which various melodic formulas and rhythmic patterns are gradually introduced. As expected, his treatment of intervals within and between melodic lines is the direct application of his two fundamental series. Seeger, by contrast, is content to provide a sketch of a contrapuntal regimen in part 2 of the treatise, to be augmented, one assumes, by the teacher and/or student. More important, Seeger's aesthetic focus shifts dramatically between parts 1 and 2; for example, when he considers the limitations on pitch and rhythmic materials in three-part counterpoint, he is addressing a specific dissonant idiom as opposed to the general compositional approach to which Hindemith aspires.

Finally, Seeger's and Hindemith's work can be distinguished by their internal theoretical structure. Hindemith's treatise is more of a genuine theory in that all his proposals and observations are generated and thus unified by a single thesis: the physical properties of sound. Seeger's work, on the other hand, is more of a speculative exploration of theory in which he experiments with several theses and proposals. For example, his ideal of a balance between the six musical functions is not an end in itself but rather a stimulus for discovering new uses of neglected functions, as witnessed in the third movement of Crawford's String Quartet.

In sum, when viewed from within either the New York experimental community in the late 1920s or the radical spirit prevalent in Europe and America before World War II, Seeger's ideas are as eclectic as they are idiosyncratic. The pedagogy of mediation not only distin-

guished Seeger's thought from that of his New York and German con-
temporaries but also added a new chapter in the history of American
musicology.

Conclusion

Chapters 5 and 6 of this study have focused on a distinguishing feature
of *Tradition and Experiment in the New Music:* Seeger's desire to unite
speculative theory and musical practice. Seeger himself underlines
this aim in a comment drawn from the introductory chapter:

> The object of the present undertaking is, first, to bridge the gap that we find
> today between the old discipline and the new practice; second, to contribute
> to the organization of a new discipline and a new method that will displace
> the old and serve the future development of music as the old, in the day of
> their usefulness, served its past.[99]

Seeger is saying two things in this passage. When he vows to "bridge
the gap" between old and new, he means that, despite his commitment to exploring and promoting experimental composition, he will
never completely abandon the musical traditions of the past. Considering what traditions Seeger revives in the treatise—such as the
eighteenth-century aesthetic of balance and the nineteenth-century
principle of organic unity—he certainly lived up to his word.

Seeger's second assertion here is much more controversial. He
hopes that his version of a new theory, whether it be called a "discipline" or a "method," not only will mold future composers but also, in
the process, will influence the course that modern composition eventually takes. In plain terms, Seeger argues that "theory" not only can,
but must, precede practice. One could easily object that Seeger is
putting the proverbial "cart before the horse": instead of theorizing
about a past musical tradition, he is trying to develop theories for a
tradition that does not yet exist. Seeger's answer to such a hypothetical objection is evident in the way that philosophy intersects with the
musical fields he addresses in the treatise: criticism, compositional
theory, and speculative musicology.

To better appreciate this interdependence, it is useful to borrow a
typology devised by Claude Palisca in 1963 in the course of his investigation of the relation between music history and music theory.[100] He

distinguishes four subfields of theoretical inquiry, "analytical," "creative," "pure," and "pedagogical," each of which he then demonstrates, drawing from a broad range of treatises. Palisca defines the four types as follows: "analytical theory" denotes theoretical systems inferred from existing musical works; "creative theory" includes the practical training of composers and draws upon music of the past; "pure theory" is more rare, comprising philosophies of music that are not necessarily confirmed by practice; and "pedagogic theory" concerns the general training of musicians. It is no surprise that Seeger's treatise does not fit into any single category in Palisca's scheme but rather is a mixture of three. First and foremost, *Tradition and Experiment in the New Music* qualifies as "creative" theory, for throughout much of part 1 and all of part 2 Seeger is speaking to experimental composers. At the same time, in his attempt to lay a foundation for new music, Seeger frequently revives or adapts older theoretical systems that were, in turn, "inferred" from previous musical traditions—for example, his reliance on the principles of organicism and harmonic dualism. His attempt to bring together "analytical" and "creative" theory is nowhere more apparent than in the musical examples he chooses to illustrate his theory of melody. Whereas all of the excerpts in chapters 7–9 are drawn from eighteenth- and nineteenth-century compositions, the examples for the manual of dissonant counterpoint are either invented by Seeger or culled from music of the early twentieth century.[101] Finally, the treatise's first two chapters illustrate well the category of "pure" theory in that he addresses faculties of the mind more than theories of music.

One obvious result of this exercise in classification is to highlight the multiple aims that Seeger pursues in the treatise. At various junctures in the treatise he wears the hat of a critic, a compositional theorist, and a music historiographer. Seeger's work might best be described as a cross between Frederico Busoni's manifesto of a new aesthetic, Milton Babbitt's logical studies of combinatoriality, and Carl Dahlhaus's essays on historical explanation. Ultimately, Seeger's interdisciplinary appetite was an outgrowth of his desire to use philosophy as a practical tool. The reason he felt justified in putting theory before practice is directly related to his theory of human knowledge that mediates between the extremes of intuitive insight and logical reflection. Using this broad-based principle, he cast new light on a wide range of problems in various musical disciplines. Instead of continuing the study of human knowledge as an end in itself—a pure form of philosophical speculation—he was convinced that philosophy, properly applied, could help solve practical problems that arose in composition and criticism. In the following chapter, we will see to what degree Seeger's ideal conception of musicology also relied on his philosophical ideals.

Chapter Seven

· · · · ·

Seeger's Vision of Musicology

Introduction

In his celebrated collection of essays on American music, Henry
Cowell characterized Charles Seeger as "the greatest musical explorer
in intellectual fields which America has produced, the greatest experimental musicologist."[1] Taking into account Cowell's unabashed enthusiasm for his former mentor, his comment nevertheless provides
an important clue if we are to understand the true significance of
Seeger's thought. While it is true Seeger certainly "explored" many
fields that grow out of musical experience, namely, composition, criticism, and speculative theory, one of his greatest gifts was that of a
mapmaker. This attribute is especially evident in Seeger's ideal vision
of musicology, or "unified field theory," that he proposed in his later
writings, which brought together a host of scientific and humanistic
fields into one grand scheme of musical knowledge. To illustrate this
abstract scheme, Seeger developed a series of diagrams or maps of musical knowledge. In constructing these elaborate diagrams, Seeger's
ultimate goal was to develop a universal explanation of musical experience, that is, a theory that would account for music from any historical period or performing tradition, such as folk, popular, or art music.
Even more important, these conceptual maps reflect the degree to
which his musical and philosophical ambitions were intertwined. In
all his musings about musicology, he was as much a musical cartographer as an explorer, venturing boldly into uncharted, speculative lands
and surveying the borders of new fields of knowledge.

This chapter is devoted to tracing the evolution of Seeger's scheme
of musical knowledge, beginning with its initial version as a theory of

criticism in 1931 and continuing with his final obiter dicta published in the 1970s. Although his personal and professional life underwent enormous changes right after he finished the treatise, the philosophical views propounded there continued to guide his search for a comprehensive scheme during the rest of his life. The following four essays chronicle the gradual shift in Seeger's scheme of musical knowledge:

"Systematic and Historical Orientations in Musicology" (1939);[2]

"Systematic Musicology: Viewpoints, Orientations, and Methods" (1951); revised version (1977).[3]

"Sources of Evidence and the Criteria for Judgment in a Critique of Music" (1977);[4]

"Toward a Unitary Field Theory" (1970); revised version (1977).[5]

Three underlying themes can be identified in these essays: (1) Seeger's belief that the discipline of musicology depends on a balance between opposing forces; (2) his aspiration to develop a truly universal scheme of musicology that could be applied to a broad range of musical cultures and traditions; and (3) a gradual shift in Seeger's attitude toward the proper role of history within his scheme of musicology.

The roots of the first theme can be traced to the proposals about music criticism and compositional theory that initially appeared in the revised draft of the treatise in 1931. In Seeger's early writings the idea of balance, originally borrowed from Goethe, served as the basis for a new compositional aesthetic, an equilibrium among the six elements of music. In his later writings, however, he adapted it as the organizing principle for an interdisciplinary map of musicology. The second theme, Seeger's search for a universally valid scheme of musicology, had two motivations. To begin with, his philosophical compass was of early nineteenth-century origin, the time when German idealism was at its peak. Just as the idealist philosophers believed that human reason could solve the problems of human knowledge, so, too, did Seeger argue that a universal foundation for musical experience was within our reach. In addition, in the years following 1931 Seeger became increasingly sensitive to the provincial tendency among musicologists to concentrate on a single tradition—Western European art music— at the expense of the rich spectrum of folk and popular traditions in Eastern as well as Western culture. Although the philosophical ideas developed in the treatise grew out of his fascination with experimental art music, in two of the four essays considered here he protests vehemently against the hegemony of influence that the Western "common practice" period had exercised among music scholars, and he urges musicologists to expand their musical and cultural curiosity. The third theme concerns a gradual shift in the priority that Seeger assigns the activities of "history" and "system" within his abstract scheme of musicology. Initially, his preoccupation with "system" was a by-product of his passion for contemporary music; later this preoccupation became even stronger as a result of his growing interest in the field of structural linguistics. In his final essays, however, this bias against history softened, and he returned to a more balanced and more comprehensive vision of musicology.

In this chapter I shall explore each of these three themes, not only focusing on its initial presentation but also tracing how it evolved in the course of his later writings. In all three the same pattern emerges: Seeger's philosophical reflections in the early treatise strongly influenced his later attempts to redefine the discipline of musicology. Despite the profound changes his musical and intellectual tastes underwent following 1931, his vision of a comprehensive and unified atlas of musical thought first took root in the same soil that produced his philosophical theory of criticism and his neumatic theory of melody.

Historical Overview

My interpretation of Seeger's scheme of musical knowledge begins by locating it within a broader historiographical context, that is, the various theories of music history that emerged during the late nineteenth and early twentieth centuries in Europe and America. The development of the modern science of musicology, or *Musikwissenschaft* (musical science), owes its internal classifications to no single source, but rather to a whole tradition of thinkers that includes Guido Adler, Waldo Pratt, Hugo Riemann, Otto Kinkeldey, Oscar Sonneck, Curt Sachs, Carl Engel, Edward Dent, Paul Henry Lang, and Glen Haydon.[6] In the interest of brevity, I will focus on the contributions of Adler and Pratt, for their writings form a backdrop against which Seeger's philosophical reflections stand out in relief. It is ironic that, on the whole, Seeger was rather naive about the history of the very discipline that he was trying to renew.

Any portrayal of the development of music historiography must begin with the pioneering work of Guido Adler, the leading Austrian musicologist of the period. After earning his doctorate at the University
of Vienna in 1880, he succeeded Edward Hanslick there as a chaired
professor of musicology in 1898 and later founded the *Musikwissen-
schaftliches Institut,* the first graduate program for musicology in the
world. Among his many accomplishments are serving as general editor of the *Denkmäler der Tonkunst in Österreich,* a groundbreaking
series devoted to preserving editions of monumental works from the
past, as well as his leadership role in various academic societies such
as the International Musicological Society.

Adler's most famous piece of writing is the monumental essay "Umfang, Methode und Ziel der Musikwissenschaft" (The scope, method,
and purpose of musicology), which was published in the inaugural issue of a music journal he cofounded in 1885 with Friedrich Chry-
sander and Phillip Spitta.[7] As the title suggests, Adler combined a
sweeping overview of the newly emerging field of *Musikwissenschaft*
with a personal commentary on a range of subjects, including music
aesthetics. Much of this essay's influence is based on the *Gesamtge-
bäude,* or comprehensive scheme, in which musical knowledge is divided initially into two branches, called historical and systematic, and
each of these is then subdivided into further categories (see figure 14).
Finally, a number of auxiliary fields are listed that serve each branch.
Strictly speaking, the distinction between historical and systematic
did not originate with Adler but can be traced back to the eighteenth
century in Johann Forkel's famous bibliography, *Allgemeine Litteratur
der Musik* (1792). Adler's achievement was to revive and clarify this
dichotomy as the basis for his vision of musical science.

To understand Adler's place in the development of music historiography, it is necessary to consider briefly another scheme of a much
older vintage devised by Aristides Quintilianus. Along with Aristoxenus and Ptolemy, Quintilianus is considered one of the greatest au-
thorities on ancient Greek music theory. In his only extant work, *Peri
Mousike (On Music),* most likely written between the first and third
centuries, Quintilianus summarizes and organizes the musical teachings of a range of Greek and Hellenistic authors within a single unifying framework, reproduced here in figure 15. Quintilianus's classification of knowledge occupies a strategic location in the "Umfang" essay,
for Adler juxtaposes it immediately beneath his own classification.

In tabellarischer Übersicht ergiebt sich das Gesammtgebäude[1] also:
Musikwissenschaft.

I. Historisch.
(Geschichte der Musik nach Epochen, Völkern, Reichen, Ländern, Gauen, Städten, Kunstschulen, Künstlern).

A. musikalische Paläographie (Notationen).	B. Historische Grundklassen (Gruppirung der musikalischen Formen).	C. Historische Aufeinanderfolge der Gesetze.	D. Geschichte der musikalischen Instrumente.
		1. wie sie in den Kunstwerken je einer Epoche vorliegen, 2. wie sie von den Theoretikern der betreffenden Zeit gelehrt werden. 3. Arten der Kunstausübung,	

Hilfswissenschaften:
Allgemeine Geschichte mit Paläographie, Chronologie, Diplomatik, Bibliographie, Bibliotheks- und Archivkunde. Litteraturgeschichte und Sprachenkunde.
Geschichte der Liturgien.
Geschichte der mimischen Künste und des Tanzes.
Biographistik der Tonkünstler, Statistik der musikalischen Associationen, Institute und Aufführungen.

II. Systematisch.
Aufstellung der in den einzelnen Zweigen der Tonkunst zuhöchst stehenden Gesetze.

A. Erforschung und Begründung derselben in der			B. Aesthetik der Tonkunst.	C. Musikalische Pädagogik und Didaktik (Zusammenstellung der Gesetze mit Rücksicht auf den Lehrzweck)	D. Musikologie (Untersuchung und Vergleichung zu ethnographischen Zwecken).
1. *Harmonik* (tonal od. tonlich).	2. *Rhythmik* (temporär oder zeitlich).	3. *Melik* (Cohärens von tonal und temporär).	1. Vergleichung und Werthschätzung der Gesetze und deren Relation mit den appercipirenden Subjecten behufs Feststellung der *Kriterien des musikalisch Schönen.* 2. Complex unmittelbar und mittelbar damit zusammenhängender Fragen.	1. Tonlehre, 2. Harmonielehre, 3. Kontrapunkt, 4. Compositionslehre, 5. Instrumentationslehre, 6. Methoden des Unterrichtes im Gesang und Instrumentalspiel.	

Hilfswissenschaften:
Akustik und Mathematik.
Physiologie (Tonempfindungen).
Psychologie (Tonvorstellungen, Tonurtheile und Tongefühle).
Logik (das musikalische Denken).
Grammatik, Metrik und Poetik.
Pädagogik
Ästhetik etc.

Figure 14. Guido Adler's conspectus of *Musikwissenschaft*, "Umfang, Methode und Ziel der Musikwissenschaft"

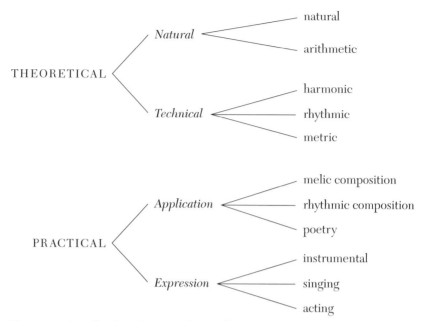

Figure 15. Aristides Quintilianus's scheme of music, *On Music* (c. 3rd century?)

Indeed, we can learn as much from the resemblances between the two schemes as we can from the differences.

To begin with, Adler's reference to Quintilianus emphasizes the former's respect for the authority of ancient learning. By including an excerpt from such a venerable source of Greek music theory, Adler establishes a link between nineteenth-century Germany and classical antiquity and, at the same time, confers a kind of imprimatur on his own work. Seeger, too, would later show a certain respect for the ideas of his musicological predecessors, even if he was more determined than Adler to refute them.

The structure of the two epistemological maps is strikingly similar in that both are dualistic. Quintilianus, too, divides musical knowledge into two branches, which he calls the theoretical and the practical, each of which is then further subdivided into two categories. Appearances to the contrary, Adler preserves almost all of Quintilianus's four subcategories except that he reorganizes them under a single branch. For example, Quintilianus's category "technical" reappears intact as "Systematic" II:A; likewise the two subcategories "application" and "expression" are collapsed into a single subcategory of "Systematic" II:C entitled "Musical Pedagogics and Didactics."

The greatest difference between the two schemes is the importance each author assigns to the discipline of history. Whereas history does not appear as a category in Quintilianus's classification, its absence is illusory, for the notion of historical judgment is implicit in virtually every category of the map: indeed, throughout much of his treatise Quintilianus was addressing a musical tradition that had long since died away and that had to be reconstructed through the interpretation of written documents. By defining history as one of the two principal branches of musical knowledge, Adler draws special attention to a form of musical inquiry that was implicit but never directly stated in his predecessor's scheme. Indeed, it could be argued that Adler's two branches are, in fact, "historical" and "nonhistorical"; that is, the only thing that "systematic" pursuits have in common is that none are "historical." According to this interpretation, systematic thought would ultimately be subordinate to historical scholarship.

As will become clear in the following, Seeger was strongly opposed to this implied priority among the historical and systematic branches of knowledge. While in his own scheme Seeger preserved Adler's two basic categories of knowledge, he reacts against the ranking that Adler had established between them. Indeed, a common theme running throughout Seeger's later philosophical writings was his desire to compensate for what he regarded as Adler's unjustified bias in favor of history.

Two other aspects of Adler's essay are significant in that they reveal a thread of continuity between his and Seeger's conception of musicology. First, Adler attaches great importance to the activity of critical judgment, which for him serves as a means of determining the "mood-content" or "aesthetic-content" of a piece of music. Although Adler never elaborates on which procedures will reveal "mood content," he explicitly warns his readers that most of the time it is futile to try to express it in words.[8] Any reader familiar with Seeger's writings would immediately recognize the parallel between this comment and Seeger's fascination with the "linguo-centric predicament." Indeed, the entire process of searching for "mood-content" seems analogous to the ideal process of critical judgment that Seeger introduces in the first two chapters of the treatise.

The second connecting thread between the two thinkers' ideas is Adler's belief that the science of musicology must remain "in living contact" with the art it serves. In short, the two are cut from the same cloth: "Art and the study of art are not separate areas whose dividing line is sharply drawn; rather they are the same area, and it is just that the way of adaptation is different."[9] Following this comment, Adler draws an analogy between the correspondence between composer as architect and musicologist as engineering consultant. Though architects alone have the creative gift, they cannot realize their aesthetic visions unless the materials they have chosen and the designs they have created satisfy the practical criteria of the engineer. Consultants not only protect and maintain buildings from the past as a resource for the architect's ongoing activity but also contribute to the creative framework for designing new buildings. As will become clear, this line of reasoning was echoed in Seeger's later writings. Although Seeger objected to the importance Adler confers upon studying music of the past, Seeger, too, would end up arguing that the only justification for musicology is as a resource for compositional practice.

During the early twentieth century a handful of American musicologists continued to speculate about the nature of the young discipline, advancing their own revisions of Adler's conspectus. The most influential of them was Waldo Selden Pratt. Originally trained in the classics, Pratt served for over forty years as a professor of ecclesiastical music and hymnology at the Hartford Theological Seminary.

Pratt's principal writings on the nature and purpose of musicology include a speech he delivered before the annual meeting of the Music Teachers National Association in 1888 and his article for the inaugural issue of *The Musical Quarterly* in 1915. Like Adler before him, Pratt establishes a historical context by presenting his ideas in the form of a comparison with the other leading schemes written during the previous twenty-five years. Instead of unveiling yet another ideal plan, he proposes something less rigid: "My aim in the present essay is not to advocate a particular scheme of scientific thought about music, but only to discuss the usefulness of the kind of thinking that leads to the formation of such schemes."[10] The irony in this remark is that elsewhere in the essay Pratt reiterates ideas he had already proposed in his 1888 speech, which, in fact, constitute a comprehensive and innovative scheme of musical study. This comment underlines an important similarity between Pratt and Seeger. Both were as passionate about devising the preliminary stages of a comprehensive scheme of knowledge, what may be called a "prolegomena," as they were about creating the scheme itself.

Two themes in Pratt's thought are germane to Seeger's writings on musicology: his belief that musicology should emulate the natural sciences, and his specific scheme of musicology. In Pratt's mind, the emergence of a science devoted to the study of music was long overdue. His notion of "science" concentrates on the "objective" aspects of various activities of musical life, such as composition and performance; the general methods he advocates are "analysis, classification, and definition."[11] The impartiality of the scientific point of view is needed, he feels, to compensate for the individual biases and eccentricities that are common among musicians and students of music alike, what he calls the "heedless impetuosity of the heart." Finally, the scientist's approach also serves an elevated purpose in that it lays a "basis for a nobler moral ambition" and will bring a sorely needed "intellectual culture and power" to the art.[12]

The second theme in Pratt's writings is his distinction between the process of investigating musical phenomena and the product of that process. As he says "The word 'science' embraces both the act of finding what there is to know, with whatever further processes of thought may be needed to coordinate and interpret what is discovered, and also the total result—the body of knowledge secured."[13] The first meaning of the word, the processes employed by musicologists, is quite similar to those of the scientist: establishing hypotheses, gathering and interpreting empirical evidence, and so forth. By contrast, the second meaning, the "total result," refers more to the classification of knowledge already discovered that Pratt refers to as an "encyclopedic" activity. In his essay Pratt presents a theory for both aspects of musical "science." Musical knowledge can be divided into seven basic areas: Musical Physics or Acoustics, Musical Psychics, Musical Poetics (i.e., Composition and Theory), Musical Aesthetics, Musical Graphics or Notation, Musical Technics (e.g., Performance Practices), and finally Musical Practics or the Organization of Musical Activity. In a later section of the essay Pratt presents four distinct methods by which any of these areas may be investigated: Historical, Systematic, Critical or Judicial, and Pedagogical. The crucial point is that the various processes and products Pratt enumerates are interwoven into a comprehensive network; all seven categories of knowledge can be examined by any or all of the four methods of treatment, yielding a total of twenty-eight configurations in all, as shown in the visual model of figure 16.[14]

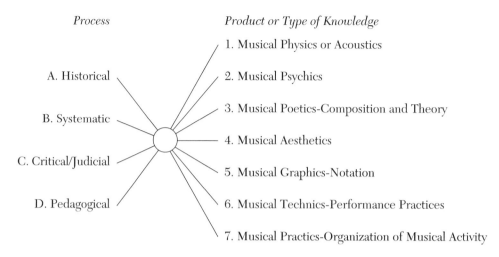

Figure 16. Pratt's ideal scheme of musicology (1915)

At this point it is helpful to mention several conclusions concerning Pratt's ideas. First of all, unlike Adler, he does not dwell on the vital connection between the academic discipline and the art itself. He not only echoes Adler's call for a scientific spirit in musicological studies, he magnifies it. In simple terms, musicologists who employ the methods and purpose of science are following a higher calling. Second, his distinction between "process" and "product," that is, between a method of investigation and the body of knowledge such an investigation yields, is a useful critical tool. By defining which one various musicologists emphasize in their writings, we can clarify the overall development of the philosophical foundation of musicology during the nineteenth and early twentieth centuries. It will become clear that one of the sources of confusion in Seeger's work is that he was not always clear about the difference between these two concepts.

Systematic and Historical Orientations

The genesis of *Tradition and Experiment in the New Music* coincided with a tumultuous period in Seeger's personal and professional life. While he had already been moved by the plight of migrant workers in California during the teens, his social conscience was further awakened by witnessing the Great Depression in New York during the early 1930s. Thus, his interest in politics, particularly socialism, began to dictate in what ways he would continue to pursue music. Understandably, his passion for avant-garde composition and, for that matter, the fine art tradition as a whole, began to wane, initially in favor of music criticism and of music traditions outside the mainstream, particularly the folk and popular music of North and South America. In general, the scope of his curiosity about musical experience was much more wide-ranging than during the period leading up to the composition treatise. Between 1934 and his death in 1979, he published articles on such disparate subjects as three-voice shape-note hymns, folklore, the Appalachian dulcimer, children's music, music as a means of political change, the unitary field theory of musicology, and the "melograph," an instrument for transcribing melody. Yet, despite this stunning diversity of interests, the question Seeger kept returning to over and over again was the philosophical foundation on which the entire discipline depended. He became intent on discovering a vision of musicology that would embrace the traditions of folk and popular music and of Western European art music as equals.

Seeger's essay "Systematic and Historical Orientations in Musicology" was his first published view regarding the state of musicology since he had put aside the treatise in the early 1930s.[15] Unlike Adler and Pratt before him, Seeger's interest in the tradition of music historiography is quite limited. Even though he seems aware of his predecessors' writings on the subject, he refers to them only indirectly, focusing instead on the specific philosophical questions they addressed without ever reviewing the chronology of the controversy. He writes as though he were continuing a conversation that had already begun, answering questions that someone had already raised, yet never bothering to identify his fellow interlocutor.

In the essay Seeger makes two basic claims: (1) that despite various unavoidable differences in approach and/or subject matter, all musicologists share common goals and obey the same fundamental principles of knowledge; and (2) that in the tradition of musicological studies two leading approaches have emerged, the historical and the systematic, and, furthermore, that the latter has been neglected in favor of the former. By vigorously promoting the virtues of the systematic approach, Seeger hopes in the long run to restore the balance between the two. Seeger's linking of these two themes is significant, for they would reappear in different versions and variations throughout many of his later works.

Seeger is disturbed by what he regards as an inordinate amount of attention directed toward the differences in method and purpose among musicologists. Although he mentions in passing the disparity between historical and comparative musicologists (the latter are now commonly referred to as "ethnomusicologists"), his main interest is in Adler's categories of history and system. He declares that "the distinction between systematic and historical musicology as separate branches of learning should be regarded as fictitious. . . . There is a real problem here: how to make clear the existence of one entity—musicology—where a most undesirable schism has existed between two supposed branches."[16]

To overcome this schism, Seeger suggests a new understanding of the opposition. Instead of treating history and system as two separate studies with their own unique perspectives, he views them as two distinct but interdependent "orientations" within a single study. In his mind, the choice of a particular "orientation" is closely tied up with a vast network of other questions concerning the aim, point of view, method, and means of expressing the results of a given investigation. To bolster his argument, Seeger examines the development of the field of history proper, tracing briefly the changes in method from the medieval period to the present. He concludes that neither the historical nor the systematic approach can ever truly exist in isolation from one another, that both are inextricably bound: "History became a study of the relationships of former systems; and system, a study of the relationships of various historical strands."[17] In his remarks, Seeger proves convincingly that the division between history and system is a gross simplification of an intricate critical process, and to do justice to this process requires the logical rigor and finesse of a philosopher.

In the second half of the essay Seeger changes his focus; instead of contemplating the entire continent of musicological thought, he limits his attention to a single province, namely, that of systematic study. In short, he transforms Adler's rather amorphous category of "system" into his own peculiar methodology, which mixes in equal proportions the scientist's objectivity and the subjective impressions of the music critic. Seeger's reflections are motivated by musicologists' general tendency to neglect the music of the present: there is "a great gap between the creative musical life of our day and the creative linguistic approach to music we call musicology."[18] He feels that the profession as a whole has relinquished its responsibility to study a whole gamut of questions sparked by developments of the previous twenty-five years (since the onset of World War I). Examples include the explosive changes in compositional technique; the resulting gap between contemporary composers and the general audience who cannot comprehend their music; and the defense of critical standards in the face of the mechanization of musical life (by which he probably means the recording industry).[19] To meet the challenges posed by the plethora of contemporary styles, Seeger exhorts musicologists to cultivate new methods of work, namely, the critic's "subjective" approach to musical understanding.

Of the many intriguing questions raised by the essay, I will focus on two: (1) What does Seeger mean by "systematic" orientation, and, more important, how can it be realized in practice? and (2) How can we account for the contradiction between his grandiose vision of musicological unity and his desire to cultivate a rivalry between two different interpretive approaches?

When one searches Seeger's previous writings for clues to explain what he means by "system," the treatise turns out to be a most fruitful resource. In fact, there are several strong threads of continuity between Seeger's 1939 essay and the early chapters of the treatise. Since he neglects to illustrate his notion of "system" with any concrete examples,[20] there is every reason to believe that his model for the ideal of "systematic" musicology in 1939 was the unique convergence of criticism, compositional theory, and philosophy that he had achieved eight years before.

Let us review the evidence that supports such a conclusion. First there is a similarity in terminology. According to the *Oxford English Dictionary,* the word "system" can be used to mean "a comprehensive and methodical exposition of or treatise on a subject."[21] In common parlance, a "systematic" study is general in the sense of being a rational and exhaustive investigation of some object, whether the natural phenomenon of lightning or an artistic portrayal of lightning such as appears in the "storm" movement of Beethoven's Pastoral Symphony. According to such a definition, Seeger's discussion throughout the essay could justly be described as "systematic"; that is, the object of investigation is neither nature nor art but a field of knowledge devoted to an art. From this perspective, a "systematic" approach toward musicology would mean a philosophical analysis of the discipline, an encyclopedic form of classification.[22]

In his 1939 essay, however, Seeger employs the term "system" in a more personal and idiosyncratic way that echoes the very modus operandi of several chapters of the composition treatise. In his words, the "systematic orientation could, in its purest form, be defined as the viewing of things *as they are*" as contrasted with the historical orientation, which views things *"as they were."*[23] While these two approaches are not mutually exclusive, he believes that the academic community on the whole has virtually ignored the musical life of the present. One essential characteristic of systematic researchers is that they experiment with the tools of the composer. A systematic musicologist

should be an actual worker in the field he is studying. . . . We need not expect him to excel, but he should at least try, with sufficient seriousness, to handle the materials and technique of the present day situation. He must also try, with trained skill, to account for this process in language.[24]

These sentiments are highly reminiscent of Seeger's idealistic tone in the introduction to *Tradition and Experiment in the New Music,* where he contrasts his aims with those of previous musical scholars. When viewed as a whole, the German musicological community "has not thoroughly grasped a present situation in the light of its history, decided what is best to do, and then, *as a worker in it,* organized materials and methods in a system for the future conduct of the art" (emphasis added).[25] While Seeger falls short of demanding that every musicologist master the fields of composition and instrumental performance, he nevertheless expects them to think like practitioners.

The other main similarity resides in the methods Seeger suggests musicologists adopt in order to participate more fully in contemporary musical life. Seeger recommends that they place a greater emphasis on the "subjective" element of their work.[26] This remark shows that he expects them to behave more like the "scientific" critics he describes in the treatise than true empirical scientists. Seeger's reliance throughout the essay on the opposition between science and criticism betrays the influence of his ideal theory of criticism, as discussed in chapter 4 of this study. For him, a "systematic" study is *by no means* a strictly rational process but rather a vestige of the sympathetic convergence of intuition and logic that he had proposed in the treatise. Thus, Seeger's notion of "science" is not the model of musical science propounded by Pratt but is closer to the ideal of philosophy outlined by Bertrand Russell in his meditations on religion (see chapter 2).

Since in the essay Seeger is reticent about what ways his ideal of "systematic" musicology can be realized in practice, his earlier compendium *Tradition and Experiment in the New Music* is invaluable because it helps illuminate the underlying philosophical beliefs on which his ideal rests.

Perhaps Seeger's peculiar notion of "system" is best understood in the context of the late nineteenth- and early twentieth-century developments in music historiography. In his 1885 essay, Guido Adler originally coined the term "system" as a negation, using it to refer to a wide range of musical studies that are unified by the fact that they are *not* history. Seeger's conception of "system" is quite different, and these differences are underlined by Pratt's distinction between "process" and "product," as summarized earlier. By focusing his attention on the categories of history and system, Seeger appears to be interested only in method: the "processes" musicologists employ when they study music. Yet, this is not entirely true. In fact, throughout this essay, Seeger is as interested in a single "product" or body of knowledge— contemporary composition as it continues to unfold—as he is in any scholarly "process" of investigating it. Appearances to the contrary, Seeger has two goals in mind: to promote compositional activity in the present and, at the same time, to catalogue and develop methods for investigating a wide range of musical styles and traditions. The reason he links the two goals under the category of "system" is that he believes both are indispensable in the study of contemporary musical life.

The second question raised by Seeger's 1939 essay concerns an apparent contradiction between its two central claims. On the one hand, he preaches a message of unity. It is as if he imagined the discipline of musicology as a vast genealogical network in which all scholarly studies, whether historical or systematic in method, European or non-European in focus, grow from a common source. By showing that even the most ideologically opposed approaches in musicology share a common ancestral heritage, he hopes to lay a foundation for interpretive and, indeed, political reconciliation.

Yet, on the other hand, Seeger also sows seeds of antipathy and distrust between proponents of the principal methods of investigation. With characteristic indignation, he expresses his outrage about musicologists' general neglect of the systematic orientation in favor of historical interpretation. The preferential treatment that historians have traditionally received within the discipline offends him deeply, for, in his mind, the two approaches are entitled to equal rights—as if citizens in some Athenian democracy of music academics. In sum, when viewed as a whole, the essay seems at cross purposes. At times Seeger pleads for musicologists to leave behind their differences and unite toward a common goal; at other times he cultivates these same methodological differences, thereby suggesting that any true unity within the discipline will be difficult to achieve.

This apparent ambivalence in Seeger's thinking can be accounted for by considering how he believes each claim can be realized in practice. His vision of harmonious unity is a lofty ideal, a distant goal that is by no means a present state of affairs. On the contrary, his plea to encourage more "systematic" research is more practical in nature, a specific path which he believes might, in the long run, help achieve the ideal of balance. When he recommends that musicologists behave more like critics and take contemporary music more seriously, he hopes to help shape the direction of their daily work. The reason he preaches both messages in the same essay is that he believes a renewed interest in contemporary music will help restore balance to a musicological community that has become too preoccupied with music of the past. His vision of a balanced musicology is a means of *compensating* for previous historical and interpretive imbalances.

That said, Seeger's enthusiasm for promoting a particular area of knowledge sometimes results in methodological "excesses" of his own. His plea that "system" should be the heart and soul of the discipline is tantamount to claiming that the telescope is an indispensable tool for any scientific field of endeavor. When the focus of study is the heavenly bodies and their motion through space, such a claim makes perfect sense. But if a biologist were to use a telescope to study the life cycle of a mold or a psychologist to examine the causes of human dementia, then the claim becomes ludicrous. It makes more sense to choose a method or a critical tool, whether in musicology or any other field, that is appropriate to the subject being studied.

Furthermore, in the course of challenging the priority that Adler assigns to the historical branch of musicology, Seeger ends up questioning the basis for historical interpretation. If one of Seeger's primary aims is to engender a new sensitivity toward contemporary musical life, is it necessary to abandon entirely the discipline of history and all music of the past? At times one wonders whether his "systematic" remedy is worse than the original disease itself. As we will see later, in his 1951 essay on musicology Seeger would find new sources of authority to renew his bias against history.

"Systematic" Musicology Revisited

Seeger's next attempt at surveying the discipline of musicology, published in 1951, was entitled "Systematic Musicology: Viewpoints, Orientations, and Methods" (hereafter abbreviated as "Systematic Musicology"). Although in this essay Seeger reiterates some of the basic claims he had made in his speculative writings during the 1920s and 1930s, he adds enough new philosophical twists that it can be considered an independent statement of his views about musicology. My overview of this work focuses on three themes: (1) the dualistic structure of Seeger's "conspectus," or atlas, of musicology; (2) a reformulation of the dichotomy between art and science that draws its inspiration from modern theoretical physics; and (3) his reliance on recent developments in linguistic theory to justify his preference for the "systematic" approach. Considered as a whole, these themes reflect well the evolution in Seeger's conception of musicology during his later years; the longer it matured, the more it was nourished from disciplines and sources outside of music.

The heart of Seeger's thesis is the diagram reproduced in figure 17, in which all the approaches that musicologists employ in their daily work are classified according to three pairs of opposites:

Viewpoints:	Musical versus general (or nonmusical)
Orientations:	Systematic versus historical
Methods:	Scientific versus critical

For Seeger, this catalogue is not only comprehensive but also hierarchical, that is, one member of each pair enjoys a privileged status over the other. He uses a different term to emphasize each level in this hierarchical framework: "viewpoint," "orientation," and "method." The overall structure of this model is binary, with each point within a given level representing the fusion of exactly two other points from a different level.

Despite the appearance of a few new terms, in fact none of the oppositions contained in the hierarchy is new. Many of Seeger's basic

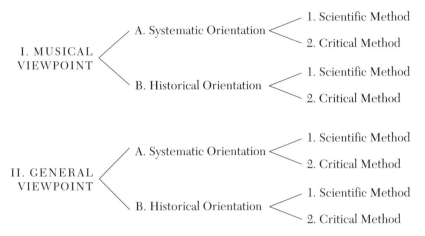

Figure 17. Seeger's conspectus of musicology, "Systematic Musicology . . ." (1951)

ideas can be found in writings over the previous twenty years. Specifically, two of the three oppositions—systematic versus historical and
critical versus scientific—had already appeared in the 1939 essay
"Systematic Musicology." In addition, the same three dichotomies illustrated by the scheme in figure 17 had also shaped Seeger's theory
of music criticism, as presented in the revised draft of the treatise,
which he completed in 1931 (see figure 4 in chapter 4). "General" experience is juxtaposed against "musical" experience by the braces at
the top; the second opposition appears twice, as the pair of categories
under General Science—"Current" versus "Historical Ethos"—and
Musical Science—"Current Mandate" versus "Music Historical Mandate"; finally, the third opposition is implied by the intersection between the individual's "intuitive" taste and the two forms of "collective" taste.

The organization of this essay bears a strong resemblance to that of
chapter 2 of the treatise, entitled "Critique": a complex diagram accompanied by a series of comments and observations. As before, this
dual format allows Seeger to present a central idea while indulging his
curiosity about a host of secondary issues and problems. Indeed, he
spends as much time in the essay exploring asides, marginalia, and
nagging doubts as he does explaining the intricate framework outlined
in the diagram.

Yet in the end, the differences between the 1951 diagram and its
precursor in the treatise outweigh the similarities. One such difference

is that Seeger's attitude toward language is less skeptical than before. At first glance, he seems to be reiterating a warning that had pervaded almost all of his previous writings about music: the dangers posed by the "linguo-centric predicament," that is, the fact that musicologists must rely on a verbal medium to describe a nonverbal art. Likening any verbal account of musical experience to "a kind of lens through which we observe and report upon music," he warns, "We cannot pretend to measure the distortion. But neither can we assume there is no distortion."[27] Taken at face value, such an observation could easily lead to musicological nihilism and a philosophy of despair. Yet the difference between his attitude toward language in the 1920s and in 1951 is that what was once an insurmountable philosophical paradox is now merely one of the accepted parameters of doing musicological work. His skepticism toward language becomes a framework for critical practice rather than a reason for critical paralysis. Now he reconciles himself with possible discrepancies between a musical event and a verbal account of it, and he carries on with the job at hand—unveiling his new vision of musicology.

A more significant difference between the two is the degree of closure Seeger seeks in each model, for this underlines his newfound aspiration to develop a truly general model of musical scholarship. The diagram in figure 4, which is reproduced from the treatise, is provisional and open-ended, as is indicated by the dotted lines and question mark beneath the bottom brace; by contrast, the diagram in figure 17, which is drawn from the essay, is closed and complete. Whereas Seeger's idealism in the early work was tempered by a certain cautious tone, in the later effort he throws caution to the wind. Early on in the 1951 essay he announces, "It is hoped that this apparatus will serve as the base for the description of any music with maximum objectivity."[28] He believes not only that a universal scheme of musical description and, by extension, musical knowledge is possible but also that he has taken the first steps toward developing it. Seeger has two motivations for seeking such a universal scheme: the specific philosophical sources that inspire his approach to human knowledge, in general; and his desire to account for non-Western musical traditions. Surprisingly enough, both are evident, though to different degrees, in the 1931 version of *Tradition and Experiment in the New Music.*

In the essay "Systematic Musicology" Seeger finally reveals his reliance on an "idealist" model of philosophy that had been present, though latent, since his earliest publications. As I have outlined in part 1, Seeger borrowed generously from the writings of Bergson and Russell, philosophers who themselves revived the assumptions and methods of eighteenth- and nineteenth-century traditions of epistemology. Once Seeger had developed a model of human knowledge with which he was content, the next step was to use it as a basis for an architectonic scheme of musicology. Such things as the opposition between "system" and "history" become building blocks with which he constructs a vast edifice of musical knowledge, an "idealist" homage to the powers of human reason. In his famous historical overview, Frederick Copleston describes the "idealist" metaphysical movement that developed during the early nineteenth century as follows:

> With the great German idealists we find a superb confidence in the power of the human reason and in the scope of philosophy.
>   For each of the leading philosophers of the period professes to solve the riddle of the world, to reveal the secret of the universe and the meaning of human existence.[29]

For Seeger, articulating an integral vision of musicology became an end in itself, more important than defending either a new technique of interpretation or a new repertory waiting to be interpreted. Though writing more than 150 years after the early German idealist philosophers, Seeger fell under the same spell in which the powers of human reason seemed virtually infinite.

Seeger's other principal motivation for developing a universal scheme stems from his desire to broaden the scope of musicology to include music outside the Western European tradition. His dream was to generalize the commonly accepted theories of musical knowledge and stylistic interpretation by expanding the pool of empirical data they were intended to explain. By 1951 he had become disturbed by a provincial tendency in musicology to concentrate on a single tradition—Western European art music—at the expense of the rich spectrum of folk and popular traditions in America and around the world. Thus, part of Seeger's motivation in devising his conspectus was to raise a protest against the hegemony of eighteenth- and nineteenth-century western European art music, or what has become known as the "common practice."

Seeger's curiosity about non-Western music first manifested itself in his introduction to the treatise:

It is to be hoped that eventually, with a more adequate knowledge of the various non-European musics, no very extensive alteration would be necessary to bring [part 1] to the point of being useful in connection with revolutionary composition in any music—Chinese, Japanese, or Indian, as well as European—that employs an *articulated* technique.[30]

While at this stage Seeger does not pretend that his theories of criticism and melodic composition are as relevant for Eastern as for Western music, he certainly believes the potential exists for some kind of intercultural application.

By the time he completed the 1951 essay, his intercultural aspirations had multiplied. He says emphatically that musicologists must "cease analyzing and evaluating other musics, or even other idioms of our own music, in terms of the Occidental fine art alone." As before, he cautions that his descriptive apparatus needed to be tested on music outside the Western European tradition before its "universal validity" could be confirmed.[31] Yet the model of musical scholarship he unveils here is considerably closer to attaining such a "universal" standard. At one point he compares musicology with linguistics, warning his readers to avoid the mistakes made by previous studies of non-Western grammar: "The last attempt to account for the non-European languages in terms of Latin grammar . . . was before 1800." For example, European musicologists who study Balinese music must not expect it to follow the norms of European folk traditions such as that of Bohemia. Aware of the potential for Western bias, he believed his conspectus was within reach of achieving a "universally valid foundation" for studying music.[32]

Time and Space

One of the most striking aspects of the essay is Seeger's desire to enrich his conception of musicology by drawing from a scientific field outside of music: theoretical physics. To help explain the basis for his opposition between history and system, Seeger turns to the basic dimensions of the physical world: space and time. Inspired by the theory of special relativity, Seeger proposes a fusion of these two dimensions he calls "spacetime." As is well known, the interdependence of space and time that Albert Einstein originally hypothesized in the early 1900s affects human perception of physical reality only under limited conditions, such as when an object or an observer approaches the speed of light. When these extreme conditions occur, the temporal and spatial dimensions undergo a dramatic transformation: time slows to a crawl, and objects literally change their shape, lengthening in the direction of their motion. However, when an object is not traveling at such a high velocity, the dimensions of time and space can be measured and understood in traditional ways, that is, separately.

It is fair to say that although Seeger was eager to borrow some of Einstein's specialized vocabulary, he did not share the physicist's "high speed" aspirations. Indeed, Seeger's fusion of space and time is, at the very best, only roughly analogous to the theory of special relativity. Instead he is searching for some framework to justify his belief that the artist's perception of musical time and of space is interdependent, and, above all, that it differs from the perceptions of the scientist. His approach is to revive the distinction between "function" and "resource" that he had first coined in the treatise, but to dress it in the guise of modern physics.[33] "General spacetime" corresponds with his previous concept of "function" and is associated with the scientist's and historian's view of music; "music spacetime," by contrast, corresponds with the intuitive world of the artist and is associated with the systematist's experience of music. He then invents yet another pair of terms to emphasize the different points of view: when perceived in "general spacetime" a musical work is a natural "phenomenon"; when perceived in "music spacetime" the same work is referred to as a musical "normenon." By the term "normenon" Seeger refers to the fact that music is man-made, and that it conforms to the "patterns or norms of tradition."[34] He then develops this difference between general and musical "spacetime" by briefly considering seven factors that apparently help shape it, including occurrence, provenience (or origin), identity, continuity, degree of control, measurability, and variability.[35] Seeger's discussion of these various factors, however, is so brief that it is not altogether clear whether they are fundamental to his basic thesis or rather newly conceived speculations.

Seeger's attempt to link the distinction between systematic and historical studies with the ways in which humans perceive time and space warrants a few comments. In the 1951 essay Seeger assumes that these two dimensions can be fused, and that the resulting spatial/temporal fusion can guide musicians and musicologists in their daily lives. It is by no means clear, however, that the fusion of time and space Seeger envisions is perceivable or, what is more important, *measurable*. In the treatise he advances the same idea of fusion, but in a much more tentative and cautious way. This idea initially appears in the sections of part 1 devoted to the theory of melodic form, where he reveals the insight that since a melodic line progresses through musical space while it is unfolding through time, a true theory of melody must take both into account.[36] But it is one thing to imagine an ideal union of time and space and quite another to actually measure both dimensions at the same time. As a first step toward developing a dual descriptive model, he proposes a new melodic unit of measure: the "tone-beat."[37] In principle, at least, tone beats offer a means of simultaneously measuring a given melody's intervallic shape and durational value. Yet, after suggesting this new unit, Seeger abandons it and resorts to measuring musical space and time in the conventional way—as separate and autonomous phenomena.

By contrast, in his later essay Seeger writes as though the ideal fusion of space and time were a fait accompli, and that musicologists could calculate it as easily as calibrating tempi on a metronome. The underlying tone of "Systematic Musicology" is that perceiving music in a framework of "spacetime" is not only possible, it is in fact what distinguishes musicians and music scholars from mere scientists who study music. The problem is that understanding musical artworks as a manifestation of Seeger's category of "spacetime," whether "musical" or "general," is exceedingly difficult to achieve. To use an analogy, it would be like my trying to convince a painter that the theory of primary colors is flawed, and that the basic triad of red, blue, and yellow in fact depends on only two fundamental colors that require new names: "bled" and "rue." If I can produce no physical confirmation that this new pair of pigments exists, nor any proof that they explain the phenomenon of color better than the old theory, then any descriptive method based on this dual-color modal is suspect. Likewise, since Seeger cannot confirm that music "spacetime" exists and can be measured as effectively as each dimension can on its own, then a theory based on this ideal is speculative fancy, however intuitively appealing or provocative it may be.

In the end, Seeger's hypothetical extrapolations from Einstein's concept of "spacetime," as well as his earlier distinction between "function" and "resource," all suffer from the same basic problem: a categorical separation of art and science. This strict dichotomy can be traced back to the thought of Henri Bergson. While Bergson's influence is most clearly evident in Seeger's early epistemological writings, it can also be recognized, though less overtly, in his later studies of musicology.

Seeger's fascination with Einstein also influenced the way he referred to his ideal map of musicology. To highlight the parallel between science and musicology, Seeger borrowed the term, the "unified field theory," which was Einstein's dream of a single science that would help unify the separate and, to some extent, mutually exclusive branches of theoretical physics: quantum mechanics and Newtonian mechanics. It is telling that Einstein died before he could witness such a unifying vision come to fruition.

Parallels with Linguistics

During his final thirty years Seeger also turned to the field of structural linguistics to further refine his vision of musicology. While Seeger's comparison of the internal division of musicology with developments in linguistic theory appears in both the original essay of 1951 and its revision of 1977, it is more clearly articulated in the latter, where he observes a strong, though apparently accidental, resemblance between his own philosophical ideas and those of the revolutionary Swiss linguist Ferdinand de Saussure. In his words, his early musings about musicology were "in accord" with the "broader and more precise" teachings of Saussure.[38] For the purposes of this overview, I am more interested in the parallel between Seeger's and Saussure's aversion toward history than in various other correspondences that exist between their theoretical approaches.

In order to appreciate fully Seeger's contribution, we must briefly summarize Saussure's principal work, *Cours de linguistique générale*, which was compiled posthumously from his lecture notes by two former students. As is well known, Saussure understood the sign, whether neume or noise, as the central fact of language. Three oppositions are associated with his theory of signs. The first is the distinction between the linguistic form itself, the "signifier," and the idea being referred to, the "signified." A sign is nothing more than the union of these two constituents. The remaining two oppositions have to do with the process by which language and, as Seeger believed, music undergo change. Saussure distinguishes between the linguistic system in the abstract from its actual manifestation by a particular speaker. Employing French terms that have no English equivalents, Saussure named the system itself, *langue*, and its execution, *parole*. The linguist's and, in turn, the music analyst's job was to study the units and rules of combination belonging to the *langue*, not merely isolated acts of speech.

The third and most important opposition, at least as far as Seeger is concerned, must be viewed in the context of the evolution of linguistic theory between the eighteenth and nineteenth centuries. As Hans Aarsfell notes:

It is universally agreed that the decisive turn in language study occurred when the philosophical, a priori method of the eighteenth century was abandoned in favor of the historical, a posteriori method of the nineteenth. The former began with mental categories and sought their exemplification in language, as in universal grammar, and based etymologies on conjectures about the origin of language. The latter sought only facts, evidence, demonstration; it divorced the study of language from the study of mind.[39]

One of the essential aspects of Saussure's work is the degree to which he reacted against the historical conception of language study that prevailed during the early nineteenth century and, in the process, revived some of the preoccupations of the eighteenth century. In particular, he proposed a distinction between two ways of understanding language: the "synchronic" view, as it exists at a given time, and the "diachronic" view, as it evolves through time. Since he believed that any historical judgment about language was in essence a comparison between two synchronic descriptions completed at different moments in time, then diachronic statements depend on and are subordinate to synchronic statements. The American linguist Leonard Bloomfield explains further the nature of this dependence:

All historical study of language is based upon the comparison of two or more sets of descriptive data. It can be only as accurate and only as complete as these data permit it to be. In order to describe a language one needs no historical knowledge whatever; in fact, the observer who allows such knowledge to affect his description, is bound to distort his data.[40]

What is particularly significant about Bloomfield's comment is that Seeger quotes it in a footnote of his essay "Systematic Musicology."[41] Looking back at his earlier critique of musicology, Seeger was struck by the resemblance between his objections against the methods of nineteenth-century musicologists and Saussure's critique of nineteenth-century linguists. He draws a one-to-one correspondence between "synchronic" and systematic, on the one hand, and between "diachronic" and historical, on the other. In drawing this parallel, Seeger is not saying that the historical approach to music is bankrupt or superficial but that it ultimately depends on the process of analytical description.

In order to evaluate the significance of this purported resemblance, let us compare the two theories more closely. Saussure's argument with the past is clear. The fascination among nineteenth-century linguists for purely empirical studies gradually led to a neglect of such philosophical questions as the process by which language actually changes and the relation between language and mind. Frustrated by what he regarded as philosophical blindness, Saussure presented his own theories as a means of compensating for his predecessors' oversights.

Seeger, too, was frustrated by the explosive growth of historical studies of music during the late nineteenth century and the blindness toward contemporary musical life epitomized in the abstract schemes of the German musicologist Guido Adler. But, what Seeger fails to make clear is which music historians were sinning and exactly what sins they were committing. Because he never spells out the philosophical and methodological approaches adopted by nineteenth-century historians, one is never sure against whom his strong polemical attacks are directed. The reader is forced to speculate: Did he believe that there was a comparable fascination with atomistic and confirmable facts among music historians at the expense of more fundamental questions of compositional technique? Or was their oversight more with respect to theoretical principle and critical value?

One thing is clear. Whatever specific grievances Seeger had toward his musicological predecessors, these resulted in a deep bias against history that manifested itself throughout his later writings. Seeger's discovery of Saussure toward the end of his life only strengthened a "structuralist" attitude that had already been established by the 1930s. Finally, the parallel between the two thinkers suggests a broader pattern in early twentieth-century intellectual history: a convergence in philosophy and method among different disciplines. It will remain for future intellectual historians to judge the ultimate significance of such interdisciplinary correspondences.

Considering the abstract character of Seeger's ideal vision, it is useful to illustrate the different facets of musicology with a specific, though hypothetical, example. Let us imagine a collection of essays all devoted to the third movement of Ruth Crawford's String Quartet, with each essay embodying one of the eight approaches prescribed in Seeger's scheme. By imagining how a team of musicologists might implement the methods, orientations, and viewpoints that Seeger outlines in figure 17 in relation to a specific work, we immediately bring to life what is otherwise a cold and clinical scheme. Since some of this movement's innovative techniques have already been discussed in some detail in chapter 6, here readers can focus less on the piece itself and more on the relationships within Seeger's plan.

According to the scheme, the musicologist's point of departure is a systematic study of the piece's internal organization (I.A.1). Technical questions to be addressed would include Crawford's treatment of dynamics, rhythm, pitch, and timbre, as well as the interdependence of neume, phrase, and whole, the movement's function within the entire work, and so forth. The second essay (I.A.2) would submit that description to a critique based on the author's own preconceptions of internal structure and any inherent biases in the methods of description employed. An example of such a bias might be the expectation that patterns within different parameters should coincide, such as recurring pitch motives reflecting in some way the rhythmic patterns formed by the ordering among instruments' crescendi. Ellie Hisama has written a probing essay explaining how two different analytical techniques of measuring the movement's climax can be reconciled with an understanding of Crawford's social position.[42] The next essay under I.B.1 would consider to what historical and stylistic traditions the quartet belonged, comparing it with other chamber works written between the wars. The contrast between a traditional genre, such as the string quartet, and Crawford's highly experimental compositional language gives her work an unusual stature among American composers. The fourth essay, I.B.2, would likewise submit that historical analysis to a critique, focusing not only on whether the style and genre are appropriate for this piece but also on the merits and shortcomings of the very process of categorizing music according to style. In addition, the historian would explore the motives for seeking a musical counterpart to Goethe's aesthetic of balance, and whether this aesthetic had been achieved in the quartet. The remaining four essays, which I will not elaborate here, would adopt the same methods and orientations of the first four, but from the vantage point of a nonmusician, or what Seeger calls a "non-carrier."

This hypothetical exercise dramatizes several limitations of Seeger's scheme. First, he assumes that the tasks must follow a predetermined order. However, some projects may warrant doing several tasks in tandem or emphasizing a historical more than a systematic orientation. For instance, Seeger asserts that musicologists who try to conduct a historical study without first having completed the systematic description of the music itself will find themselves with nothing to study. While this observation, when taken at face value, is irrefutable, it is nevertheless possible for someone to explore significant and profound historical questions having completed only a preliminary analysis of a work. The question is a matter of emphasis; whereas systematists typically cultivate analytical description as an end in itself, historians are usually more interested in the place a given work occupies within a broader context of aesthetic and stylistic change. Second, by assigning an inherent priority among the eight "provinces" of his musicological map, Seeger ends up encouraging, if unwittingly, the very division of intellectual labor that he elsewhere abhors. If Seeger truly wishes to champion a holistic view of music in which the two basic orientations are complementary and interdependent, as he says in the opening sentence,[43] he is undermining his own argument. The very binary structure of the model tends to emphasize the *differences* rather the similarities between the various approaches and methods. If systematic musicologists must, by definition, take into account the historical point of view and vice versa, there would be no need to endow the model with inherent preferences and priorities as does Seeger.

"Sources of Evidence"

In order to complete this historic panorama of Seeger's views on musicology, it is necessary to consider briefly his speculations published during his final years. "Sources of Evidence and Criteria for Judgment in the Critique of Music" (hereafter abbreviated as "Sources of Evidence") is a representative example, for it was one of the last written projects completed before Seeger's death in 1979. This short, dense work is a revised version of part 3 of an earlier and much more involved essay, "Preface to a Critique of Music," which he wrote in 1963.

"Sources of Evidence" is significant in two respects. On the one hand, it reveals the degree of continuity in the philosophical questions Seeger pursued: he was as eager to study the cognitive process by which music is understood as he was to develop a model of the discipline as a whole. For him, what works, styles, or musical traditions musicologists choose to think about are ultimately bound up with the very ways they think. On the other hand, his understanding of the basic philosophical questions musicologists face and the solutions he recommends contain some new and significant twists.

The essay's format conforms to that of the other two essays under discussion: a comprehensive diagram accompanied by extensive verbal commentary. The subject of his study, however, differs slightly from that of the 1939 and 1951 essays. Rather than continuing his meditations on the internal divisions of the discipline as a whole, he explores the nature of critical judgment, whether that judge be a composer, performer, listener, or musicologist. While this focus is a throwback to the philosophical questions he pursued in the treatise, the solutions he offers have since matured.

Seeger illustrates his ideas using two visual models. The first is a circle, reproduced in figure 18, of eight different "sources" that all participate in the process of musical judgment. The list includes "individual valuer," "general arbitrage," "musical arbitrage," "general historics," "musical historics," "general systematics," "musical systematics," and "law." Because Seeger's penchant for creating new terms is not always balanced by a desire to clarify them, it is helpful to discuss these sources in more detail.

He begins with the individual in order to emphasize that idiosyncrasies of each judge, that is, "preferences, indifferences, prejudices and even suppressions," are instrumental in shaping the judgments he or she makes.[44] By the term "arbitrage" Seeger means models or standards that influence an individual's process of judgment; Seeger then considers sources outside of music—such as the teachings of religion, ethics, and folklore, or the financial success at the box office—as well as within music. In the treatise, Seeger labeled the latter category as "Collective Musical Taste," which included music critics, teachers, and so forth.[45] The familiar opposition between history and system is now expressed in slightly broader terms. The term "historics" is intended to refer to the content of history, that is, what historians investigate, as well as the process of historical investigation itself. The

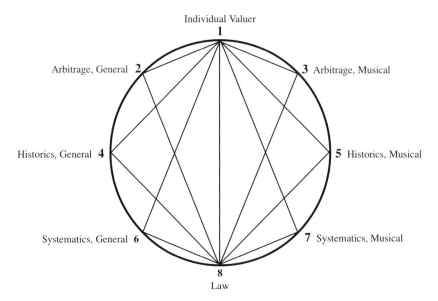

Figure 18. Sources of musical value, "Sources of Evidence . . ."

latter includes such specialized fields as historiography, iconography, and paleography. Likewise, the concept of "systematics" is somewhat broader than before, embracing a wide range of fields such as physiology, psychology, sociology, and anthropology. The final source, "law," can be understood as a subcategory of nonmusical "systematics" in which musical judgment is influenced by some sort of legal tradition, whether political, moral, or religious.

The most striking difference between the essay "Sources of Evidence" and chapters 2 and 3 in the treatise is that Seeger changed his mind regarding the priority among the various sources of influence. Instead of presenting them in a so-called tree diagram and thereby identifying patterns of internal grouping that such a structure requires, Seeger arranges them in a circle. This is particularly evident in a later diagram from the same essay reproduced in figure 19. The circular structure implies equality among all eight sources, with each one leading directly to the final outcome of judgment located at the center. It should be stressed that vestiges of the binary model of musical knowledge remain; for example, the distinction between musical and nonmusical organizes six of the eight sources. Yet this diagram is substantially different from its predecessors in that the members of perhaps the most crucial pair, system and history, are conceived not

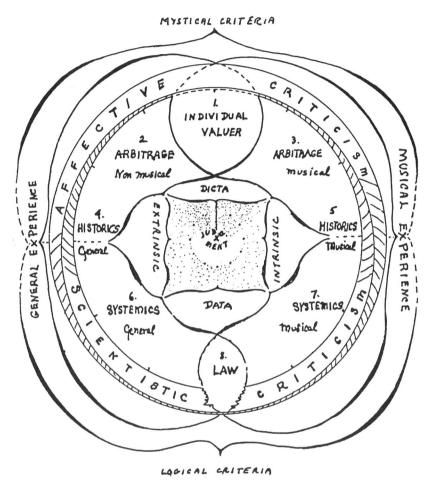

Figure 19. Alternate model of sources of musical judgment, "Sources of Evidence . . ."

as opposites but as complements. The ideal for musicologists is to decrease

the use of dichotomies as each others' irreconcilable opposites and [increase] their use as each others' complements, thus placing less reliance upon the predominantly structural formal logic and more upon the dialectic of functions.[46]

On the whole, compared with the 1951 conspectus, Seeger's categories in the 1977 version are not as rigid, the process through which categories or methods are combined is not as strict, and the order of steps within the process is not as fixed.

Seeger's diagram warrants two final comments. First, in choosing a circular visual model, he revives an idea he had introduced as an aside in the treatise but ultimately had rejected. In a footnote to his original diagram of the music-critical process, he imagines a hypothetical set of circumstances in which the circle would be closed—he refers specifically to ancient Chinese culture, where apparently the state had enormous influence over the development of the arts.[47] Although in 1931 he finally settled on another visual model to illustrate his theory, he nevertheless included the circular design as a passing speculation. By the time he reconsidered his theory in 1977, Seeger had changed his mind; the circle now served as an apt tool for visualizing the process of judgment in the present, not in some remote time and place. In sum, the appearance of the same diagram in two separate meditations on music criticism more than thirty-five years apart shows that the philosophical questions Seeger originally posed in the treatise continued to occupy him for the rest of his life.

Second, Seeger's model of judgment also revives, though unwittingly, the ideas that Waldo Pratt had initially propounded in 1915. As will be recalled, in the essay "On Behalf of Musicology" Pratt describes a network of musical knowledge in which four processes are interlinked with seven different fields, making a total of twenty-eight combinations in all. After all, his purpose in that essay was to offer a foundation on which any musicological investigation could be based, not a method of investigation itself. In "Sources of Evidence" Seeger's aim conforms more closely to that of Pratt; he is content to *describe* what orientations are possible, instead of trying to *prescribe* what orientations musicologists ought to adopt, as a means of compensating for unnamed scholarly excesses of the past.

A Scheme of Schemes

The final chapter in the evolution of Seeger's ideal vision of musicology appears in *Studies in Musicology, 1935–1975*. This volume does not present a single unified statement of his views; instead, it is a music-critical scrapbook, including essays that address a wide range of topics—from the fretted zither to the philosophical foundation of musicology. What is noteworthy is Seeger's decision to revise and reprint sixteen essays that he had already published elsewhere.[48] Thus, even though he rewrote large sections of and renamed many essays so as to reflect his latest thinking, he did not entirely eliminate all differences between them. In many respects much of this collection reads like a set of variations on the common themes in Seeger's philosophical and historiographical thought.

The most significant work in the collection, at least as far as Seeger's speculations about music are concerned, is "Toward a Unified Field Theory for Musicology," which is a dialogue, in the tradition of Plato, between Seeger and two imaginary interlocutors. Seeger's choice of an open-ended dialogue format is fortuitous, since it is so well suited to his subject matter (one also suspects that he was responding to complaints about his dense writing style.)[49] In his study *Contemplating Music,* Joseph Kerman refers to this essay as "a sort of self-review . . . which is as illuminating as it is entertaining."[50]

In this dialogue Seeger introduces a new way of understanding the discipline, which he dubs "the musicological juncture." Instead of beginning with predetermined abstract categories—namely, Adler's two branches of knowledge—Seeger explores what things that a musicologist encounters when beginning to examine some aspect of music: "the situation you put yourself in when you start to use one means of communication, speech, to deal with another, music, in the middle of things."[51] By the "middle of things," Seeger means that his philosophical approach has a certain pragmatic cast, that is, is related to a particular time, place, and individual. He then develops a list of five things that arise in this "situation": speech, music, individuality, culture, and physics. He describes their inner connections as follows:

Musicology is (1) *a speech study,* systematic as well as historical, critical as well as scientific . . . ; whose field is (2) *the total music* of man . . . ; whose cultivation is (3) *by individual students* who can view its field as musicians [and] . . . nonmusical specialists . . . whose aim is to contribute to the *understanding of man,* in terms both (4) of human *culture* and (5) of his relationships with the *physical universe.*[52]

Next Seeger illustrates all the possible relations between the various categories in this "juncture" in a set of five diagrams (see figure 20). The remarkable feature of these diagrams is that they are conceived as a single network or totality; no diagram can be isolated or given special status over any other. Seeger's term for the network of relations within each diagram is "inclusion," which is a somewhat misleading allusion to the mathematical theory of sets. For example, an individual

Figure 20. Musicological juncture: five possible relations among speech (S), music (M), individual (I), human culture (C), and physical universe (P)

"includes" the other four categories in the sense that each musicologist's physical, musical, cultural, and linguistic experience is unique and solipsistic. Speech "includes" the other four in that it represents and, to some extent, generalizes them in language.[53] A simpler way of visualizing the multiple connections among the five categories is as a pentagonal star (see figure 21). The symmetrical shape of this model reflects the equality among all five, with no single category enjoying priority over the other four.

As important as the "musicological juncture" is for Seeger, it is merely a preliminary stage in the exposition of his scheme of musicology, the ground upon which his theory proper rests. He unveils his "unified field theory" in the form of a two-page, fold-out diagram entitled "Conspectus of the Resources of the Musicological Process."[54] At first glance, the diagram appears like yet one more installment in the ongoing series of Seeger's models of musicology. But the caption accompanying the diagram explains that it synthesizes materials from this paper as well as five others.[55] Hence, this diagram encapsulates all of Seeger's previous visions of musicology; it is a scheme of schemes, a music-cartographic extravaganza—indeed, a consummation of years of theoretical speculation.

Seeger arranges six categories of musical experience in a complex chain from top to bottom:

1. World View
2. Music
3. Speech
4. Musicology
    a. The Audiocommunicatory Event
    b. The Biocultural Event [Context]
5. The Musicological Event
6. Application

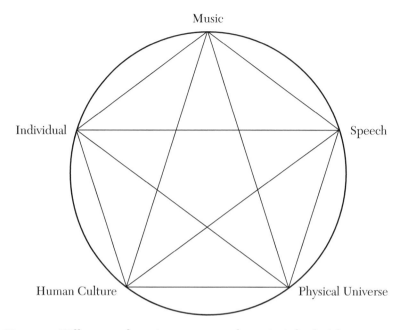

Figure 21. Different configuration among speech, music, individual, human culture, and physical universe

Most of these categories are divided into two subcategories, each of which is then split into various number of further divisions, as needed.

However, as meticulously detailed as this diagram is, Seeger confesses that he is not content with it: in particular, he is troubled by its binary structure, inherited from Adler, which "dangerously oversimplifies."[56] He muses that, if he only knew how to draw it, a three- or four-dimensional model might be more appropriate. To compensate, he suggests the following:

In limiting myself to the two dimensions of the conspectus, the best I can do is to ask you to begin at the top and as you read down to remember that you are tracing your own progress over the terrain. When you come to a fork, you must decide which path to follow first but not to stay on it so long that you forget to go back and follow the other fork; for it is the drawing of the two together that is essential to the reading of the table.[57]

A telling metaphor in this comment helps us interpret not only his final conspectus but also the very impulse for developing a philosophy of music.

Seeger refers to the scheme as a conceptual map over which one can trace one's "progress" over the music-intellectual "terrain." This comment is in keeping with our approach toward Seeger's various conspecti of musical knowledge as they evolved from 1931 to 1977. Each serves as a kind of diary of Seeger's own music-intellectual journey as he traveled through the provinces of avant-garde composition, criticism, folk music, and philosophy. One of the participants in Seeger's dialogue even acknowledges this point.[58]

Yet the conspectus is as much an exercise in fantasy as in memory. Seeger's ideal of mediation is nowhere more apparent than in his exhortation that musicologists should try to "draw together" each member of an opposition. Seeger is silent about how this mediation can be accomplished, hoping that each individual will discover it for himself or herself. Like many nineteenth-century maps of the American West, some areas are charted in detail, while others are simply left blank. Perhaps Seeger hoped his indefatigable mapmaking would induce musicologists to approach the borders of *musica terra incognita,* and, equipped with his *principia musicologica,* dare to venture beyond.

Conclusion

When considering Seeger's writings on musicology as a whole, it is useful to draw an analogy with the world of archaeology. In some ancient cultures it was common to reuse writing materials such as parchment or tablets made of stone or brass by effacing the previous message and then inscribing a new one on top of the old. This kind of multilayered artifact is known as a "palimpsest." In some cases the original message is not entirely removed, and the resulting linguistic jumble combines fragments from two or more messages. To the archaeologist, such a mosaic can yield clues not only about the messages themselves but also about the historical evolution of the culture that gave birth to them.

If we borrow this interpretive technique from archaeology, the four essays discussed here all serve as a "palimpsest" of Seeger's views about musical understanding and its implications for the field of musicology. In each one, two separate messages are juxtaposed so as to form a rich interpretive mosaic: Seeger's ideal vision of musicology is the newest one, scrawled in the foreground; the old message—his theory of music criticism—is still visible, but only in bits and pieces. This image of old and new messages presented together also helps highlight the fact that, while some aspects of Seeger's thought underwent a dramatic evolution, others never changed at all.

Yet certain hazards result from Seeger's desire to combine old and new messages. Chief among these is the failure to separate two different ways of characterizing the field of musicology: relatively neutral taxonomic description and self-interested prescription. Seeger succumbs to the temptation of letting his protests on behalf of new music get in the way of his panorama of the discipline. When mixed together, the two messages never fuse into a whole, each one dulling the impact and significance of the other. The result may be likened to the compositional ideals of "heterophony" and "diaphony" that Seeger outlined in his younger days, in which separate lines within a texture achieve the maximum possible independence. The difference here is that what may be a stimulating idea for an avant-garde composer does not always succeed as a model for an entire discipline.

Despite this shortcoming, it is still possible to resurrect Seeger's twin aims of protesting the nineteenth-century view of musicology and of presenting his own new panorama without sacrificing the fundamental spirit of either. To achieve this end, the two messages must be separated and each must be evaluated in its own right. Surely his frustration at the public indifference toward new music has merit. Indeed, composers and advocates of new music during the 1990s face neglect and hostility comparable to what Seeger must have faced in New York during the 1920s. In the end, had Seeger removed his plea for new music from its philosophical moorings, it would have gained in clarity and impact. After all, if his ultimate goal was for historians to harken to the music of their own time, a full-scale philosophical study of the discipline was hardly the best means of achieving it.

Likewise, had Seeger separated his plea for contemporary music from his comprehensive atlas of musicology, the latter would have been a more honest picture of the field. What is questionable is to criticize previous schemes and to construct an alternative scheme of the discipline sheerly on the basis of one individual's musical taste and biases. Seeger was so concerned with compensating for what he regarded as his predecessors' narrow musical taste that he *underestimated* the value of studying the past and *overestimated* the importance of studying the present. In an ideal conspectus of musicology, both forms of scholarship deserve an equal place.

I began this chapter with an analogy between philosophical speculation and the tradition of exploring and making maps of the frontier.
In the end the truly challenging cartographic questions within the
landscape of musicology involve finding where and how the various
provinces of music history, criticism, and compositional theory meet.
If Seeger's various philosophical maps can be understood as a record
of his own music-intellectual journeys, the ultimate challenge is to
fashion a map on which we *all* can chart our own journeys, whether
they be intuitive, logical, historical, or systematic.

Epilogue

Neume, New Music, New Musicology

To survey the writings of Charles Seeger is to embark on a vast music-intellectual journey. In this study my journey has involved two stages: one was to trace the metaphysical springs that feed into the river of Seeger's musical philosophy; the other to follow the course of the river and locate where it divides into the streams and tributaries of various musical disciplines. Now that both stages are complete, it is appropriate to assess the merits and shortcomings of Seeger's contributions and then to contemplate what other journeys may lie ahead.

In his book on aesthetics the English philosopher R. G. Collingwood provides a distinction for evaluating Seeger's philosophical contributions. In his view, there are two kinds of people who pursue aesthetics: artists with a taste for philosophy and philosophers with a taste for art.[1] If Collingwood's two "profiles" serve as opposite ends of a hypothetical aesthetic spectrum, the idiosyncrasies of Seeger's philosophical thought and its gradual evolution can be better understood. During the early part of his career, Seeger undeniably fit the first aesthetic profile. Despite a growing propensity for theoretical speculation, he never considered himself a philosopher. In his mind, philosophers were so busy trying to establish a comprehensive basis for criticizing the fine arts that they neglected the arts themselves, a point which Collingwood himself admits: philosophers "are admirably protected against talking nonsense: but there is no security that they will know what they are talking about."[2] Seeger's earliest writings grew out of a profound discontent with the music-intellectual traditions he had inherited from the nineteenth century. He believed that since most musicologists ignored the intrinsic nature of musical experience, the discipline as a whole was crippled. Inspired by the ideas of Bergson, Seeger argued that any interpretation of music was necessarily limited by the incompatibility between music and language: a verbal report could never do justice to a nonverbal art form. As a response to this predicament, he exhorted musicologists to question the use of scientific methods as a means of interpreting compositional practice and instead harken to their own musical intuitions.

Seeger's enthusiasm for the theories of Ralph Perry shows that during the late 1920s he slowly moved toward the center of my music-aesthetic spectrum. In constructing his philosophical edifice, Perry began with the concept of ethical value and then generalized it in order to embrace a wide range of disciplines such as aesthetics, religious studies, and political theory within a single framework. Although Seeger, too, was fascinated by the concept of value, he insisted on narrowing its scope so as to include matters pertaining only to music. Instead of searching for a single source of human value, Seeger developed a dualistic approach to knowledge in which musical value was achieved through a process of mediating among opposite mental faculties. In this respect, his loyalty to the integrity of musical intuition still outweighed his desire to create a comprehensive philosophical system.

Considering how much admiration Seeger had for Bertrand Russell, it is curious that at the beginning of their respective careers they belonged to opposite ends of my hypothetical spectrum. Usually an ultrarationalist, Russell was compelled by his discovery of spirituality to temper his reliance on logic and facts with the power of mystical belief. Although, strictly speaking, Russell never applied his model of balance to aesthetic questions, if he had, the results would have placed him somewhere near the center. Seeger, too, arrived at the middle but from the opposite direction. By the time he completed a draft of his enormous compendium, *Tradition and Experiment in the New Music*, in 1931, his love of rational explanation had become strong enough to counterbalance his faith in spontaneous intuition. In that work he proposed an outline for a theory of criticism that would help musicologists overcome the discrepancy between music and words. Influenced by Russell's recent religious writings, Seeger proposed an ideal synthesis between the faculties of intuition and reason that could be likened to a process of mediation: the music critic's initial intuition would subsequently be tested and compared with other intuitions until a final judgment of value was reached. In sum, Seeger's aesthetic philosophy evolved from one end of the spectrum to the center: from the youthful extremes of antirationalism toward a philosophy of mediation in which logical discourse was balanced against intuitive immediacy.

Because part of my study has been devoted to explaining a theory of critical judgment, it seems only fitting to submit Seeger's own musical contributions to the same process of judgment. The aspects of his work that were surveyed in part 2 can be encapsulated by the epithet "Neume, New Music, New Musicology." Not only does each term in this list refer to a different field of music, but the nesting relation among the sounds themselves symbolizes the interconnections among Seeger's profuse and, in some cases, profound contributions to music.

The medieval term "neume" symbolizes Seeger's interest in the craft of composition and in developing theories that composers could actually use. This term also underlines his ambivalent attitude toward musical traditions of the past. On the one hand, he cherished older musical styles, as witnessed by his revival of an eighteenth-century ideal of counterpoint and his desire to fuse it with a thoroughly nineteenth-century principle of organic unity. On the other hand, he also reacted passionately against the past by developing new aesthetic models that would highlight musical functions which he felt previous composers had neglected, such as dynamics or accent. Readers may wonder whether Seeger's historical attitude, developed over sixty years ago, is out of step with the present. Yet in a musical climate in which composers of the 1990s have been known to mix the gestures of rock and roll with the musical language of Webern, such historical ambivalence seems more the rule than the exception.

From a composer's perspective, it is unfortunate that the technical sections of Seeger's *Tradition and Experiment in the New Music* lay unpublished for so many years. As it stands, the only composers who knew Seeger's theories of composition were either his students, colleagues, or students of students.[3] Had more musicians been able to read or hear about his theories of composition, his work may have had greater historical impact in avant-garde circles. However, the area in which the treatise may well have the most impact in the future is the use of Seeger's notion of melodic contour and its various extensions to other parameters as analytical tools.

During the twentieth century the slogan "New Music" has known many interpretations—from a sense of honor among experimental composers themselves to a sense of horror among their less charitable listeners. As a composition teacher and critic, Seeger certainly took seriously the creation and evaluation of new musical works. Beginning in the 1930s, he simultaneously tried to put two different ideals into practice: a theory of balanced criticism, and a compositional aesthetic mixing balance and experimentation. Since Seeger believed that Ruggles, Cowell, and Crawford were on the verge of discovering a new style of composition, one way he could contribute to that discovery would be to submit his colleagues' latest efforts to sympathetic but honest judgment.

In evaluating the success of Seeger's critical writings, two aspects must be considered. To begin with, Seeger's handful of critical reviews are worthwhile in themselves as historical documents that help portray the newly emerging American avant-garde. His close association with all three ultramodernists allowed him to assess their creative temperaments as much as their musical creations. Second, despite his hopes of developing a general theory of music criticism, in the end the only person likely to ever master the numerous principles and criteria is Seeger himself. While the framework of his critical method is highly appealing, the details of its application are not always clear. Thus, Seeger's exposition of his theory of criticism is more effective as a summary of his own philosophical assumptions than as a primer for apprenticing critics.

The last term in my epithet "New Musicology" refers to Seeger's writings in speculative musicology. In his controversial contemplations about musicologists Joseph Kerman puts his finger on one of Seeger's basic motivations: "It was the idea of studying all musics that appealed to Seeger, not those musics themselves as subjects for actual study."[4] While over the course of his life Seeger wrote about an enormous range of musical subjects—from dulcimers and dissonance to linguistic predicaments—in his later years the one topic he kept returning to was an ideal scheme of the discipline of musicology. As will be recalled from chapter 7, a theme running through most of Seeger's various schemes is his desire to protest the nineteenth-century conception of musicology as much as to reveal his own new panorama. He developed dichotomies that would emphasize his plea for contemporary music and scolded those musicologists who used their professional specialization to justify their indifference toward music of the present. Taken together, his intellectual "maps" describe a holistic vision of musicology as a truly interdisciplinary form of study.

Yet there is a paradox in Seeger's maps of musicology that is symptomatic of his thought as a whole. On the one hand, he possessed a deep faith in dichotomies and dualistic models. His fascination with oppositions between such things as system and history, science and criticism, and the faculties of logic and intuition at times seems overly strict and anachronistic. In choosing these dichotomies, Seeger had absorbed the philosophical controversies of the pre–World War I era and had adapted them to the study of music. Some modern readers may have little patience with a dualistic approach that divides the mind into two hemispheres and debates the priority between them. Yet I wonder what really has changed since Seeger's time: our desire to make dichotomies or those dichotomies that happen to be desirable.

On the other hand, his personal style of thinking was anything but strict in that he transcended traditional divisions between fields of knowledge. His knack for blending ideas and methods from a broad range of disciplines and professions such as criticism and performance, compositional theory and philosophy, musicology and ethnomusicology into a single project has had no parallel in the landscape of twentieth-century American music. Indeed, the story of how Seeger's philosophical ideals helped shape his study of American popular music, particularly folk song, remains to be told.

There are signs in recent musicological writings, however, that Seeger may have left some legacy after all. First and foremost is the relationship between musicology and philosophical inquiry. Examples of musicologists who draw inspiration from contemporary developments in philosophy are legion: Carolyn Abbate, Scott Burnham, Thomas Christensen, Brian Hyer, and Susan McClary come to mind.[5] Although the ideas of these authors bear little resemblance to those that occupied Seeger, all share a common interest in using philosophical reflection as a springboard for questioning the traditional assumptions of musical scholarship. Most important, while Seeger consistently relied on two-part models, he also placed enormous emphasis on the value of trying to overcome conflicts between opposing points of view. This spirit of reconciliation is especially important when one considers the number of oppositions that suffuse today's academic presses and music journals: theory versus history, formalist versus post-modernist, and feminist versus nonideological, and vernacular versus cultivated. The question is whether we will be as devoted as was Seeger to the ideal of mediation and, if so, what strategies we will invent to fulfill it.

Perhaps it is Seeger's view of criticism that will be his ultimate legacy for musicologists. What I have in mind is less the model of alternating between the mind's internal faculties than his insistence that we must begin by listening to our own intuitions about listening. In this day of professionalization, when methods, ideologies, even entire disciplines are treated as ends in themselves, it is all too easy to forget that our common point of departure is the overwhelming, emotionally charged sensation that some musical works evoke in us. That is a message Seeger never tired of delivering.

In closing, I wish to mention a recent study by the French philologist Pierre Hadot, *Philosophy as a Way of Life,* that provides a telling insight into Seeger's penchant for combining theory and practice.[6] Hadot argues that the modern preconception of philosophy as a purely intellectual activity, far removed from everyday life, runs counter to the original intentions of its founders in ancient Greece. Beginning with Socrates, the purpose of philosophy was not to contemplate theories or analyze texts for their own sake. Instead, the skills needed for sustaining intricate verbal dialogues were treated as a forensic means of achieving a higher spiritual end. Philosophers of many different traditions tried to perfect a set of "spiritual exercises," which Hadot describes as follows:

Rather than aiming at the acquisition of a purely abstract knowledge, these exercises aimed at realizing a transformation of one's vision of the world and a metamorphosis of one's personality. The philosopher needed to be trained not only to know how to speak and debate, but also to know how to live. . . . Hence, the teaching and training of philosophy were intended not simply to develop the intelligence of the discipline, but to transform . . . [the philosopher's] intellect, imagination, sensibility, and will. . . . Spiritual exercises were exercises because they were practical, required effort and training. . . . they were spiritual because they involved the entire spirit, one's whole way of being.[7]

Although this philosophical ideal of classical antiquity may be quite distant in time from Seeger's ultramodernist musings during the 1920s and 1930s, it captures well the unique fusion of theory and practice that he hoped to realize. This is abundantly clear in a comment drawn from one of Seeger's earliest essays. Following a diagnosis of the various ills which he believed were afflicting contemporary composers, he proposes a provisional but nonetheless profound solution:

Hence, our main occupation should be to allow for the commensurate development of all the essential resources by outlining a set of preparatory disciplines by which we may hope to correct the disparity now existing and prepare a way for their more balanced articulation at the hands of someone who is able and at a time ripe for the undertaking.[8]

While Seeger prescribes this "set of disciplines" for a limited segment of the musical community—avant-garde composers—his philosophical writings as a whole can be viewed as a set of "spiritual disciplines" of much larger dimensions. For Charles Louis Seeger, the concept of theory—whether compositional, musicological, or philosophical—was never far removed from the practice of music. The ultimate measure of success for Seeger's many ideas in criticism, compositional theory, musicology, and philosophy was that they enhance the art of living as much as the living art of music.

Notes

Introduction

1. Joseph Kerman, *Contemplating Music: Challenges to Musicology* (Cambridge, Mass.: Harvard University Press, 1985), p. 162.

2. For a comprehensive bibliography of Seeger's writings, editions, and compositions, see Ann M. Pescatello, *Charles Seeger: A Life in American Music* (Pittsburgh: University of Pittsburgh Press, 1992), pp. 317–29.

3. From her birth in 1901 until she married Charles in 1932, she called herself "Crawford"; thereafter she added her husband's surname: "Crawford Seeger." For convenience, I will refer to her as "Ruth Crawford." In a flyer announcing the formation of the New Music Society in 1925, Henry Cowell wrote: "It is seldom that Los Angeles has the opportunity to hear presented the works of the most discussed composers of so-called ultra-modern tendencies, such as Stravinsky, Schoenberg, Ruggles, Rudhyar, etc." See Rita Mead, *Henry Cowell's New Music 1925–1936, The Society, The Music Editions, and the Recordings* (Ann Arbor: UMI Research Press, 1981), p. 31. Throughout this study I use the term "ultramodern" to refer to American experimental composers during the 1920s and 1930s.

4. Gilbert Chase, "An Exagmination [*sic*] Round His Factification for Incamination of Work in Progress (Review Essay and Reminiscence)," *Yearbook of the International Folk Music Council* 11 (1979): 138–44.

5. Bruno Nettl, "The Dual Nature of Ethnomusicology in North America: The Contributions of Charles Seeger and George Herzog," in *Comparative Musicology and Anthropology of Music: Essays on the History of Ethnomusicology,* ed. Bruno Nettl and Philip V. Bohlman (Chicago: University of Chicago Press, 1991), p. 269.

6. Michael Broyles, review of *Charles Seeger: A Life in American Music,* by Ann M. Pescatello, *American Music* 12 (Fall 1994): 336.

7. George List alludes to this remark that Seeger made in his oral presentation; see "On the Non-Universality of Musical Perspectives," *Ethnomusicology* 15 (September 1971): 399.

8. Ann M. Pescatello, *Charles Seeger: A Life in American Music* (Pittsburgh: University of Pittsburgh Press, 1992).

9. Frances Sparshott, "Aesthetics of Music—Limits and Grounds," *What Is Music? An Introduction to the Philosophy of Music,* ed. Philip Alperson (University Park: Pennsylvania State University Press, 1987), p. 35.

10. Hermann Pfrogner, *Musik: Geschichte ihrer Deutung* (Freiburg: 1954), p. 352; cited and translated by Edward Lippman in *A History of Western Musical Aesthetics* (Lincoln: University of Nebraska Press, 1992), p. 394.

11. Ibid., pp. 35–36.

12. The one exception to this observation is Seeger's essay "Tractatus Esthetico-Semioticus," which is a comprehensive synoptic theory of human communication. In this study music is merely one among many forms of communication.

13. All told, Seeger considered at least three other titles for the treatise, including *Tradition and Experiment in Musical Composition, Tradition and Experiment in the Musical Idiom,* and *Tradition and Invention in Musical Composition in the Occidental World.*

14. Charles Louis Seeger, "Reminiscences of an American Musicologist," ed. Adelaide Tusler and Ann Briegleb, The Oral History Program (Los Angeles: University of California, 1972), p. 209.

15. Seeger writes: "In 1930 I wrote a book, *Tradition and Experiment in Music Composition* . . . that was strictly structuralist in the sense of the current vogue of the term. . . . But the almost explosive force of the Great Depression, with its bringing to my attention my ignorance of folk and popular music and the musics of the non-European cultures, made me realize that I had told only half the story. The other half was in comparative musicology: and I knew precious little of that. So I never published the thing." See Chase, "An Exagmination," p. 139.

16. Charles Louis Seeger, *Studies in Musicology II: 1929–1979,* ed. Ann Pescatello (Berkeley: University of California Press, 1994), p. 6.

17. Mark D. Nelson, "In Pursuit of Charles Seeger's Heterophonic Ideal: Three Palindromic Works by Ruth Crawford," *The Musical Quarterly* 57 (1986): 458–75.

18. David Nicholls, *American Experimental Music, 1890–1940* (Cambridge: Cambridge University Press, 1990).

19. Charles Louis Seeger, "On Dissonant Counterpoint," *Modern Music* 7, no. 4 (June/July 1930): 25–31.

20. Joseph N. Straus, *The Music of Ruth Crawford Seeger* (Cambridge: Cambridge University Press, 1995).

21. Judith Tick, *Ruth Crawford Seeger: A Composer's Search for American Music* (New York: Oxford University Press, 1997).

22. Ruth Crawford, letter to Charles Seeger, September 20, 1930; cited

in Matilda Gaume, *Ruth Crawford Seeger: Memoirs, Memories, Music* (Metuchen, N.J.: Scarecrow Press, 1986), p. 152. For more details regarding the genesis of the treatise, see Tick, *Ruth Crawford Seeger,* pp. 131–33.

23. Item #18, Charles Seeger Archive, Music Library, University of California, Berkeley. Pescatello included Crawford's comments in the endnotes to the treatise. See *Studies in Musicology II, 1929–1979,* pp. 267–73.

24. However, in a 1974 interview with Matilda Gaume, Seeger said, "I think it was that summer that knocked her out, knocked me out too. It knocked us out from my making the examples for the book and her continuing composition of the fine art of music." See Gaume, *Ruth Crawford Seeger,* p. 86.

25. For a more detailed biography, see Pescatello's *Charles Seeger.* Much of what follows is based on her study.

26. For a brief biography of Charles's brother, see William Archer's introduction in Alan Seeger, *Poems* (New York: Scribner, 1916), pp. xi–xlvi.

27. Seeger, "Reminiscences," p. 41.

28. The reason Seeger graduated with honors was the high caliber of his senior composition, an orchestral overture entitled *The Shadowy Waters,* not his cumulative grade point average! See Seeger, "Reminiscences," pp. 50–53.

29. Ibid., pp. 85–86.

30. Ibid., p. 88.

31. Ibid., pp. 88–90, 109–13.

32. In an unpublished foreword to *Principia Musicologica,* Seeger remembers reading the Veda with the help of A. W. Ryder. See Charles Seeger Collection, Music Library, Library of Congress, Box 51.

33. Seeger, "Reminiscences," p. 112.

34. Charles Louis Seeger, "Henry Cowell," *Magazine of Art* 33 (May 1940): 288.

35. Seeger, "Reminiscences," p. 106.

36. The relationship between Cowell's *New Musical Resources* and Seeger's *Tradition and Experiment in the New Music* is somewhat complex. On the one hand, although Cowell never mentions his mentor in his own treatise, it seems certain that the concept of "dissonant counterpoint" grew out of their private composition lessons in the teens. In a 1940 essay devoted to Cowell, Seeger claimed that his former student "swiped many of his best (and some of his worst) 'ideas' from me, and occasionally acknowledges it." Yet, on the other hand, Cowell may well have participated in the creative process. Later in the same essay Seeger describes their teaching rapport as follows "Suggestion is the rule; precept, taboo. This works beautifully where one of the collaborators is prolific of ideas but too lazy to use them, while the other is exceptionally energetic in the use not only of his own but of any and all within hailing distance." See "Henry Cowell," *Magazine of Art* 33 (May 1940): 288. The answers to the question of influence must wait until there is greater access to Cowell's private papers on deposit at the New York

Public Library, especially the revised manuscript of *New Musical Resources* and the unpublished study of melody he wrote while in prison.

37. Interview with Vivian Perlis, March 16, 1970. Oral History Project, Music Library, Yale School of Music, p. 21.

38. Marilyn Ziffrin, *Carl Ruggles: Composer, Painter, and Storyteller* (Urbana: University of Illinois Press, 1994), p. 64.

39. Letter from Ruth Crawford to Alice, quoted in Matilda Gaume, "Ruth Crawford: A Promising Young Composer in New York, 1929–30," *American Music* 5 (1987): 79.

40. Obituary by Archie Green, *Journal of American Folklore* 92 (1979): 394.

41. They include *Our Singing Country* (1941), *Folk Song U.S.A.* (1947), *American Folk Songs for Children* (1948), *Animal Folk Songs for Children* (1950), and *American Folk Songs for Christmas* (1953).

42. Charles Louis Seeger, "Versions and Variants of 'Barbara Allen' in the Archive of American Song to 1940," In *Studies in Musicology, 1935–1975* (Berkeley: University of California Press, 1977), pp. 273–320.

43. Pescatello, *Charles Seeger*, pp. 252–56.

44. Ibid., p. viii.

45. "Charles Seeger," in *American Composers on American Music*, ed. Henry Cowell (Stanford, Calif.: Stanford University Press, 1933), p. 120.

46. Tick, *Ruth Crawford Seeger*, p. 221. For this dichotomy Tick relies on an essay by Daniel J. Singal, "Toward a Definition of American Modernism," *American Quarterly* 39 (Spring 1987): 10, who, in turn, borrows and adapts T.J. Jackson Lears's notion of "antimodernism" in *No Place for Grace: Antimodernism and the Transformation of American Culture, 1880–1920* (Chicago: University of Chicago Press, 1981).

Chapter 1:
Bergson's Intuition and Seeger's Predicament

1. Bertrand Russell, *The Basic Writings of Bertrand Russell: 1903–1959*, ed. Robert E. Egner and Lester E. Denonn (New York: Simon and Schuster, 1961), p. 262.

2. According to Pescatello, Seeger was the first American to offer a university course not only in the history of Western music but also in the discipline of musicology. See Ann M. Pescatello, *Charles Seeger: A Life in American Music* (Pittsburgh: University of Pittsburgh Press, 1992), pp. 57, 72.

3. Interview with Vivian Perlis, March 16, 1970, Oral History Project, Yale School of Music, p. 20. Strictly speaking, Seeger couldn't have read the essay before he graduated from Harvard in 1908 because Russell wrote it in 1914.

4. See Charles Louis Seeger, "Reminiscences of an American Musicologist," ed. Adelaide Tusler and Ann Briegleb, The Oral History Program. Los

Angeles: University of California, 1972, p. 426; and unpublished foreword, *Principia Musicologica,* Charles Seeger Collection, Music Division, Library of Congress, Box 51, p. iii.

5. In the collection as a whole Russell addresses a variety of topics in logical theory and outlines his vision of a scientific approach to philosophy.

6. Ralph Barton Perry, *The Present Conflict of Ideals: A Study of the Philosophical Background of the World War* (New York: Longmans, Green, 1918), pp. 348–63. In the preface dated August 15, 1918, Perry writes: "The following lectures were delivered at the University of California while I had the honor and good fortune to be Lecturer on the Mills Foundation from January to May of the present year. I am publishing them in virtually the same form as that in which I delivered them . . ." (p. iii).

7. Seeger, "Reminiscences," pp. 111–12.

8. Michel-Dimitri Calvocoressi, *The Principles and Methods of Musical Criticism* (London: H. Milford, 1923), p. 109.

9. Leszek Kolakowski, *Bergson* (Oxford: Oxford University Press, 1985), p. 1.

10. Ibid., p. 1.

11. These two terms are drawn from Sanford Schwartz's penetrating essay "Bergson and the Politics of Vitalism," in *The Crisis in Modernism: Bergson and the Vitalist Controversy,* ed. Frederick Burwick and Paul Douglass (Cambridge: Cambridge University Press, 1992), pp. 277–305.

12. They were Jules Lachelier (1832–1918) and Emile Boutroux (1845–1921).

13. Henri Bergson, "Philosophical Intuition," in *The Creative Mind,* English trans. Mabelle L. Andison (New York: Greenwood Press, 1968), p. 132.

14. Kolakowski makes the same point in his short but eloquent overview of Bergson's thought. See *Bergson,* p. 2.

15. Henri Bergson, *Introduction to Metaphysics,* trans. T. E. Hulme (Indianapolis: Bobbs-Merrill, 1949), p. 24.

16. Ibid., p. 114–15.

17. As it turns out, Bergson's utilitarian conception of the rational intellect was to exercise an enormous influence on the ideas of the American philosopher William James.

18. Paul Edwards, ed., *Encyclopedia of Philosophy* (New York: Macmillan, 1967), 1:291.

19. Bergson, *Introduction to Metaphysics,* pp. 23–24.

20. A. R. Lacey, *Bergson* (London: Routledge, 1989), p. 153.

21. Bergson, *Introduction to Metaphysics,* p. 51.

22. Bergson, *The Creative Mind,* p. 127.

23. Edwards, ed., *Encyclopedia of Philosophy,* 1: 290.

24. For an English translation of an excerpt from *Laughter* see Melvin Rader, ed., *A Modern Book of Esthetics: An Anthology,* rev. ed. (New York:

Henry Holt, 1952), pp. 114–26. Other excerpts that address aesthetic issues include *Time and Free Will* (1910), pp. 11–18 and *The Creative Mind* (1968), pp. 159–63.

25. Rader, *A Modern Book of Esthetics,* p. 114.

26. Ibid., p. 118.

27. Ibid., p. 116.

28. Ibid., p. 115.

29. Ibid., p. 117.

30. Ibid., pp. 117–18.

31. Charles Louis Seeger, "On the Principles of Musicology," *The Musical Quarterly* 10 (1924): 244–50. According to Seeger's biographer, Ann Pescatello, he completed a draft of this essay between 1918 and 1920, long before it was published. See Pescatello, *Charles Seeger,* p. 90. Pescatello also quotes generously from an earlier unpublished manuscript entitled "Toward an Establishment of the Study of Musicology in America" (pp. 55–7) which I have not been able to locate.

32. Charles Louis Seeger, "Prolegomena to Musicology: The Problem of the Musical Point of View and the Bias of Linguistic Presentation" *Eolus* 4 (1925): 12–24.

33. Seeger, "Principles," p. 244.

34. Considering his own ignorance of previous writings about musicology as a discipline, it is ironic that he blames musicologists for their blindness toward method. He later observed that all of his early work was written under the influence of Guido Adler's 1887 essay. See *Studies in Musicology, 1935–1975* (Berkeley: University of California Press, 1977), p. 2.

35. Seeger, "Principles," p. 244.

36. Ibid., p. 247.

37. Seeger, "Prolegomena," p. 13.

38. Ibid., p. 16.

39. Ibid.

40. Seeger, "Principles," p. 245.

41. Ibid., p. 247.

42. Ibid.

43. Ibid., pp. 245–46.

44. The final section of "Principles" and the entire essay entitled "Prolegomena" are devoted to the problem of music and language.

45. Seeger, "Principles," p. 246.

46. Ibid.

47. The first appearance of this term is in "Prolegomena," p. 18, but the dilemma is strongly suggested in his other article on musicology, "Principles."

48. Victor E. Harlow, *A Bibliography and Genetic Study of American Realism* (Oklahoma City: Harlow, 1931), p. 20.

49. This principle of logic was first coined by Mill in his compendium *Sys-*

tem of Logic (1843). See J. L. Mackie, "Mill's Methods of Induction," in Edwards, *Encyclopedia of Philosophy*, 3:324–32.

50. Ralph Perry, *Present Philosophical Tendencies: A Critical Survey of Naturalism, Idealism, Pragmatism, and Realism with a Synopsis of the Philosophy of William James* (New York: Longmans, Green, 1912), p. 130.

51. Seeger, "Prolegomena," pp. 14–15.

52. In all fairness to Seeger, although he uses the term "intuition" sporadically in his two early essays, he never explicitly claims that his standard of musicological truth, the "musical" point of view, is a product of the faculty of intuition. Nevertheless, their common reliance on the concept of immediacy provides overwhelming evidence that Seeger's theory is intuitionist in nature. In addition, Bergson's philosophy can be interpreted in part as a repudiation of Charles Darwin's theory of natural selection. Since there were no revolutions in musicology comparable to Darwin's in biology, Seeger's antirational spirit reflects indirectly his reaction against the ideas of Darwin.

53. George Santayana, *Winds of Doctrine* (New York: Scribner, 1913), p. 58.

54. Ibid., p. 73.

Chapter 2:
Russell's Synthesis of Mysticism and Logic

1. Charles Louis Seeger, *Studies in Musicology II: 1929–1979*, ed. Ann Pescatello (Berkeley: University of California Press, 1994), p. 52.

2. In all fairness to Seeger, hints of this balanced view are already evident in his early essay: "We cannot, I think, avoid the assumption that if any particular instance of talking or writing about music is logically sound (allowing for reasonable possibility for error) it may benefit the conduct of the art of music." See Charles Louis Seeger, "On the Principles of Musicology," *The Musical Quarterly* 10 (1924): 245.

3. Charles Louis Seeger, "Preface to a Critique of Music," *Primera Conferencia interamericana de etnomusicologia: Trabajos presentados*, Cartagena de Indias, Colombia, 24–28 February 1963 (Washington, D.C.: Pan American Union, 1965).

4. Richard A. Reuss, "Folk Music and Social Conscience: The Musical Odyssey of Charles Seeger," *Western Folklore* 38 (October 1979): 225. Pescatello also quotes from a letter that Seeger wrote to Reuss in which he expresses his admiration of Russell's pacifist views. See *Charles Seeger*, p. 80.

5. Frederick Copleston, *A History of Philosophy*, vol. 8, *Bentham to Russell* (Westminster, Md.: Newman Press, 1966; reprint, New York: Doubleday, 1967), p. 425.

6. Bertrand Russell, *The Collected Papers of Bertrand Russell*, vol. 12, ed.

Richard Rempel, Andrew Brink, and Margaret Moran (London: George Allen and Unwin: 1985), pp. xx–xxii.

7. Ibid., p. xxiii.

8. Ibid., pp. 97–101.

9. The only record of their joint collaboration is a series of outlines and fragments of the manuscript. See ibid., pp. 102–09.

10. Ibid., p. xxv.

11. See Bertrand Russell, "Spinoza's Moral Code," Unsigned review of J. Allanson Picton, *Spinoza: A Handbook to the Ethics, The Nation* 1 (April 13, 1907): 276; and Bertrand Russell, "Spinoza," review of Spinoza, *The Ethics,* Eng. trans. W. Hale White, *The Nation* 8 (November 12, 1910): 278, 280.

12. Russell, *Collected Papers*, p. xxvii.

13. In his American tour Russell read the speech to gatherings in Greenwich, Connecticut; Wellesley College, Wellesley, Massachusetts; and Madison, Wisconsin.

14. Bertrand Russell, "Mysticism and Logic," *Hibbert Journal* 12 (July 1914): 780–803.

15. Russell, *Collected Papers*, p. 158.

16. This lecture was later published along with a reply in Bergson's defense by H. Wildon Carr, followed by a rejoinder from Russell. See *The Philosophy of Bergson* (Cambridge: Bowes and Bowes, 1914). Interestingly enough, two years later Russell delivered an early version of "Mysticism and Logic" at the very same forum.

17. Russell, *Collected Papers*, p. 166.

18. Ibid., pp. 166–67.

19. Ibid., p. 168.

20. Ibid., p. 165.

21. Ibid., p. 168.

22. Ibid., p. 164.

23. Ibid., p. 165.

24. Alan Wood, *Bertrand Russell: The Passionate Sceptic* (London: George Allen and Unwin, 1957), pp. 61–62.

25. Apparently Russell himself regarded T. S. Eliot's review of the set of essays as the only one that "showed any understanding" (ibid., p. 95). Unfortunately, though Eliot praises the collection as a whole, his remarks throw little light on the essay itself. Eliot claims that Russell was an "emancipated Puritan," by which he meant that, although Russell was eager to deny God, he was adamant about enforcing a strict moral code. See Thomas Stearns Elliot, Review of Bertrand Russell, *Mysticism and Logic and Other Essays, The Nation* 22 (March 23 1918): 768, 770.

26. Russell, *Collected Papers*, p. xx.

27. Charles Louis Seeger, "On the Principles of Musicology," *The Musical Quarterly* 10 (1924): 248.

28. Charles Louis Seeger, "Prolegomena to Musicology: The Problem of the Musical Point of View and the Bias of Linguistic Presentation," *Eolus* 4 (1925): 19.

29. Ibid., p. 14.

30. Ibid.

31. Ibid.

32. Ibid., p. 13.

33. Ibid., p. 15.

34. Ibid.

35. Ibid., p. 18.

36. Charles Louis Seeger, *Studies in Musicology, 1935–1975* (Berkeley: University of California Press, 1977), p. 2.

37. Seeger, "Prolegomena," p. 20.

38. Ibid., p. 21.

39. Ibid., p. 22.

40. In a later article Seeger experiments with new versions of Aristotle's three laws of logic (identity, contradiction, and the excluded middle) that, he believes, are more appropriate for the art of music. See "On the Moods of a Music Logic," in *Studies in Musicology, 1935–1975*, pp. 69–73.

41. Seeger, "Prolegomena," pp. 14–15.

42. Ibid., p. 23.

43. Ibid., p. 19.

44. Ibid., p. 23.

45. Charles Louis Seeger and Edward Griffith Stricklen, *Harmonic Structure and Elementary Composition: An Outline of a Course in Practical Musical Invention,* rev. ed. (Berkeley: n.p., 1916).

46. In his article on "dialectic," Roland Hall explains that in the late dialogues Plato employs a method of dividing "more general notions into less general ones, as a way of arriving at a definition when no further division is possible." See Paul Edwards, ed., *Encyclopedia of Philosophy* (New York: Macmillan, 1967), 2:386.

47. Robert Grogin, *The Bergsonian Controversy in France 1900–1914* (Calgary: University of Calgary Press, 1988), p. 2.

48. Seeger, "Reminiscences," p. 110.

49. Ernest Nagel, introduction to *The Grammar of Science* by Karl Pearson (New York: Meridian Books, 1957), p. vi.

50. Ibid., p. 46.

51. Ibid., p. 37.

52. Ibid., p. 110.

53. Ibid., p. 31.

54. Ibid., p. 12.

55. William James, *Pragmatism* (Cambridge, Mass.: Harvard University Press, 1975), p. 11.

56. Ibid., p. 12.

57. Ibid., p. 17.

58. Ibid., p. xxxi.

59. Ibid., p. 28.

60. Ibid., p. 31.

61. Arthur O. Lovejoy, "The Thirteen Pragmatisms," *Journal of Philosophy* 5 (1908): 29–39.

Chapter 3: Perry's Philosophy of Value

1. Stephen C. Pepper, "A Brief History of General Theory of Value," in *A History of Philosophical Systems,* ed. Vergilius Ferm (New York: Philosophical Library, 1950), p. 496.

2. David Hume, *A Treatise of Human Nature,* ed. L. A. Selby-Bigge (Oxford: Clarendon Press, 1975), p. 469.

3. Charles R. Pigden, "Naturalism," in *A Companion to Ethics,* ed. Peter Singer (Oxford: Basil Blackwell, 1991), pp. 421–31.

4. A. Richard Konrad, "There Is No 'Fact-Value Gap' for Hume," *Journal of Value Inquiry* 4 (Summer 1970): 126–33.

5. Wilbur Marshall Urban, *Valuation, Its Nature and Laws, Being an Introduction to the General Theory of Value* (London: Swan Sonnenschein, 1909), p. 2.

6. Nicholas Rescher, *Introduction to Value Theory* (Englewood Cliffs, N.J.: Prentice-Hall, 1969), p. 50.

7. Ibid.

8. Ralph Barton Perry, *General Theory of Value* (New York: Longmans, Green, 1926), pp. 115–16.

9. Ibid., p. 3.

10. J. Prescott Johnson, "The Fact-Value Question in Early Modern Value Theory," *Journal of Value Inquiry* 1 (1967–68): 64–65.

11. Perry's source for behaviorism was the writings of E. C. Tolman. See Pepper, "A Brief History of Value," p. 497.

12. Ira S. Steinberg, *Ralph Barton Perry on Education for Democracy* (Columbus: Ohio State University Press, 1970), p. 47.

13. Pepper, "A Brief History of Value," p. 498.

14. Ralph Barton Perry, "Realism in Retrospect," in *Contemporary American Philosophy: Personal Statements,* ed. George Adams and William Montague (New York: Macmillan, 1930), vol. 2, p. 189.

15. Pepper, "A Brief History of Value," p. 497.

16. Perry, *General Theory of Value,* p. 667.

17. In the years since Perry unveiled his theory, the philosophical study of values has steadily fallen out of favor. Some critics charge that his initial definitions and framework are too vague. For instance, James Ward Smith ar-

gues that while everyone would agree that human beings have preferences, feelings, beliefs, and so forth, problems arise when someone tries to verify that these actually exist using traditional methods of empirical confirmation. Smith concludes that the study of these preferences, feelings, and so forth, belongs more to the field of psychology, and that such psychological description "can offer no satisfactory account of any actual 'values,' nor can it answer the simple question whether there *are* any actual 'values.' Indeed it is, as such, devoid of any distinctively philosophical subject matter" (p. 288). See Smith, "Should the General Theory of Value Be Abandoned?" *Ethics* 57 (1947): 274–88.

18. Charles Louis Seeger, "On the Principles of Musicology," *The Musical Quarterly* 10 (April 1924): 250.

19. Although Seeger unveils the notion of value only in the conclusion of the article, he implies it at various stages along the way. Such an organizational strategy gives a whole new meaning to Hume's aphorism "No 'ought' from 'is'"!

20. Charles Louis Seeger, "Prolegomena to Musicology: The Problem of the Musical Point of View and the Bias of Linguistic Presentation," *Eolus* 4 (1925): 15.

21. Ibid., p. 23.

22. Charles Louis Seeger, *Studies in Musicology II: 1929–1979*, ed. Ann Pescatello (Berkeley: University of California Press, 1994), p. 63.

Chapter 4: Seeger's Theory of Music Criticism

1. Charles Louis Seeger, *Studies in Musicology II: 1929–1979*, ed. Ann Pescatello (Berkeley: University of California Press, 1994), p. 52.

2. Seeger originally intended to reproduce an additional copy on the inside cover of the treatise for easy reference. See ibid., p. 71.

3. Ibid., p. 82.

4. Ibid., p. 79. Seeger's comment suggests that some aspects of his theory are intended as a stimulus for thought more than as a handbook for critical practice.

5. Ibid., p. 67.

6. Ibid., p. 65.

7. Ibid., p. 67.

8. Bertrand Russell, *The Collected Papers of Bertrand Russell*, vol. 12, *Contemplation and Action, 1902–14*, ed. Richard Rempel, Andrew Brink, and Margaret Moran (London: George Allen and Unwin, 1985), p. 165.

9. Ibid., p. 158.

10. Charles Louis Seeger, *Studies in Musicology, 1935–1975* (Berkeley: University of California Press, 1977), p. 105.

11. Seeger, *Studies in Musicology II: 1929–1979*, p. 66.

12. Ibid.

13. *Oxford English Dictionary,* vol. 17, p. 61.

14. It is curious that, after going to the trouble of coining a separate word to reflect the unique character of critical value, in the chapters that follow Seeger seldom uses it again.

15. Seeger, *Studies in Musicology II: 1929–1979,* p. 69.

16. Ibid., p. 71.

17. Ibid., p. 70.

18. Charles Louis Seeger, "On Style and Manner in Modern Composition," *The Musical Quarterly* 9 (1923): 427.

19. Ibid., p. 428.

20. See Paul Hindemith, *A Composer's World: Horizons and Limitations* (Cambridge, Mass.: Harvard University Press, 1952), pp. 1–13.

21. Although the diagram in figure 4 does not explicitly show it, Seeger hopes that, in exploring the question of "ethos," critics will also take advantage of the analysis of musical phenomena that is offered by modern science. In the diagram the category "General Science" appears in parenthesis next to the word "Reason." But what is not made clear is the relation that scientific knowledge has with Seeger's version of "ethical" significance. Regrettably, this question underlines the greatest point of ambiguity in Seeger's entire theory of criticism.

22. See "Tractatus Esthetico-Semioticus: Model of the Systems of Human Communication," in *Current Thought in Musicology,* ed. John W. Grubbs, Symposia in the Arts and Humanities, No. 4 (Austin: University of Texas Press, 1976), pp. 1–39.

23. Seeger, *Studies in Musicology II: 1929–1979,* p. 82.

24. Monroe C. Beardsley, review of *A Humanistic Philosophy of Music,* by Edward Lippman, *The Musical Quarterly* 66 (1980): 305–8.

25. Michel-Dimitri Calvocoressi, *The Principles and Methods of Musical Criticism* (London: H. Milford, 1923), p. 91.

26. Ralph Barton Perry, *General Theory of Value* (New York: Longmans, Green, 1926), p. vii.

27. Seeger, *Studies in Musicology II: 1929–1979,* p. 67n.

28. Ralph Barton Perry, in *Contemporary American Philosophy: Personal Statements,* ed. George P. Adams and William P. Montague (New York: Macmillan, 1930), vol. 2, pp. 198–99.

29. Ibid.

Chapter 5:
A Philosophy in Practice: Music Criticism

1. Charles Louis Seeger, "Carl Ruggles," *The Musical Quarterly* 18 (1932): 591.

2. Interview with Vivian Perlis, 16 March 1970. Oral History Project, Music Library, Yale School of Music, p. 65.

3. In his study of *Essays Before a Sonata,* J. Peter Burkholder argues that a fondness for dualism was one of three fundamental elements in Ives's aesthetic philosophy. Examples include "absolute" versus "program" music and "manner" versus "substance." The philosophical framework that embraced these dichotomies was ultimately inspired by the American transcendentalists Emerson and Thoreau. See Burkholder, *Charles Ives: The Ideas Behind the Music* (New Haven, Conn.: Yale University Press, 1985).

4. Both titles refer to Aeolus, the Greek god of the wind.

5. Dane Rudhyar, "Carl Ruggles and the Future of Dissonant Counterpoint," Part 1 of "Revolt of the Angels," *Eolian Review* 3, no. 1 (November 1923): 13–16; Charles Louis Seeger, "Reviewing a Review," Part 2 of "Revolt of the Angels," *Eolian Review* 3, no. 1 (November 1923): 16–23. The first version of *Angels* was completed in 1920–21 as part of a multimovement work entitled *Men and Angels.* Originally scored for five trumpets and 1 bass trombone, it was subsequently arranged for four trumpets and three trombones.

6. Charles Louis Seeger, "Carl Ruggles," in *American Composers on American Music,* ed. Henry Cowell (Stanford, Calif.: Stanford University Press, 1933), p. 15. In the original version Seeger used the phrase "with common fury." See Seeger, "Carl Ruggles," p. 578.

7. Seeger, "Reviewing a Review," p. 23.

8. Ibid., p. 16.

9. Ibid., p. 23.

10. It is particularly ironic that Seeger felt compelled to chastise Rudhyar for his neglect of intuition, for the latter had already become and would continue to be one of the leading American proponents of a mystical approach to musical experience. For a detailed study of Rudhyar's writings on music and their relationship to other ultramodernist composers, see Carol Oja, *Experiments in Modern Music: New York in the 1920s* (forthcoming).

11. Seeger, "Carl Ruggles," 578–92; "Charles Ives and Carl Ruggles," *Magazine of Art,* 32 (July 1939): 396–99; 435–37; and "In Memoriam: Carl Ruggles (1876–1971)," *Perspectives of New Music* 10 (1972): 171–74.

12. Seeger, "In Memoriam," p. 172.

13. Ibid., p. 173.

14. Ibid., pp. 172–73.

15. Seeger, "Carl Ruggles," p. 590.

16. Seeger, "In Memoriam," p. 172.

17. Seeger, "Charles Ives and Carl Ruggles," p. 397.

18. Seeger, "Carl Ruggles," p. 585.

19. Ibid., pp. 584–85, 587.

20. Ibid., p. 590.

21. In his article "Henry Cowell" Seeger recalls that when he first met

Cowell in 1913, the prodigy had already completed opus 110. Since Cowell's numbered works had reached only opus 50 by that time, Daniel S. Augustine concludes that Seeger's recollection is wrong by one year. See Augustine, "Four Theories of Music in the United States, 1900–1950: Cowell, Yasser, Partch, Schillinger" (Ph.D. diss., University of Texas, Austin, 1979), p. 4.

22. Charles Louis Seeger, "Reminiscences of an American Musicologist," interviewed by Adelaide Tusler and Ann Briegleb, Oral History Program, University of California at Los Angeles, 1972, p. 106.

23. Henry Cowell, *New Musical Resources* (New York: Something Else Press, 1969).

24. Charles Louis Seeger, "Henry Cowell," *Magazine of Art* 33 (May 1940): 288–89, 322–25, 327.

25. Ibid., p. 323.

26. Ibid., p. 288.

27. Ibid., p. 323.

28. Augustine, "Four Theories of Music in the United States," pp. 3–4.

29. Seeger, "Henry Cowell," p. 324.

30. Ibid., p. 325.

31. Two composers on whom Cowell's theories exercised a profound influence were Lou Harrison and Conlon Nancarrow, the latter of whom took Cowell's approach to rhythmic subdivision as a point of departure for his own music.

32. Seeger, "Henry Cowell," p. 325.

33. Charles Louis Seeger, "Ruth Crawford," in *American Composers on American Music,* ed. Henry Cowell (Stanford, Calif.: Stanford University Press, 1933), pp. 110–18.

34. Four works that explore specific ways in which Crawford's music interacts with Seeger's theoretical ideals are Mark Nelson, "In Pursuit of Charles Seeger's Heterophonic Ideal: Three Palindromic Works by Ruth Crawford," *The Musical Quarterly* 57 (1986): 458–75; Judith Tick "Dissonant Counterpoint Revisited: The First Movement of Ruth Crawford's String Quartet 1931," in *Words and Music in Honor of H. Wiley Hitchcock,* ed. Richard Crawford, R. Allen Lott, and Carol Oja (Ann Arbor: University of Michigan Press, 1990); and Joseph Straus, *The Music of Ruth Crawford Seeger* (Cambridge: Cambridge University Press, 1995); and Judith Tick, *Ruth Crawford Seeger: A Composer's Search for American Music* (New York: Oxford University Press, 1997).

35. Seeger, "Ruth Crawford," pp. 116, 118.

36. Johann Wolfgang von Goethe, "The Collector and His Circle," in *Essays on Art and Literature,* trans. Ellen von Nardroff and Ernest H. von Nardroff (New York: Suhrkamp, 1986), pp. 121–59. Seeger explicitly mentions Goethe as his source in his explanation of the importance of showmanship in contemporary music; see Seeger, "Ruth Crawford," p. 117.

37. For a detailed description of the entire scheme, see *Essays on Art and Literature*, pp. 153–59.

38. Seeger, "Ruth Crawford," p. 117.

39. Ibid., p. 113.

40. Crawford's application for a Guggenheim Foundation fellowship includes the following two aims: "To write one major work of the general magnitude of a symphony, for full orchestra, and various minor works for smaller combinations." During her year abroad she achieved only the second aim. See Matilda Gaume, *Ruth Crawford Seeger: Memoirs, Memories, Music* (Metuchen, N.J.: Scarecrow Press, 1986), p. 74.

41. Judith Tick, "Ruth Crawford's 'Spiritual Concept': The Sound-Ideals of an Early American Modernist," *Journal of the American Musicological Society* 44 (Summer 1991): 223.

42. Seeger, "Charles Ives and Carl Ruggles," p. 397; also see Seeger, "Reviewing a Review," p. 19.

43. Charles Louis Seeger, *Studies in Musicology II: 1929–1979*, ed. Ann Pescatello (Berkeley: University of California Press, 1994), p. 52.

44. Seeger, "Reviewing a Review," p. 21.

45. Seeger, *Studies in Musicology II*, pp. 146–47, 160.

46. Seeger, *Studies in Musicology II*, p. 192.

47. In this respect, it is curious that Seeger gave Stravinsky so little credit for the rhythmic innovations displayed in such works as *Le Sacre du printemps* and *L'Histoire du soldat*. While by no means as systematic as Cowell's *Quartet Romantic*, these two works clearly explore new dimensions of rhythmic organization that cannot be found in the traditions of late romanticism.

Chapter 6:
A Philosophy in Practice: Compositional Theory

1. Charles Louis Seeger, *Studies in Musicology II: 1929–1979*, ed. Ann Pescatello (Berkeley: University of California Press, 1994), p. 52.

2. Ibid., p. 57.

3. Ibid., p. 5. Ann Pescatello quotes this source as part of her rationale for which of Seeger's essays she chose to include in her collection.

4. Ibid., p. 57.

5. Gilbert Chase provides an excerpt from a letter Seeger wrote to him about the treatise's failure to address non-Western music. See Chase, "An Exagmination [*sic*] Round His Factification for Incamination of Work in Progress (Review Essay and Reminiscence)," *Yearbook of the International Folk Music Council* 11 (1979): 139.

6. See Charles Louis Seeger, "On the Moods of a Music Logic," in *Studies in Musicology, 1935–1975* (Berkeley: University of California Press, 1977), pp. 64–101.

7. Seeger, *Studies in Musicology II*, p. 90 n.

8. Ibid., p. 86.

9. Ibid., p. 87.

10. Ibid., p. 94.

11. James Tenney, *A History of "Consonance" and "Dissonance"* (New York: Excelsior, 1988).

12. Ibid., pp. 95–97.

13. Seeger concludes: "The chief fault of the Schönberg school, as of all the others, seemed to lie not in the handling of dissonance, but of consonance. All went well as long as a thoroughly dissonant structure was maintained, but upon the first introduction of consonance, a feeling of disappointment, of defeat, frequently occurred. It was as if there were holes in the fabric." See Charles Louis Seeger, "On Dissonant Counterpoint," *Modern Music* 7, no. 4 (June/July 1930): 26.

14. Ibid., p. 25.

15. Seeger, *Studies in Musicology II*, p. 85.

16. Ibid., p. 94.

17. Regarding timbre, Seeger observes that "consonant" tone quality is the rule in single melodic lines, whereas "dissonant" tone quality has become fashionable in polyphonic textures during the nineteenth and early twentieth centuries. He finally concludes that until a concept of gamut is developed for this function, it is premature to describe the phenomenon of timbre with pitch-based terms. See ibid., pp. 100–101.

18. This chart appears in *Studies in Musicology II*, p. 102.

19. Ibid., p. 79. In his assessment of Henry Cowell's version of a proportional analogue to the harmonic series, Daniel S. Augustine argues that, since the perception of rhythm is fundamentally different from that of pitch, the analogy is bankrupt. See Augustine, "Four Theories of Music in the United States, 1900–1950: Cowell, Yasser, Partch, Schillinger" (Ph.D. diss., University of Texas, Austin, 1979), pp. 54–58.

20. Schoenberg argues that through the evolution of music composers have exploited intervals whose ratios are higher and higher in the overtone series. See *Theory of Harmony*, trans. Roy E. Carter (Berkeley: University of California Press, 1978), p. 21.

21. Seeger, *Studies in Musicology II*, p. 104.

22. Johann Wolfgang von Goethe, "The Collector and His Circle," in *Essays on Art and Literature*, trans. Ellen von Nardroff and Ernest H. von Nardroff (New York: Suhrkap, 1986), pp. 121–59. For further discussion of this scheme, see chapter 5.

23. The "serious" manners include "imitators," "characterizers," and "miniaturists"; the "playful" manners include "phantomists," "undulators," and "sketchers."

24. Seeger initially introduced the distinction in one of his first publica-

tions: "On Style and Manner in Modern Composition," *The Musical Quarterly* 9 (July 1923): 423–31. Elsewhere he explicitly mentions Goethe as his source in his discussion of showmanship in contemporary music; see Seeger, "Ruth Crawford," *American Composers on American Music*, ed. Henry Cowell (Stanford, Calif.: Stanford University Press, 1933), p. 117.

25. Seeger also employed Goethe's dichotomy between "style" and "manner" to diagnose what he felt was wrong with the leading European composers after World War I. Stravinsky epitomized the "Neo-Classical" manner; Scriabin typified the "Neo-Romantic" manner; and Schoenberg represented a third unnamed manner. See Seeger, *Studies in Musicology II*, pp. 51–52, 73–74.

26. Ibid., p. 98.

27. Interview with Vivian Perlis, March 16, 1970. The Oral History Collection of American Music, Yale University, School of Music, p. 38.

28. Matilda Gaume, *Ruth Crawford Seeger: Memoirs, Memories, Music* (Metuchen, N.J.: Scarecrow Press, 1986), p. 71.

29. This movement has been discussed at length by the following commentators: David Nicholls, *American Experimental Music, 1890–1940* (Cambridge: Cambridge University Press, 1990), pp. 119–21; Joseph Straus, *The Music of Ruth Crawford Seeger* (Cambridge: Cambridge University Press, 1995), pp. 158–72; Ellie M. Hisama, "The Question of Climax in Ruth Crawford's String Quartet, Mvt. 3," in *Concert Music, Rock, and Jazz Since 1945: Essays and Analytical Studies* ed. Elizabeth West Marvin and Richard Hermann (Rochester, N.Y.: University of Rochester Press, 1995), pp. 285–312; and Judith Tick, *Ruth Crawford Seeger: A Composer's Search for American Music* (New York: Oxford University Press, 1997), pp. 212–22, 357–60.

30. This interest in the rate at which a musical parameter changes, whether it be pitch, tempo, or dynamics, was an ongoing theme in Seeger's writings beginning with the treatise. See "Prescriptive and Descriptive Music Writing," *Studies in Musicology, 1935–1975*, pp. 168–81.

31. These integers should not be construed as a "contour segment" as defined by Elizabeth West Marvin and Paul Laprade. See "Relating Musical Contours: Extensions of a Theory for Contour," *Journal of Music Theory* 31 (1987): 225–67.

32. For example, if the cellist sits to the left of the violist, to the right of the second violinist, and across from the first violinist, then a repeated pattern of rotation could be perceived in a live performance.

33. Letter to Edgard Varèse, May 29, 1948; cited in Carol Neuls-Bates, ed., *Woman in Music: An Anthology of Source Readings from the Middle Ages to the Present* (New York: Harper and Row, 1982), pp. 308–11.

34. Seeger, "On Dissonant Counterpoint," p. 28. Joseph Straus aptly describes the aesthetic contradiction that arises: "Ultra-modern music, then, is characterized by two deep, and deeply contradictory, impulses: one toward

heterogeneity and multiplicity, the other toward integration and unification. It pushes both terms of the dichotomy to their outermost limits." Straus, *The Music of Ruth Crawford Seeger,* pp. 219–20.

35. Charles Louis Seeger, "On Style and Manner in Modern Composition," *The Musical Quarterly* 9 (1923): 430.

36. Seeger, "On Dissonant Counterpoint," p. 26.

37. For more detailed studies of the relation between Seeger's theoretical speculations and Crawford's music, see Nicholls, *American Experimental Music,* pp. 89–133; Judith Tick, "Dissonant Counterpoint Revisited: The First Movement of Ruth Crawford's String Quartet 1931," in *Words and Music in Honor of H. Wiley Hitchcock,* ed. Richard Crawford, R. Allen Lott, and Carol Oja (Ann Arbor: University of Michigan Press, 1990), pp. 405–22; and Straus, *The Music of Ruth Crawford Seeger.*

38. *Studies in Musicology II,* p. 114.

39. In d'Indy's version the symmetry exists between the ascending C major scale and the descending Phrygian mode. See Vincent d'Indy, *Cours de composition musicale,* 3 vols. (Paris: Durand et fils, 1903), 1:101–2. While Seeger never directly acknowledges that he borrowed the idea from the French composer, he does briefly assess d'Indy's treatise in the introduction to *Tradition and Experiment in the New Music.* See *Studies in Musicology II,* p. 55.

40. Seeger, *Studies in Musicology II,* pp. 114–15.

41. Henry Cowell, *New Musical Resources,* with preface and notes by Joscelyn Godwin (New York: Something Else Press: 1969), p. 150.

42. *Tradition and Experiment in the New Music,* Charles Louis Seeger Archives, University of California, Berkeley, Music Library, Item no. 18, p. 58.

43. Charles Louis Seeger and Edward Stricklen, *Harmonic Structure and Elementary Composition: An Outline of a Course in Practical Musical Invention* (Berkeley: n.p., 1916), pp. 12–13. Seeger and Stricklen's formulation bears a strong resemblance to Riemann's dualistic model of harmony.

44. See Adolf Weidig, *Harmonic Material and Its Uses: A Treatise for Teachers, Students, and Music Lovers* (Chicago: Clayton F. Summy, 1923).

45. The theory of harmonic dualism was flourishing in American harmony textbooks long before Seeger took up his pen. Richard Devore explores various adaptations of dualism by two American authors, John C. Fillmore and Carl W. Grimm, in his essay "Nineteenth-Century Harmonic Dualism in the United States," *Theoria* 2 (1987): 85–100.

46. *Studies in Musicology II,* pp. 215–16.

47. Ibid., p. 137.

48. Ibid.

49. Ibid.

50. *Tradition and Experiment in the New Music,* Item #18, Seeger Archives.

51. For example, in his final collection of essays he referred to the scientist's perspective as a "phenomenon" in "general spacetime" and the artist's as a "normenon" in "music timespace." Apparently, in choosing these terms, he was inspired by developments in modern physics. See *Studies in Musicology, 1935–1975*, pp. 6–11.

52. Since one of Seeger's aims is to simplify his critical vocabulary, he forwent other neumatic signs such as the "porrectus" or "climacus." One infers that his reason for excluding them is either they contain too many notes (the "porrectus" contains four) or can be explained as the transformation of one of the two essential neumes (a "climacus" is a gestural inversion of a "scandicus").

53. It is curious that in his catalogue of neumes and neume-analogues Seeger neglects to take into account the "poise" inflection. This oversight stems from the original definition of the neume, which does not take into account a static melodic gesture (i.e., one that repeats the same pitch).

54. Seeger's source for his understanding of Cicero is the French theorist Jules Combarieu, who in turn was highly influenced by the writings of the German musicologist Rudolph Westphal. Combarieu's influence on Seeger will be discussed in greater depth below.

55. Seeger, *Studies in Musicology II*, p. 138.

56. Ibid., pp. 158–59.

57. See Charles Seeger, "On the Moods of a Music-Logic," *Journal of the American Musicological Society* 13 (1960): 224–61.

58. A representative sampling of research in this area can be found in the following works: Michael Friedmann, "A Methodology for the Discussion of Contour: Its Application to Schoenberg's Music," *Journal of Music Theory* 29 (1985): 223–48; Robert Morris, *Composition with Pitch-Classes: A Theory of Compositional Design* (New Haven, Conn.: Yale University Press, 1987); Elizabeth West Marvin and Paul Laprade, "Relating Musical Contours," 225–67; and Elizabeth West Marvin, "The Perception of Rhythm in Non-Tonal Music: Rhythmic Contours in the Music of Edgard Varèse," *Music Theory Spectrum* 13 (1991): 61–78. For a historical survey of theories of contour during the past thirty years, see Elizabeth West Marvin, "A Generalization of Contour Theory to Diverse Musical Spaces: Analytical Applications to the Music of Dallapiccola and Stockhausen," in *Concert Music, Rock, and Jazz Since 1945: Essays and Analytical Studies*, ed. Elizabeth West Marvin and Richard Hermann (Rochester, N.Y.: University of Rochester Press, 1995), pp. 135–171.

59. Seeger, *Studies in Musicology II*, p. 150.

60. Ibid.

61. Ibid., p. 151.

62. Seeger, "On Style and Manner in Modern Composition," pp. 423, 428.

63. Seeger, *Studies in Musicology II*, p. 157.

64. Ibid., p. 140.

65. An example of this redundancy is that the "intension" and "ellipsis" operations both denote a reduction of pitch and/or rhythmic material at a neume's beginning, middle, or end. Although Seeger does identify an eighth operation, "cancrizans," it is identical with the last of his four conversions. See Seeger, *Studies in Musicology II*, pp. 150–53.

66. Ibid., pp. 144–46.

67. Ibid., p. 146.

68. Analyses of this movement appear in Nicholls, *American Experimental Music*, pp. 108–9; and Straus, *The Music of Ruth Crawford Seeger*, pp. 7–8, 28–30, 42–45, 48–50, 54–56. The reader is encouraged to consult the original score.

69. Straus refers to Seeger's concept of "phrase-neume" as "motivic projection." See Straus, *The Music of Ruth Crawford Seeger*, pp. 57–59.

70. The reference to Combarieu is in the context of Seeger's attempts to define the musical phrase. Although Seeger and Combarieu both refer to Cicero's notion of an oratorical "period," neither adapts it to music. Compare Seeger, *Studies in Musicology II*, p. 138, and Jules Combarieu, *Théorie du rythme dans la composition musicale moderne* (Paris: Picard, 1897), p. 75.

71. D'Indy, *Cours de composition musicale*, 1:29 (translation mine).

72. " . . . une inégalité réelle dans la durée, dans l'intensité ou dans l'acuité des sons." Ibid., 1:25 (translation mine).

73. Ibid. D'Indy cites this particular work by Riemann.

74. Ibid., 1:29–46.

75. " . . . on peut considérer comme une sorte de syllabe musicale, servant à établir le discours musical, par le moyen des groupes et des périodes mélodiques." Ibid., 1:26 (translation mine).

76. Ibid., 1:25.

77. See Seeger, *Studies in Musicology II*, pp. 100, 135, 147, 150, 160, 217.

78. "I'd taken a seminar on Kant, but I hadn't been able to make any headway with his *Reinen* [*sic*] *Vernunft*. The sentences were too long and too verbose, and my German wasn't up to it, and I didn't have a translation." Charles Louis Seeger, "Reminiscences of an American Musicologist," ed. Adelaide G. Tusler and Ann M. Briegleb. Oral History Program, The University of California at Los Angeles, 1972, p. 112. Seeger mentions that a work by Freud, *Drei Abhandlungen*, was too difficult in the original German. See interview with Vivian Perlis, March 16, 1970, p. 12.

79. There are only three references to German sources. See Seeger, *Studies in Musicology II*, pp. 55–56. Also, on p. 79 Seeger cites the first historical survey of aesthetics to appear in English, Bernard Bosanquet's *A History of Aesthetic*.

80. Arnold Schoenberg, "Theory of Form" (1924), "Tonality and Form" (1925), and "Opinion or Insight?" (1926), all in *Style and Ideas*, ed. Leonard Stein, trans. Leo Black (Berkeley: University of California Press, 1975). An

English translation of "Tonality and Form" appeared in the *Christian Science Monitor* on December 19, 1925.

81. Arnold Schoenberg, "Problems of Harmony," trans. Adolph Weiss, *Modern Music* 11, no. 4 (May–June 1934): 167–87.

82. Arnold Schoenberg, *The Musical Idea and the Logic, Technique, and Art of Its Presentation,* edited, translated, and with a commentary by Patricia Carpenter and Severine Neff (New York: Columbia University Press, 1995).

83. See Alfred Einstein, "The Newer Counterpoint," *Modern Music* 6, no. 1 (November–December 1928): 29–34; Erwin Stein, "Schönberg's New Structural Form," *Modern Music* 7, no. 4 (June–July 1930): 3–10; Willi Reich, "Schönberg's New Männerchor," *Modern Music* 9, no. 2 (January–February 1932): 62–66; Richard S. Hill, "Schoenberg's Tone-Rows and the Tonal system of the Future," *The Musical Quarterly* 22 (1936): 14–37.

84. The following summary of the April 27 meeting appears in the *New York Musicological Society Bulletin,* no. 1 (November 1931): 4: "The presentation was held adequate, but exception was taken to the use of the word 'systematic' in connection with the subject. The consensus of opinion was that a romantic phantasy characterizes the 'composition in twelve tones' as well as the earlier work of the master. The question of the validity of the distinction between consonance and dissonance, and its relation to the propaedeutical discipline of preparation and resolution was sharply contested." One imagines that Seeger was doing most of the "contesting."

85. Adolph Weiss, "The Lyceum of Schönberg," *Modern Music,* vol. 9, no. 3 (March–April 1932): 100.

86. Arnold Schoenberg, *Fundamentals of Musical Composition,* ed. Gerald Strang and Leonard Stein (New York: St. Martin's Press, 1967), p. 8.

87. Arnold Schoenberg, "Schoenberg's Tone-Rows," in *Style and Idea,* ed. Leonard Stein, trans. Leo Black (Berkeley: University of California Press, 1975), p. 214.

88. Schoenberg, *The Musical Idea and the Logic, Technique, and Art of Its Presentation,* pp. 20–21.

89. Robert Fleisher, "Dualism in the Music of Arnold Schoenberg," *Journal of the Arnold Schoenberg Institute* 12 (June 1989): 22–42.

90. For a fascinating discussion of the role that theosophy and the occult played in Schoenberg's development, see John Covach, "Schoenberg and the Occult: Some Reflections on the Musical Idea," *Theory and Practice* 17 (1992): 103–18.

91. Camille Saint-Saëns, *Outspoken Essays on Music,* trans. Fred Rothwell (Freeport, N.Y.: Books for Libraries Press, 1969), pp. 9–10.

92. For more information about the American avant-garde in the early twentieth century, see Michael Broyles, *Mavericks and Other Traditions in American Music* (New Haven, Conn.: Yale University Press, forthcoming). For an insightful overview of musical theories at the turn of the century in

Europe and America, see Allen Forte, "Theory," *Dictionary of Contemporary Music,* ed. John Vinton (New York: E. P. Dutton, 1971), pp. 753–61.

93. Charles Seeger, review of *The Schillinger System of Musical Composition* by Joseph Schillinger, *Music Library Association Notes,* 2nd ser., 4, no. 2 (March 1947): 183–84.

94. "Combination," or "resultant," tones are an acoustical phenomenon in which two different tones, when sounding loudly, produce a third tone. The frequency of this third tone is the difference or sum of the frequencies of the two sounding tones or of their multiples.

95. David Neumeyer, *The Music of Paul Hindemith* (New Haven, Conn.: Yale University Press, 1986), p. 25.

96. Ibid., p. 30.

97. Victor Landau argues that the harmonic theories in the first volume of Hindemith's treatise are not reflected in a representative sampling of his chamber works; see Landau, "Paul Hindemith, a Case Study in Theory and Practice," *Musical Review* 21 (1960): 38ff. However, Neumeyer, drawing on ideas from the later writings such as *Traditional Harmony* (1943), presents an intricate and persuasive interpretation of a number of Hindemith's own works. See Neumeyer, *The Music of Paul Hindemith.* Seeger recalls that when Henry Cowell visited Germany on a Guggenheim fellowship in 1931–32, he claimed he saw copies of Seeger's course syllabus outlining the theory of dissonant counterpoint on the desks of Schoenberg and Hindemith. Seeger, however, had doubts about the truth of the story. See Seeger, "Reminiscences of an American Musicologist," p. 107.

98. Paul Hindemith, *The Craft of Musical Composition,* vol. 2, *Exercises in Two-Part Writing,* translated by Otto Ortmann (New York: Associated Music, 1941), p. viii.

99. Seeger, *Studies in Musicology II,* p. 54.

100. Claude Palisca, "American Scholarship in Western Music," in Frank L. Harrison, Mantle Hood, and Claude Palisca, *Musicology* (Englewood Cliffs, N.J.: Prentice-Hall, 1963), pp. 112–16. According to Palisca, "The musicologist is concerned with music that exists, whether as an oral or a written tradition, and with everything that can shed light on its human context" (p. 116).

101. This is why in my overview of Seeger's two theories of melody I counterbalanced works by Brahms and Beethoven with the first movement of Ruth Crawford's Diaphonic Suite #1. If Seeger's neumatic understanding of melody is to have the general properties he envisioned, then one should be able to apply it as effectively to tonal as to nontonal styles.

Chapter 7: Seeger's Vision of Musicology

1. Henry Cowell, "Charles Seeger," *American Composers on American Music,* ed. Henry Cowell (Stanford, Calif.: Stanford University Press, 1933), p. 118.

2. Charles Louis Seeger, "Systematic and Historical Orientations in Musicology," *Acta Musicologica* 11 (1939): 121–28.

3. Charles Louis Seeger, "Systematic Musicology: Viewpoints, Orientations, and Methods," *Journal of the American Musicological Society* 4 (Fall 1951): 240–48.

4. Charles Louis Seeger, "Sources of Evidence and Criteria for Judgment in the Critique of Music," in *Essays for a Humanist: An Offering to Klaus Wachsmann*, ed. Charles Seeger and Bonnie Wade (New York: Town House, 1977), pp. 261–76.

5. Charles Louis Seeger, "Toward a Unitary Field Theory," *Studies in Musicology, 1935–1975* (Berkeley: University of California Press, 1977), pp. 102–38.

6. For a comprehensive bibliography of the development of music historiography, see Ernst C. Krohn, "The Development of Modern Musicology," in *Historical Musicology: A Reference Manual for Research in Music*, ed. Lincoln B. Spiess (New York: Institute of Mediaeval Music, 1963), pp. 153–72.

7. Guido Adler, "Umfang, Methode und Ziel der Musikwissenschaft," *Vierteljahrschrift für Musikwissenschaft* 1 (1885): 5–20.

8. Ibid., p. 8 (translation mine).

9. Ibid., p. 17 (translation mine).

10. Waldo S. Pratt, "On Behalf of Musicology," *The Musical Quarterly* 1 (January 1915): 5.

11. Waldo S. Pratt, "The Scientific Study of Music," *Music Teachers' National Association: Proceedings of the Annual Meeting* (1890): 53.

12. Ibid.

13. Pratt, "On Behalf of Musicology," p. 5.

14. It should be emphasized that even though in his essay Pratt never provides a visual model of his scheme, he does provide a detailed account of the relationship between the categories "process" and "product." Figure 16 is based on that account.

15. In fact Seeger actually delivered this paper in 1935 at an annual meeting of the American Musicological Association in Philadelphia. See Seeger, "Systematic and Historical Orientations in Musicology," p. 121n.

16. Ibid., p. 121.

17. Ibid., pp. 123–24.

18. Ibid., p. 124.

19. Ibid., p. 125.

20. The only example he does offer is an image of musicology as a layer cake that can be cut either horizontally or vertically. The purpose of this hypothetical example is to illustrate the *interdependence* of systematic and historical orientations. See ibid., p. 122.

21. *The New Shorter Oxford English Dictionary* (Oxford: Clarendon Press, 1993), p. 3193.

22. In his 1951 essay "Systematic Musicology: Viewpoints, Orientations, and Methods," Seeger occasionally uses the term in this sense. My use of "encyclopedia" is somewhat different from the way Waldo Pratt uses the expression "Music Encyclopedia." See Pratt, "On Behalf of Musicology," p. 9.

23. Seeger, "Systematic and Historical Orientations in Musicology," pp. 122–23.

24. Ibid., pp. 126–27.

25. Charles Louis Seeger, *Studies in Musicology II: 1929–1979,* ed. Ann Pescatello (Berkeley: University of California Press, 1994), p. 56.

26. Seeger, "Systematic and Historical Orientations in Musicology," p. 126.

27. Seeger, "Systematic Musicology," p. 242.

28. Ibid., p. 241.

29. Frederick Copleston, *A History of Philosophy,* vol. 7, *Fichte to Nietzsche* (Westminster, Md.: Newman Press, 1963; reprint, New York: Doubleday, 1965), p. 1.

30. Seeger, *Studies in Musicology II,* p. 57.

31. "Systematic Musicology," p. 241.

32. Ibid., p. 245.

33. For a detailed account of these two terms and the role they play in the Seeger's early treatise, see the opening section of chapter 6.

34. Seeger, "Systematic Musicology," p. 244.

35. Ibid., pp. 243–44.

36. Seeger, *Studies in Musicology II,* p. 139.

37. Ibid., p. 138.

38. Charles Louis Seeger, *Studies in Musicology, 1935–1975* (Berkeley: University of California Press, 1977), p. 2. Seeger admits that his primary source for Saussure's theory was a book by the American linguist Leonard Bloomfield entitled *Language,* which he read sometime during the 1940s. See Seeger, "Systematic Musicology," p. 245.

39. Hans Aarsfell, *The Study of Language in England, 1780–1860* (Princeton: Princeton University Press, 1967), p. 127.

40. Leonard Bloomfield, *Language* (New York: Holt, Rinehart and Winston, 1933), pp. 19–20.

41. See Seeger, "Systematic Musicology," p. 245n.

42. See Ellie M. Hisama, "The Question of Climax in Ruth Crawford's String Quartet, Mvt. 3," in *Concert Music, Rock, and Jazz Since 1945: Essays and Analytical Studies,* ed. Elizabeth West Marvin and Richard Hermann (Rochester, N.Y.: University of Rochester Press, 1995), pp. 285–312.

43. Seeger, "Systematic Musicology," p. 240.

44. Seeger, "Sources of Evidence," p. 263.

45. Seeger, *Studies in Musicology II,* pp. 66, 69–70.

46. Seeger, "Sources of Evidence," p. 275.

47. Seeger, *Studies in Musicology II,* pp. 67–68.

48. In fact, there are seventeen, if one counts the introduction, which is a revised version of "Systematic Musicology: Viewpoints, Orientations, and Methods" (1951).

49. At the beginning of the dialogue he intimates that the literary conceit of a running conversation will be easier to understand than traditional expository prose. See Seeger, *Studies in Musicology, 1935–1975* p. 102.

50. Joseph Kerman, *Contemplating Music: Challenges to Musicology* (Cambridge, Mass.: Harvard University Press, 1985), p. 158.

51. Seeger, *Studies in Musicology, 1935–1975* p. 103.

52. Ibid., p. 108.

53. Ibid., pp. 108–10.

54. Ibid., insert between pp. 114 and 115.

55. The essays are "On the Formational Apparatus of the Music Compositional Process"; "Factorial Analysis of the Music Event"; "Preface to the Critique of Music"; "Systematic Musicology: Viewpoints, Orientations and Method"; and "The Music Process as a Function in a Nest of Functions and as in Itself a Nest of Functions." See *Studies in Musicology, 1935–1975*, insert between pp. 114 and 115. The titles of the last two essays differ slightly from those of the published versions: for example "The Music Process as a Function in a Nest of Functions and in Itself a Nest of Functions" appears later in the same collection.

56. Ibid., p. 125.

57. Ibid.

58. Ibid.

Epilogue:
Neume, New Music, New Musicology

1. R. G. Collingwood, *Principles of Art* (Oxford: Clarendon Press, 1938), pp. 1–3.

2. Ibid., p. 3.

3. An example of the latter is the American composer Lou Harrison, who proposes a method of composing melody he calls "melodicles" that he learned from Henry Cowell. See Heidi Von Gunden, *The Music of Lou Harrison* (Metuchen, New Jersey: Scarecrow Press, 1995), pp. 7–8.

4. Joseph Kerman, *Contemplating Music: Challenges to Musicology* (Cambridge, Mass.: Harvard University Press, 1985), p. 162.

5. Carolyn Abbate, *Unsung Voices: Opera and Musical Narrative in the Nineteenth Century* (Princeton: Princeton University Press, 1991); Scott Burnham, *Beethoven Hero* (Princeton: Princeton University Press, 1995); Thomas Christensen, "Music Theory and Its Histories," in *Music Theory and the Exploration of the Past,* ed. Christopher Hatch and David W. Bernstein (Chicago: University of Chicago Press, 1993); Brian Hyer, "Before Rameau

and After," *Music Analysis* 15 (March 1996): 75–100; and Susan McClary, *Feminine Endings: Music, Gender, and Sexuality* (Minneapolis: University of Minnesota Press, 1991).

6. Pierre Hadot, *Philosophy as a Way of Life*, trans. Michael Chase (Oxford: Blackwell, 1995).

7. Ibid., introduction by Arnold Davidson, p. 21.

8. Charles Louis Seeger, "On Style and Manner in Modern Composition," *The Musical Quarterly* 9 (1923): 430.

Bibliography

Manuscripts

Charles Seeger Archives, Music Library, University of California, Berkeley
Charles Seeger Collection, Music Division, Library of Congress, Washington, D.C.

Sources

Aarsfell, Hans. *The Study of Language in England, 1780–1860.* Princeton: Princeton University Press, 1967.

Abbate, Carolyn. *Unsung Voices: Opera and Musical Narrative in the Nineteenth Century.* Princeton: Princeton University Press, 1991.

Adams, George P., and William P. Montague, eds. *Contemporary American Philosophy: Personal Statements.* 2 vols. New York: Macmillan, 1930.

Adler, Guido. "Umfang, Methode und Ziel der Musikwissenschaft." *Vierteljahrschrift für Musikwissenschaft* 1 (1885): 5–20.

Augustine, Daniel S. "Four Theories of Music in the United States, 1900–1950: Cowell, Yasser, Partch, Schillinger." Ph.D. diss., University of Texas, Austin, 1979.

Bauer, Marion. *Twentieth Century Music: How It Developed, How to Listen to It.* New York: Putnam, 1933. Reprint, New York: Da Capo Press, 1978.

Beardsley, Monroe C. *Aesthetics: Problems in the* Philosophy of Criticism. 2nd ed. Indianapolis: Hackett, 1981.

———. Review of *A Humanistic Philosophy of Music,* by Edward Lippman. *The Musical Quarterly* 66 (1980): 305–8.

Bergson, Henri. *The Creative Mind.* Translated by Mabelle L. Andison. New York: Greenwood Press, 1968.

———. *Introduction to Metaphysics.* Translated by T. E. Hulme. Indianapolis: Bobbs-Merill, 1949.

———. *Mélanges.* Paris: Presses Universitaires de France, 1972.

———. *Time and Free Will: An Essay on the Immediate Data of Conscious-ness.* Translated by F. L. Pogson. London: George Allen and Unwin, 1910.

Bloomfield, Leonard. *Language.* New York: Holt, Rinehart and Winston, 1933.

Blum, Stephen. "Towards a Social History of Musicological Technique." *Ethnomusicology* 19 (1975): 208–24.

Bosanquet, Bernard. *A History of Aesthetic.* New York: Meridian, 1957.

Broyles, Michael. "Interests in the Musicological Juncture: On the Relationship Between History, Theory, and Criticism." *College Music Symposium* 23 (1983): 177–92.

———. Review of *Charles Seeger: A Life in American Music,* by Ann M. Pescatello. *American Music* 12 (Fall 1994): 333–37.

Burkholder, J. Peter. *Charles Ives: The Ideas Behind the Music.* New Haven, Conn.: Yale University Press, 1985.

———, ed. *Charles Ives and His World.* Princeton: Princeton University Press, 1996.

Burnham, Scott. *Beethoven Hero.* Princeton: Princeton University Press, 1995.

Burwick, Frederick, and Paul Douglass, eds. *The Crisis in Modernism: Bergson and the Vitalist Controversy.* Cambridge: Cambridge University Press, 1992.

Calvocoressi, Michel-Dimitri *The Principles and Methods of Musical Criticism.* London: H. Milford, 1923.

Carr, H. Wildon. *The Philosophy of Change: A Study of the Fundamental Principles of the Philosophy of Bergson.* London: Macmillan, 1914.

Chase, Gilbert. *America's Music: From the Pilgrims to the Present.* Revised 3rd ed. Urbana: University of Illinois Press, 1987.

———. "An Exagmination [*sic*] Round His Factification for Incamination of Work in Progress (Review Essay and Reminiscence)," *Yearbook of the International Folk Music Council* 11 (1979): 138–44.

Clark, Ronald. *The Life of Bertrand Russell.* London: Jonathan Cape, 1975.

Collingwood, R. G. *The Principles of Art.* Oxford: Clarendon Press, 1938.

Combarieu, Jules. *Théorie du rythme dans la composition musicale moderne.* Paris: Picard, 1897.

Copleston, Frederick. *A History of Philosophy.* Vol. 7, *Fichte to Nietzsche.* Vol. 8, *Bentham to Russell.* Vol. 9, *Maine de Biran to Sartre.* Westminster, Md.: Newman Press, 1963–74. Reprint, New York: Doubleday, 1965–77.

Cotkin, George. *Reluctant Modernism: American Thought and Culture, 1880–1900.* New York: Twayne, 1992.

Covach, John. "Schoenberg and the Occult: Some Reflections on the Musical Idea." *Theory and Practice* 17 (1992): 103–18.

Cowell, Henry, ed. *American Composers on American Music.* Stanford, Calif.: Stanford University Press, 1933.

———. *New Musical Resources.* New York: Knopf, 1930. Reprint, New York: Something Else Press, 1969.

———. *New Musical Resources.* With notes and an accompanying essay by David Nicholls. Cambridge: Cambridge University Press, 1996.

Craige, Betty Jean, ed. *Relativism in the Arts.* Athens: University of Georgia Press, 1983.

Dahlhaus, Carl. *Analysis and Value Judgment.* Translated by Siegmund Levarie. New York: Pendragon Press, 1983.

———. *Esthetics of Music.* Translated by William W. Austin. Cambridge: Cambridge University Press, 1982.

———. *Schoenberg and the New Music.* Translated by Derrick Puffett and Alfred Clayton. Cambridge: Cambridge University Press, 1987.

Devore, Richard. "Nineteenth-Century Harmonic Dualism in the United States." *Theoria* 2 (1987): 85–100.

Dunaway, David K. "Charles Seeger and Carl Sands: The Composers' Collective Years." *Ethnomusicology* 24 (May 1980): 159–68.

———. *How Can I Keep from Singing: Pete Seeger.* New York: McGraw-Hill, 1981.

Edwards, Paul, ed. *Encyclopedia of Philosophy.* 8 vols. New York: Macmillan, 1967.

Einstein, Alfred. "The Newer Counterpoint." *Modern Music* 6, no. 1 (November–December 1928): 29–34.

Eliot, Thomas Stearns. Review of *Mysticism and Logic and Other Essays,* by Bertrand Russell. *The Nation* 22 (March 23, 1918): 768, 770.

Epperson, Gordon. *The Musical Symbol: A Philosophic Theory of Music.* Ames: Iowa State University Press, 1967.

Fleisher, Robert. "Dualism in the Music of Arnold Schoenberg." *Journal of the Arnold Schoenberg Institute* 12, no. 1 (June 1989): 22–42.

Flower, Elizabeth, and Murray G. Murphey. *A History of Philosophy in America.* 2 vols. New York: Putnam, 1977.

Friedmann, Michael. "A Methodology for the Discussion of Contour: Its Application to Schoenberg's Music." *Journal of Music Theory* 29 (1985): 223–48.

Frondizi, Risieri. *What Is Value: An Introduction to Axiology.* 2nd ed. La Salle, Ill.: Open Court Publishing, 1971.

Gaume, Matilda. "Ruth Crawford: A Promising Young Composer in New York, 1929–30." *American Music* 5 (Spring 1987): 74–84.

———. *Ruth Crawford Seeger: Memoirs, Memories, Music.* Metuchen, N.J.: Scarecrow Press, 1986.

George, William Bernard. "Adolph Weiss." Ph.D. diss., University of Iowa, 1971.

Gode–von Aesch, Alexander. *Natural Science in German Romanticism.* New York: Columbia University Press, 1941.

Goethe, Johann Wolfgang von. "The Collector and His Circle." In *Essays on Art and Literature*, translated by Ellen von Nardroff and Ernest H. von Nardroff, 121–59. New York: Suhrkamp, 1986.

Green, Archie. Obituary of Charles Seeger. *Journal of American Folklore* 92 (1979): 391–99.

Griffin, Nicholas. *The Selected Letters of Bertrand Russell.* Vol. 1, *The Private Years, 1884–1914.* London: Penguin, 1992.

Grimes, Robert R. "Form, Content and Value: Seeger and Criticism to 1940." In *Foundations of a Modern Musicology: Understanding Charles Seeger,* edited by Bell Yung and Helen Rees (forthcoming).

Grogin, Robert C. *The Bergsonian Controversy in France 1900–1914.* Calgary: University of Calgary Press, 1988.

Hadot, Pierre. *Philosophy as a Way of Life.* Translated by Michael Chase. Oxford: Blackwell, 1995.

Hanna, Thomas, ed. *The Bergsonian Heritage.* New York: Columbia University Press, 1962.

Harlow, Victor E. *A Bibliography and Genetic Study of American Realism.* Oklahoma City: Harlow Publishing, 1931.

Hatch, Christopher, and David W. Bernstein, eds. *Music Theory and the Exploration of the Past.* Chicago: University of Chicago Press, 1993.

Hill, Richard S. "Schoenberg's Tone-Rows and the Tonal System of the Future." *The Musical Quarterly* 22 (1936): 14–37.

Hindemith, Paul. *A Composer's World: Horizons and Limitations.* Cambridge, Mass.: Harvard University Press, 1952.

———. *The Craft of Musical Composition.* 2 vols. Vol. 1, *Theoretical Part,* rev. ed. Translated by Arthur Mendel. Mainz: B. Schott's Söhne, 1945. Vol. 2, *Exercises in Two-Part Writing.* Translated by Otto Ortmann. New York: Associated Music, 1941.

Hisama, Ellie M. "The Question of Climax in Ruth Crawford's String Quartet, Mvt. 3." In *Concert Music, Rock, and Jazz Since 1945: Essays and Analytical Studies,* edited by Elizabeth West Marvin and Richard Hermann, 285–312. Rochester, N.Y.: University of Rochester Press, 1995.

Hitchcock, H. Wiley. "Americans on American Music." *College Music Symposium* 8 (1968): 138–42.

Hulme, Thomas E. *Speculations: Essays on Humanism and the Philosophy of Art.* Edited by Herbert Read. New York: Harcourt, Brace, 1924.

Hume, David. *An Inquiry Concerning Human Understanding.* Edited by Charles W. Hendel. Indianapolis: Bobbs-Merrill, 1955.

———. *A Treatise of Human Nature.* Edited by L. A. Selby-Bigge. Oxford: Clarendon Press, 1975. Reprint from original edition.

Hyer, Brian. "Before Rameau and After." *Music Analysis* 15 (March 1996): 75–100.

D'Indy, Vincent, with August Sérieyx. *Cours de composition musicale.* Vol. 1. Paris: Durand et fils, 1903.

Jackson Lears, T. J. *No Place for Grace: Antimodernism and the Transformation of American Culture, 1880–1920.* Chicago: University of Chicago Press, 1981.

James, William. *Pragmatism.* Cambridge, Mass.: Harvard University Press, 1975.

Johnson, J. Prescott. "The Fact-Value Question in Early Modern Value Theory." *Journal of Value Inquiry* 1 (1967–68): 64–71.

Jorgenson, Dale. "A Résumé of Harmonic Dualism." *Music and Letters* 44 (1963): 31–42.

Kerman, Joseph. *Contemplating Music: Challenges to Musicology.* Cambridge, Mass.: Harvard University Press, 1985.

Kern, Stephen. *The Culture of Time and Space 1880–1918.* Cambridge, Mass.: Harvard University Press, 1983.

Kirkpatrick, John. "The Evolution of Carl Ruggles: A Chronicle Largely in His Own Words." *Perspectives of New Music* 6 (1968): 146–66.

Kockelmans, Joseph J. *Philosophy of Science: The Historical Background.* New York: Free Press, 1968.

Kolakowski, Leszek. *Bergson.* Oxford: Oxford University Press, 1985.

Konrad, A. Richard. "There Is No 'Fact-Value Gap' for Hume." *Journal of Value Inquiry* 4 (Summer 1970): 126–33.

Krohn, Ernst C. "The Development of Modern Musicology." In *Historical Musicology: A Reference Manual for Research in Music,* edited by Lincoln B. Spiess, 153–72. New York: Institute of Mediaeval Music, 1963.

Lacey, A. R. *Bergson.* London: Routledge, 1989.

Landau, Victor. "Paul Hindemith, a Case Study in Theory and Practice." *Musical Review* 21 (1960): 38.

Lange, Frederick A. *The History of Materialism and Criticism of Its Present Importance.* 3 vols. in 1. Translated by Ernest C. Thomas. London: Routledge and Kegan Paul, 1925.

Lippman, Edward. *A History of Western Musical Aesthetics.* Lincoln: University of Nebraska Press, 1992.

List, George. "On the Non-Universality of Musical Perspectives." *Ethnomusicology* 15 (September 1971): 399–402.

Lomax, John A., and Alan Lomax, eds. *Folk Song U.S.A.: The 111 Best American Ballads.* New York: Duell, Sloan and Pearce, 1947.

———. *Our Singing Country.* New York: Macmillan, 1941.

Lovejoy, Arthur O. "The Thirteen Pragmatisms." *Journal of Philosophy* 5 (1908): 29–39.

Mandelbaum, M. Joel. "Multiple Division of the Octave and the Tonal Resources of 19-Tone Temperament." Ph.D. diss., Indiana University, 1961.

Marvin, Elizabeth West. "A Generalization of Contour Theory to Diverse Musical Spaces: Analytical Applications to the Music of Dallapiccola and Stockhausen." In *Concert Music, Rock, and Jazz Since 1945: Essays and*

Analytical Studies, edited by Elizabeth West Marvin and Richard Hermann, 135–71. Rochester, N.Y.: University of Rochester Press, 1995.

———. "The Perception of Rhythm in Non-Tonal Music: Rhythmic Contours in the Music of Edgard Varèse." *Music Theory Spectrum* 13 (1991): 61–78.

Marvin, Elizabeth West, and Paul Laprade. "Relating Musical Contours: Extensions of Theory for Contour." *Journal of Music Theory* 31 (1987): 225–67.

McClary, Susan. *Feminine Endings: Music, Gender, and Sexuality.* Minneapolis: University of Minnesota Press, 1991.

McMahan, Robert Young. "A Brief History of *The Sunken Bell*, Carl Ruggles's Unfinished Opera." *American Music* 11 (Summer 1993): 131–57.

Mead, Rita. *Henry Cowell's New Music 1925–36: The Society, the Music Editions, and the Recordings.* Ann Arbor, Mich.: UMI Research Press, 1981.

Meyer, Leonard B. *Music, the Arts, and Ideas: Patterns and Predictions in Twentieth-Century Culture.* Chicago: University of Chicago Press, 1967.

Morris, Robert. *Composition with Pitch-Classes: A Theory of Compositional Design.* New Haven, Conn.: Yale University Press, 1987.

Münsterberg, Hugo. *The Eternal Values.* Boston: Houghton Mifflin, 1909.

Murphey, Murray G., and Ivar Berg, eds. *Values and Value Theory in Twentieth-Century America: Essays in Honor of Elizabeth Flower.* Philadelphia: Temple University Press, 1988.

Nelson, Mark D. "In Pursuit of Charles Seeger's Heterophonic Ideal: Three Palindromic Works by Ruth Crawford." *The Musical Quarterly* 57 (1986): 458–75.

Nettl, Bruno. "The Dual Nature of Ethnomusicology in North America: The Contributions of Charles Seeger and George Herzog," *Comparative Musicology and Anthropology of Music: Essays on the History of Ethnomusicology,* ed. Bruno Nettl and Philip V. Bohlman Chicago: The University of Chicago Press, 1991.

———. "'Musical Thinking' and 'Thinking About Music' in Ethnomusicology: An Essay of Personal Interpretation." *Journal of Aesthetics and Art Criticism* 52 (Winter 1994): 139–48.

Neuls-Bates, Carol, ed. *Women in Music: An Anthology of Source Readings from the Middle Ages to the Present.* New York: Harper and Row, 1982.

Neumeyer, David. *The Music of Paul Hindemith.* New Haven, Conn.: Yale University Press, 1986.

Nicholls, David. *American Experimental Music, 1890–1940.* Cambridge: Cambridge University Press, 1990.

———. Review of *Studies in Musicology II: 1929–1979* by Charles Seeger and *The Music of Ruth Crawford Seeger* by Joseph N. Straus. *Music and Letters* 77 (February 1996): 140–43.

————. "Ruth Crawford Seeger: An Introduction." *Musical Times* 124 (July 1983): 421–25.

Oja, Carol J. "Women Patrons and Crusaders for Modernist Music: New York in the 1920s." In *Cultivating Music in America: Women Patrons and Activists Since 1860,* edited by Ralph P. Locke and Cyrilla Barr, 237–61. Berkeley: University of California Press, 1997.

Palisca, Claude. "American Scholarship in Western Music." In Frank L. Harrison, Mantle Hood, and Claude Palisca, *Musicology,* 89–213. Englewood Cliffs, N.J.: Prentice-Hall, 1963.

Papanicolaou, Andrew C., and Pete Gunter, eds. *Bergson and Modern Thought: Toward a Unified Science.* Vol. 3 of *Models of Scientific Thought.* Chur, Switzerland: Harwood Academic Publishers, 1987.

Passmore, John. *A Hundred Years of Philosophy.* Rev. ed. New York: Basic Books, 1966.

Pearson, Karl. *The Grammar of Science.* 3rd ed. New York: Meridian Books, 1957.

Pepper, Stephen C. "A Brief History of General Theory of Value." In *A History of Philosophical Systems,* edited by Vergilius Ferm, 493–503. New York: Philosophical Library, 1950.

Perry, Ralph Barton. "The Ego-Centric Predicament." *Journal of Philosophy, Psychology, and Scientific Methods* 7 (1910): 5–14.

————. *General Theory of Value: Its Meaning and Basic Principles Construed in Terms of Interest.* New York: Longmans, Green, 1926.

————. *The Present Conflict of Ideals: A Study of the Philosophical Background of the World War.* New York: Longmans, Green, 1918.

————. *Present Philosophical Tendencies: A Critical Survey of Naturalism, Idealism, Pragmatism, and Realism with a Synopsis of the Philosophy of William James.* New York: Longmans, Green, 1912.

————. "The Questions of Moral Obligation." *International Journal of Ethics* 21 (1911): 291.

Pescatello, Ann M. *Charles Seeger: A Life in American Music.* Pittsburgh: University of Pittsburgh Press, 1992.

Pratt, Waldo Selden. "On Behalf of Musicology." *The Musical Quarterly* 1 (January 1915): 1–16.

————. "The Scientific Study of Music." *Music Teachers' National Association: Proceedings of the Annual Meeting* (1890): 51–55.

Putnam, Hilary. "Fact and Value." In *Reason, Truth and History,* 127–49. Cambridge: Cambridge University Press, 1981.

Rader, Melvin, ed. *A Modern Book of Esthetics: An Anthology.* Rev. ed. New York: Henry Holt, 1952.

Randall, John H., and Justus Buchler, eds. *Philosophy: An Introduction.* New York: Barnes and Noble, 1942.

Reich, Willi. "Schönberg's New Männerchor." *Modern Music* 9, no. 2 (January–February 1932): 62–66.

Rescher, Nicholas. *Introduction to Value Theory.* Englewood Cliffs, N.J.: Prentice-Hall, 1969.

Reuss, Richard A. "American Folklore and Left-Wing Politics, 1927–57." Ph.D. diss., Indiana University, 1971.

———. "Folk Music and Social Conscience: The Musical Odyssey of Charles Seeger." *Western Folklore* 38 (October 1979): 221–38.

Rothstein, Lawrence E. "What About the Fact-Value Dichotomy: A Belated Reply." *Journal of Value Inquiry* 9 (Winter 1975): 307–11.

Rudhyar, Dane. "Carl Ruggles and the Future of Dissonant Counterpoint." Part 1 of "Revolt of the Angels." *Eolian Review* 3, no. 1 (November 1923): 13–16.

Russell, Bertrand. *The Basic Writings of Bertrand Russell: 1903–1959.* Edited by Robert E. Egner and Lester E. Denonn. New York: Simon and Schuster, 1961.

———. *The Collected Papers of Bertrand Russell.* Vol. 12, *Contemplation and Action, 1902–14.* Edited by Richard Rempel, Andrew Brink, and Margaret Moran. London: George Allen and Unwin, 1985.

———. *A History of Western Philosophy.* New York: Simon and Schuster, 1945.

———. "Mysticism and Logic." *Hibbert Journal* 12 (July 1914): 780–803.

———. *Mysticism and Logic and Other Essays.* London: Longmans and Green, 1918.

———. "The Philosophy of Bergson." *The Monist* 22 (1912): 321–47. Reprinted with a reply by H. Wildon Carr, *The Philosophy of Bergson.* Cambridge: Bowes and Bowes, 1914.

———. "Spinoza." *The Nation* 8 (1910): 278, 280. Review of *The Ethics,* by Benedict de Spinoza, translated by W. Hale White.

———. "Spinoza's Moral Code." *The Nation* 1 (1907): 276. Unsigned review of *Spinoza: A Handbook to the Ethics,* by J. Allanson Picton.

Saint-Saëns, Camille. *Outspoken Essays on Music.* Translated by Fred Rothwell. Freeport, N.Y.: Books for Libraries Press, 1969.

Santayana, George. *Winds of Doctrine.* New York: Scribner, 1913.

Saylor, Bruce. "Henry Cowell." In *The New Grove Dictionary of American Music,* edited by H. Wiley Hitchcock and Stanley Sadie, 1:520–23. London: Macmillan, 1986.

———. "The Tempering of Henry Cowell's Dissonant Counterpoint." *Essays on Modern Music* 2, nos. 1–3 (1985): 3–12.

Schillinger, Joseph. *The Schillinger System of Musical Composition.* 2 vols. New York: Carl Fischer, 1946.

Schilpp, Paul A., ed. *The Philosophy of Bertrand Russell.* New York: Tudor, 1944.

Schoenberg, Arnold. *Fundamentals of Musical Composition.* Edited by Gerald Strang and Leonard Stein. New York: St. Martin's Press, 1967.

————. *The Musical Idea and the Logic, Technique, and Art of Its Presentation.* Edited, translated, and with a commentary by Patricia Carpenter and Severine Neff. New York: Columbia University Press, 1995.

————. "Problems of Harmony." Translated by Adolph Weiss. *Modern Music* 11, no. 4 (May–June 1934): 167–87.

————. *Style and Idea.* Edited by Leonard Stein; translated by Leo Black. Berkeley: University of California Press, 1975.

————. *Theory of Harmony.* Translated by Roy E. Carter. Berkeley: University of California Press, 1978.

Seeger, Alan. *Poems.* New York: Scribner, 1916.

Seeger, Anthony. "The Styles of Musical Ethnography," in *Comparative Musicology and Anthropology of Music: Essays on the History of Ethnomusicology,* ed. Bruno Nettl and Philip V. Bohlman. Chicago: University of Chicago Press, 1991, pp. 342–55.

Seeger, Charles Louis. "Carl Ruggles." *The Musical Quarterly* 18 (1932): 578–92. Reprinted in *American Composers on American Music,* edited by Henry Cowell. Stanford, Calif.: Stanford University Press, 1933.

————. "Charles Ives and Carl Ruggles." *Magazine of Art* 32 (July 1939): 396–99, 435–37.

————. "Henry Cowell." *Magazine of Art* 33 (May 1940): 288–89, 322–25, 327.

————. "In Memoriam: Carl Ruggles (1876–1971)." *Perspectives of New Music* 10 (1972): 171–74.

————. Interview with Vivian Perlis, March 16, 1970. The Oral History Collection of American Music, Yale University, School of Music.

————. "On Dissonant Counterpoint." *Modern Music* 7, no. 4 (June/July 1930): 25–31.

————. "On the Moods of a Music-Logic." *Journal of the American Musicological Society* 13 (1960): 224–61.

————. "On the Principles of Musicology." *The Musical Quarterly* 10 (1924): 244–50.

————. "On Style and Manner in Modern Composition." *The Musical Quarterly* 9 (July 1923): 423–31.

————. "Preface to a Critique of Music." In *Prima Conferencia interamericana de etnomusicologia: Trabajos presentados,* Cartagena de Indias, Colombia, 24–28 February 1963, 39–63. Washington, D.C.: Panamerican Union, 1965. Reprinted as "Preface to the Critique of Music." *Boletin Interamericano de Musica* 49 (September 1965): 2–24.

————. "Prolegomena to Musicology: The Problem of the Musical Point of View and the Bias of Linguistic Presentation." *Eolus* 4 (1925): 12–24.

————. "Reminiscences of an American Musicologist." Interviewed by Adelaide Tusler and Ann Briegleb, Oral History Program, University of California at Los Angeles, 1972.

————. "Reviewing a Review." Part 2 of "Revolt of the Angels." *Eolian Review* 3, no. 1 (November 1923): 16–23.

————. Review of *The Schillinger System of Musical Composition* by Joseph Schillinger. *Music Library Association Notes,* 2nd ser., 4, no. 2 (March 1947): 183–84.

————. "Ruth Crawford." In *American Composers on American Music,* edited by Henry Cowell, 110–18. Stanford, Calif.: Stanford University Press, 1933.

————. "Sources of Evidence and Criteria for Judgment in the Critique of Music." In *Essays for a Humanist: An Offering to Klaus Wachsmann,* edited by Charles Seeger and Bonnie Wade, 261–76. New York: Town House, 1977.

————. *Studies in Musicology, 1935–1975.* Berkeley: University of California Press, 1977.

————. *Studies in Musicology II: 1929–1979.* Edited by Ann Pescatello. Berkeley: University of California Press, 1994.

————. "Systematic and Historical Orientations in Musicology." *Acta Musicologica* 11, no. 4 (1939): 121–28.

————. "Systematic Musicology: Viewpoints, Orientations, and Methods." *Journal of the American Musicological Society* 4 (Fall 1951): 240–48.

————. "Tractatus Esthetico-Semioticus: Model of the Systems of Human Communication." In *Current Thought in Musicology,* edited by John W. Grubbs, 1–39. Symposia in the Arts and Humanities, No. 4. Austin: University of Texas Press, 1976.

————, ed. *New York Musicological Society Bulletin,* nos. 1–3 (1931–34).

Seeger, Charles Louis, and Edward Griffith Stricklen. *Harmonic Structure and Elementary Composition: An Outline of a Course in Practical Musical Invention.* Rev. ed. Berkeley: n.p., 1916.

Seeger, Ruth Crawford, ed. *American Folk Songs for Children.* New York: Doubleday, 1948.

————. *American Folk Songs for Christmas.* Garden City, N.Y.: Doubleday, 1953.

————. *Animal Folk Songs for Children.* New York: Doubleday, 1950.

Singal, Daniel. "Toward a Definition of American Modernism." *American Quarterly* 39 (Spring 1987): 7–35.

Singer, Peter, ed. *A Companion to Ethics.* Oxford: Basil Blackwell, 1991.

Smith, James W. "Should the General Theory of Value Be Abandoned?" *Ethics* 57 (1947): 274–88.

Solie, Ruth A. "The Living Work: Organicism and Musical Analysis." *19th Century Music* 4 (Fall 1980): 147–56.

Sparshott, Francis. "Aesthetics of Music—Limits and Grounds." In *What Is Music? An Introduction to the Philosophy of Music,* edited by Philip Alperson, 35–98. University Park: Pennsylvania State University Press, 1987.

Stace, W. T. *Mysticism and Philosophy.* Philadelphia: Lippincott, 1960.

Stein, Erwin. "Schönberg's New Structural Form." *Modern Music* 7, no. 4 (June–July 1930): 3–10.

Steinberg, Ira S. *Ralph Barton Perry on Education for Democracy.* Columbus: Ohio State University Press, 1970.

Stephens, H. M., and H. H. Bolton, eds. *Prolegomena to History: The Relation of History to Literature, Philosophy, and Science.* Berkeley: University of California Publications, no. 4, 1916–17.

Straus, Joseph N. *The Music of Ruth Crawford Seeger.* Cambridge: Cambridge University Press, 1995.

———. *Remaking the Past: Musical Modernism and the Influence of the Tonal Tradition.* Cambridge, Mass.: Harvard University Press, 1990.

Teggert, Frederick J. *The Theory of History as Progress.* Berkeley: University of California Press, 1925.

Tenney, James. *A History of "Consonance" and "Dissonance."* New York: Excelsior, 1988.

Tick, Judith. "Dissonant Counterpoint Revisited: The First Movement of Ruth Crawford's String Quartet 1931." In *Words and Music in Honor of H. Wiley Hitchcock,* edited by Richard Crawford, R. Allen Lott, and Carol Oja, 405–22. Ann Arbor: University of Michigan Press, 1990.

———. *Ruth Crawford Seeger: A Composer's Search for American Music.* New York: Oxford University Press, 1997.

———. "Ruth Crawford's 'Spiritual Concept': The Sound-Ideals of an Early American Modernist." *Journal of the American Musicological Society* 44 (Summer 1991): 221–61.

Underhill, Evelyn. *Mysticism: A Study in the Nature and Development of Man's Spiritual Consciousness.* London: Methuen, 1911.

Urban, Wilbur M. *Valuation, Its Nature and Laws, Being an Introduction to the General Theory of Value.* London: Swan Sonnenschein, 1909.

Urmson, J. O. *Philosophical Analysis: Its Development Between the Two World Wars.* Oxford: Clarendon Press, 1956.

Vinton, John, ed. *Dictionary of Contemporary Music.* New York: E. P. Dutton, 1971.

Von Gunden, Heidi. *The Music of Lou Harrison.* Metuchen, New Jersey: Scarecrow Press, 1995.

Weidig, Adolf. *Harmonic Material and Its Uses: A Treatise for Teachers, Students, and Music Lovers.* Chicago: Clayton F. Summy, 1923.

Weisgall, Hugo. "The Music of Henry Cowell." *The Musical Quarterly* 45 (1959): 484–98.

Weiss, Adolph. "The Lyceum of Schönberg." *Modern Music* 9, no. 3 (March–April 1932): 99–107.

West, Cornel. *The American Evasion of Philosophy: A Genealogy of Pragmatism.* Madison: University of Wisconsin Press, 1989.

Whitehead, Alfred North, and Bertrand Russell. *Principia Mathematica.* 3 vols. Cambridge: Cambridge University Press, 1910–13.

Wood, Alan. *Bertrand Russell: The Passionate Sceptic.* London: George Allen and Unwin, 1957.

Yasser, Joseph. *A Theory of Evolving Tonality.* New York: American Library of Musicology, 1932.

Ziffrin, Marilyn. *Carl Ruggles: Composer, Painter, and Storyteller.* Urbana: University of Illinois Press, 1994.

Index

Designer:	Ina Clausen
Compositor:	G&S Typesetters
Text:	11/13.5 Caledonia
Display:	Caledonia
Printer and Binder:	Braun-Brumfield